Puccini and *The Girl*

PUCCINI & THE GIRL

History and Reception of The Girl of the Golden West

Annie J. Randall and Rosalind Gray Davis

The University of Chicago Press
Chicago and London

Annie J. Randall is professor of musicology at Bucknell University.
Rosalind Gray Davis, an award-winning journalist, is an independent scholar based in Carmel, California

The University of Chicago Press, Chicago 60637
The University of Chicago Press, Ltd., London
© 2005 by The University of Chicago
All rights reserved. Published 2005
Printed in the United States of America
14 13 12 11 10 09 08 07 06 05   5 4 3 2 1

ISBN (cloth): 0-226-70389-4

A publishing subvention from Bucknell University is gratefully acknowledged.

Library of Congress Cataloging-in-Publication Data

Randall, Annie Janeiro.
    Puccini and The Girl : history and reception of The girl of the golden West / Annie J. Randall and Rosalind Gray Davis.
        p.   cm.
    Includes discography (p.   ), videography (p.   ), bibliographical references (p.   ), and index.
    ISBN 0-226-70389-4 (cloth : alk. paper)
    1. Puccini, Giacomo, 1858–1924. Fanciulla del West.   I. Davis, Rosalind Gray.
II. Title.
    ML410.P89R36   2005
    782.1—dc22

                                                                        2004009716

For the two men who changed my life
Robert M. Davis and Marvin Mitchell Gray
Rosalind Gray Davis

For my mother
Annie J. Randall

CONTENTS

ILLUSTRATIONS

Figures

Musical Examples

Plates (following page 144)

ACKNOWLEDGMENTS

Many people and institutions have contributed to the creation of this history and reception of Puccini's *Fanciulla,* but among the first to lend her expert help and encouragement was Karin Pendle of the College-Conservatory of Music, University of Cincinnati. All parts of this book benefited immeasurably from her encyclopedic knowledge of opera, careful scholarship, and detailed editing. Moreover, we had the great fortune of working with Robert Tuggle, director of the Metropolitan Opera Archives in New York, whose contributions have been substantial. Over the years we have made many visits to the Met archives, and he has graciously guided us to invaluable primary and secondary source material, photographs, and illustrations. Our fond appreciation also extends to the assistant archivist at the Met, John Pennino, who was always willing to lend his expertise in a professional and genial manner. This relationship with the Metropolitan Opera would not have been possible without Robert J. Callander and Marilyn Berg Callander; we also thank them for their encouraging and helpful commentary on all aspects of this project.

Special recognition goes to Kathleen Hansell, our editor at the University of Chicago Press, who believed in this book from the beginning and skillfully guided us through the minefields of publication, editing, and the translation of complex material. Gabriella Biagi Ravenni, one of the founders of the Centro Studi Giacomo Puccini in Lucca, Italy, also made essential contributions by providing research information, including primary source material, and assistance with the translation of several of the Puccini-Zangarini letters. Additionally, we are indebted to the late Geminino Zangarini and his wife, Noreen, who still lives in Bologna. They shared reams of untouched information on Geminino's uncle, Carlo Zangarini, which they lovingly stored in their home for years after his death. This treasure-trove of material helped us piece together the story of the letters' provenance. And research on this book could not have been completed without the help of Cosimo Cricchio and his sister, Rosie. Cosimo painstakingly worked on locating and translating challenging archival information in Italy and in the United States.

Long-term projects such as this need institutional support; we, therefore, gratefully acknowledge Bucknell University's provost, Stephen Bowen, and vice president for academic affairs, Jim Rice. And, for their assistance in transcription and for reviewing the translations of Puccini's letters, we recognize Bernhard Kuhn and Janet Clapp, also of Bucknell. Lenore Coral, Cornell University's music librarian, and Vincent Giroud, at Yale University's Beinecke Library, generously shared their knowledge concerning the provenance of *Fanciulla*'s production booklet and Puccini's autograph sketches for parts of the opera, while Allan Atlas, Distinguished Professor of Musicology at Brooklyn College and the Graduate Center, City University of New York, kindly lent us his notes on the Koch Collection autograph sketches. We are deeply indebted to Philip Gossett, Robert W. Reneker Distinguished Service Professor of Music, University of Chicago, for his invaluable contributions to the final draft of this book. He not only reviewed the transcriptions of all the letters and pertinent documents, but also made suggestions regarding the musical sketches and examples, as well as helping us to clarify various interpretations and documentation in our chapters. Marcia Citron, Martha and Henry Malcolm Lovett Distinguished Service Professor of Musicology, Shepherd School of Music, Rice University, also read our later work, and her astute advice regarding additions and revisions significantly helped to refine many points. For his wise advice during the book's early development, we recognize Jim Zychowicz of A-R Editions.

We would also like to thank Mario Armellini, Civico Museo Bibliografico-Musicale "G. B. Martini," Bologna; librarians at the Biblioteca Comunale dell'Archiginnasio, Bologna; Danilo Fullin, Archivio Storico del *Corriere della sera*, Milan; Museo Teatrale alla Scala, Milan; Stephanie Challener, *Musical America*; New York Public Library for the Performing Arts (Music Division and the Billy Rose Theatre Collection); David Gilbert, University of California, Los Angeles, Music Library; Brad Ball, Warner Bros. Entertainment; and the students at Bucknell University who participated in the seminar "Puccini's Operas in Social-Historical Perspective" (1997).

In the collaboration for this book both authors edited and commented upon the other's chapters. Annie Randall wrote chapters 1, 2, 6, 7, and 8, the introduction to chapter 5, and appendix C. Rosalind Gray Davis wrote chapters 3, 4, and 5, and appendixes A, B, D, and E. Ms. Gray Davis, who owns the Puccini-Zangarini letters, is also responsible for securing the majority of the illustrations and photographs used in the book.

From a more personal perspective, we thank Robert M. Davis and Irene Randall for their inspiration, love, and wise counsel throughout the inevitable ups and downs of a multiyear project. In 1996, Dr. Kelsey Gray introduced us to one another while still a student at Mills College; both she and Robert Davis were involved in this project from the very beginning, and we acknowledge them for their many readings of the book's various drafts and for their unwavering support through all stages of the process. Lily Gray Allen provided us with information on the provenance of the Puccini-Zangarini letters as well as valuable historical and personal information on Marvin M. Gray. We also recognize Dorke Poelz, Luke Gray, William W. Davis, Frederick and Teresa Sturdivant, Jim Pinckney, Sue Peccianti, Michael Wecker, Charles Cohen, Susan Ashelford, Judy Logan, Lyn Evans, Barbara Nelson, and Judi Chandler.

PART I

Setting the Stage

CHAPTER ONE

New Documents, New Approaches

Puccini's Letters to Zangarini: Provenance and Significance

The veteran journalist Marvin Gray sensed the historical importance of the twenty-nine Puccini letters he had just purchased from Mary Benjamin in the early 1960s.[1] Inspired by his knowledge and love of Puccini's operas and convinced that the composer's letters to Carlo Zangarini, *La fanciulla del West*'s librettist, would be of value to scholars and Puccini devotees alike, Gray planned to publish the letters in their entirety. Along with the letters and their English translations, he also intended to write a narrative account of the creation of the opera in order to place the 1907–10 correspondence in historical context.[2]

Writing about *Fanciulla* would have been a real departure for Gray, who, at the time he conceived this project, was president of southern California–based Triad Newspapers and former publisher of the *Manila Evening News*.[3] Gray's enthusiasm overcame whatever doubts he might have had about writing

---

1. Mary Benjamin (1905–1998) was among New York's most respected autograph specialists. Her book *Autographs: A Key to Collecting* (New York: R. R. Bowker, 1946; reprint, New York: Book Craftsmen Associates, 1963) is a classic text for collectors and dealers. She took over the family business, Walter Benjamin Autographs (est. 1887), in 1943.

2. Benjamin also supplied the translations.

3. The *Manila Evening News* was the largest English-language newspaper in the Far East. Gray had also written three books: *The Magsaysay Story* (with Carlos Romulo; New York: John Day, 1956); *The Abominable Snowman and Other Stories* (New York: Vantage Press, 1961); and *Island Hero* (New York: Hawthorn Books, 1965).

on an unfamiliar subject; his zeal is evident in a promotional essay he prepared, intended perhaps for perusal by a prospective book agent or publisher:

> Among all the phenomena of the opera's bizarre history, perhaps the
> most singular is that its history is less than half told. The composer's
> correspondence with his original librettist from the time he first received
> a translation of Belasco's play . . . until he put the finishing touches on
> the score in 1910, has never been seen.
>
> Until now!
>
> For I propose to publish this correspondence, the originals of which
> are in my possession, publish them for the first time. They will not only
> unveil the growth of *La fanciulla* from its inception but also, will reflect
> the stormy times through which the composition traveled.[4]

Fascinated by the sensational events in Puccini's life that ran parallel to the
creation of the opera, Gray promised to include biographical details in his
book. His essay summarizes a grim episode in the composer's life:

> Over the years, Puccini was interrupted in the composition of this opera
> by a family disaster that resulted from his wife's outrageous (yet some-
> times justified) jealousy. A female retainer killed herself after Puccini's
> wife had vilified her to the community for allegedly trying to seduce her
> husband. The post mortem determined that the unhappy servant girl
> was *virgina intacta*. A law suit followed. Puccini suffered the agonies of
> deciding whether he could hold on to his marriage under these unhappy
> circumstances, disgusted as he was by his wife's behavior. (Essay, 1)

The biographical material and the pledge to shed new light on Puccini's working relationship with Zangarini were, in Gray's view, the most compelling features of his projected book. He asserted that the letters "explode a theory
regarding the composer's embittered relationship with the original librettist. It
is generally accepted today that Puccini broke forever with his librettist. The
correspondence shows this is not true" (Essay, 2). Believing that *Fanciulla* was
an unjustly neglected masterpiece, Gray hoped that this new information
would help to establish the opera's historical uniqueness and thereby raise its
profile in the operatic repertoire. He envisioned his book as "a small volume
that contributes to history and to the unusual marriage of America's West and

---

4. Marvin Gray, unpublished essay, Los Angeles, c. 1960, 1; cited hereafter as "Essay," followed by
page number.

Americana with Italy's great, operatic genius." Ending his essay with a rhetorical flourish, Gray asked, "Should this story be told?" He answered dramatically, "I think it should . . . and must . . . be told [ellipses in the original]. And
I am ready to tell it" (Essay, 3). Unfortunately, Gray suffered a heart attack
and died shortly after describing his beloved project. His daughter, Rosalind
Gray Davis, revived the project in 1996 and is responsible for initiating this
study.

One of the first questions that needed to be addressed concerned the provenance of the material. How did Puccini's letters to Carlo Zangarini wind up
halfway around the world in southern California in the hands of Marvin Gray,
a newspaper publisher, more than fifty years after they were written? A probe
of likely Italian and American sources of information yielded only fragmen-
tary results. Neither Zangarini's descendants nor Walter Benjamin Autographs
were able to supply definitive answers: Mary Benjamin's sales records and many
others from Benjamin Autographs were no longer extant, and all of Zangarini's contemporaries had died.[5] Hence, it is unlikely that we shall ever dis-
cover exactly how the letters left Zangarini's estate upon his death in Bologna,
Italy, in 1943 or who among his heirs sold the packet of letters. Nor can we
determine to whom, if anyone, they were sold before Mary Benjamin obtained
them. However, Geminino Zangarini, Carlo's nephew and the last relative
to know the librettist, conjectured that his uncle's lifelong companion, Zita
Minghazzi, inherited the Puccini letters from Carlo and sold them after
World War II.[6]

What we do know with absolute certainty is that Marvin Gray purchased
the twenty-nine letters from the Benjamin autograph house in New York
around 1962. We speculate that no more than one dealer owned the letters before Mary Benjamin sold them to Gray. Had the letters fallen into the hands of
a mere treasure-seeker rather than a professional dealer, they probably would
have been sold one by one for quick cash. The seller, probably Minghazzi,
must have understood the historical importance of the Puccini letters and, despite the economically bleak conditions of postwar Italy, resisted the tempta-
tion to sell them off individually. Rather, she probably sought out a reputable
dealer to handle the packet of letters and may have stipulated that they be kept
together as a set. This dealer could have been Mary Benjamin, who, on a buy-
ing trip to postwar Europe, may have discovered the letters in the course of
her autograph-hunting, or an Italian who, in turn, sold them to Benjamin.

---

5. Many of the records of Walter Benjamin Autographs were apparently lost after the retirement of
Mary Benjamin, including the ones pertaining to the Puccini–Zangarini letters.

6. Geminino Zangarini died in February 1999.

Reputable dealers would have known that marketing the letters individually, while having the appeal of making them easier to sell, would have severely
compromised or completely ruined their historical value. Scattered across the
globe among voracious collectors of Puccini memorabilia, the letters would
have been nearly impossible to retrieve and to reconstitute as a set.[7] It seems
that Zita Minghazzi and the agent(s) to whom the letters were sold deferred
their profits and waited for buyers who were willing to invest a considerable
sum to acquire them as a group. Whatever the scenario might have been, it is
extremely fortunate that the set of letters from Puccini to Zangarini has been
preserved. It fills a considerable gap in Puccini's published correspondence
and provides new points of departure for historical and critical discussions
of La fanciulla. It was also fortunate that Zita Minghazzi preserved much of
Zangarini's literary archives and arranged for it to pass on to Geminino
Zangarini at her death. The documents contained therein (copies of most
of his published works, early diaries, juvenilia, opera program booklets, and
newspaper reviews of premieres) shed much-needed light on the writer's creative life.

In planning this book we felt strongly that if the letters were to be prop-
erly understood it was not enough to know only about the sender, Puccini;
rather, the recipient and his position in Italian cultural life must also be taken
into account. Unlike Adami and Carner's Letters of Puccini and other published
collections that reduce personal information on the letters' recipients to foot-
note-length descriptions, our treatment of the letters presents as fully as
possible Zangarini's point of view as well as Puccini's.[8] Knowing Zangarini's
background adds a new dimension to Fanciulla's libretto and grants us greater
precision in locating the opera within the musicoliterary aesthetics of the first
decades of the twentieth century.

Carlo Zangarini (1874–1943)

While the newly available letters from Puccini give us a glimpse into Carlo
Zangarini's life in the years from 1907 to 1910, they also arouse curiosity about
the rest of the librettist's work both before and after his career-making en-

7. One of the objectives of the Centro Studi Giacomo Puccini in Lucca is to create a database containing all of Puccini's letters.

8. Giuseppe Adami, ed., Giacomo Puccini epistolario (Milan: Mondadori, 1928), trans. and ed. Ena Makin
as Letters of Giacomo Puccini Mainly Connected with the Composition of His Operas (Philadelphia: J. B. Lippincott,
1931); Arnaldo Marchetti, ed., Puccini com'era (Milan: Curci, 1973); Eugenio Gara, ed., Carteggi pucciniani
(Milan: G. Ricordi, 1958). Future scholars enjoying free access to the Ricordi archives will, no doubt,
be able to provide an even fuller picture.

counter with the composer of *La fanciulla del West*.[9] In the seven years preceding *Fanciulla*, Zangarini's music-related work had consisted of only three translations—*Caino, Hans il suonatore di flauto*, and *Pelleas e Melisanda*—and an adaptation, *Hail, Columbia!* Yet, after word of Zangarini's collaboration with Puccini had spread, his stock in the music world skyrocketed, and between 1908 and 1915 he created eight original libretti: *Berta alla siepe, Terra promessa, Jaufré Rudel, Saltarello, I gioielli della Madonna, Nido di falco, Il santo*, and *Maria sul monte*. In this period he also completed four adaptations, *Conchita, Melenis, Capriccio antico*, and *Amore in maschera*, and two translations, *Medea* and *La principessa della czarda*. By the end of World War I Zangarini had finished one more stage work, an adaptation of James Fenimore Cooper's *Last of the Mohicans*, but he never again approached the level of productivity he had attained in the prewar years. Only five libretti are attributed to Zangarini in the twenty-five years from the war's end in 1918 to his death in 1943: *Severo Torelli, Anthony, La rosiera, Le astuzie di Bertoldo*, and *Vanda* (see appendix C).

For most of his professional life Zangarini lived in two worlds: the professional music world, in which he operated as an esteemed librettist, and the world of the public intellectual, in which he used his writing to express nationalist and fascist beliefs. He gained local fame as a writer for Bologna's *Il resto del carlino*, a newspaper for which he wrote on a variety of topics; before about 1920 his subject matter was largely confined to arts topics, but after that his attention turned increasingly toward political matters. His two worlds merged in 1934 when he was appointed chair of poetic and dramatic literature at Bologna's Liceo Musicale. The appointment recognized Zangarini's nearly forty years' worth of published work and rewarded his lifelong involvement in Bologna's civic and cultural life.[10]

Although Zangarini's work with composers such as Ruggero Leoncavallo, Pietro Mascagni, and Ermanno Wolf-Ferrari served to burnish his own reputation,[11] his association with Puccini had the greatest impact on his career. Not only did he refer to the association at every opportunity, but other

---

9. See appendix C for further information on Zangarini's libretti.

10. Zangarini was known not only for his libretti and newspaper articles, but also as a poet who created laudatory verse on widely divergent themes. He composed moving commemorative poems for World War I's fallen soldiers (which he read aloud at military hospitals) and wrote doggerel in praise of a well-known indigestion medicine that appeared in full-page advertisements in *Il resto del carlino*. Throughout his career he tried his hand at different genres; he wrote a radio play, a film script, texts for songs, and a few stage plays.

11. Leoncavallo's *Zaza* was the subject of an ugly public dispute after the work appeared in print (1900) without proper acknowledgment of Zangarini's contribution to the libretto. The experience made Zangarini particularly vigilant in contractual matters for the rest of his life. Several years later he created the libretto for Riccardo Zandonai's *Conchita* (1912) and Ermanno Wolf-Ferrari's *I gioielli della Madonna* (1912).

journalists also regularly mentioned his work with Puccini in their reviews of Zangarini's premieres. He kept their association alive through several articles he wrote about the collaboration, most notably in "Vigilia pucciniana" (Puccini Vigil), and "Un carteggio inedito del Maestro per *La fanciulla del West*" (Unpublished Correspondence of the Composer on *La fanciulla del West*).[12] In the latter article Zangarini quotes extensively from some of the letters that are now known as the Marvin Gray Collection.

Additional Sources, New Perspectives

Our approach to this material was determined by the observation that no study of *La fanciulla* had yet brought together many of the most important Italian and English sources concerning the opera's genesis, premiere, and critical reception. In an attempt to fill this gap, we have included complete texts and translations of Puccini's letters to Zangarini and quoted Italian sources. The book weaves together the letters with other material into a detailed account of events concerning the opera's creation (chapters 3, 4, and 5). In addition, it surveys the opera's narrative and musical themes (chapter 2) and examines its reception history while proposing new critical perspectives (chapters 6 and 7). Following the historical and critical treatments of the opera, we consider in chapter 8 some performance implications of this study.[13] Our objective is to blend the historical with the critical in ways that will invite fresh readings and possibly new productions of *La fanciulla del West*.

12. Carlo Zangarini, "Vigilia pucciniana," *Il resto del carlino* (Bologna), 20 September 1910; "Un carteggio inedito del Maestro per *La fanciulla del West*," *Il resto del carlino* (Bologna), 29 November 1928.

13. Although we present a thorough treatment of the Puccini–Zangarini letters and documents related to the opera's international critical reception, analysis of other types of primary sources remains another challenge. For instance, the Koch Collection of autograph sketches at Yale University's Beinecke Library and the Lehmann Collection of Puccini's early drafts of acts 1 and 2 at the Pierpont Morgan Library (both worthy of a monographs) await careful analysis that will undoubtedly link the development of musical ideas presented therein with events in *Fanciulla*'s chronology. The absence of dates on the Koch Collection sketches and paucity of information concerning their provenance makes speculation about them, at this stage, of limited value. However, once archival materials that have been severely restricted are available for study (such as those held by Casa Ricordi, Milan: *Fanciulla*'s autograph manuscript, libretto drafts, drafts of post-1910 revisions), cross-checking will be possible, probable dates can be established for currently undated sources, and autograph materials in Italy and the United States can then be analyzed and placed within the new chronological and critical frames we present here.

The quandary over Ricordi's historical archives, which have been inaccessible for several years, was resolved at the end of 2003. By agreement with the Italian Ministry of Culture, the archives are now deposited at Milan's Biblioteca Nazionale Braidense. The several collections it comprises (including 2,500 autograph scores, 15,000 letters of composers and librettists, 10,000 costume and stage designs, 9,000 opera librettos, 4,000 photographs, and original production registers) will gradually become available for consultation during the spring and summer of 2004.

This book was already in press when *Giacomo Puccini: Catalogue of the Works*, by Dieter Schickling and Michael Kaye (Kassel: Bärenreiter, 2003) was released.

CHAPTER TWO

The Opera's Story: Texts and Subtexts

The libretto and English version of *La fanciulla* published by Ricordi in 1910 present the cast of characters as follows:

Minnie	Soprano
Jack Rance, sheriff	Baritone
Dick Johnson (Ramerrez)	Tenor
Nick, bartender at the "Polka"	Tenor
Ashby, agent of the Wells Fargo Transport Co.	Bass
Sonora	Baritone
Trin	Tenor
Sid	Baritone
Handsome	Baritone
Harry	Tenor
Joe	Tenor
Happy	Baritone
Larkens	Bass
Billy Jackrabbit, an Indian redskin	Bass
Wowkle, Billy's squaw	Mezzo-soprano
Jake Wallace, a traveling camp-minstrel	Baritone
José Castro, a greaser from Ramerrez's gang	Bass

(Sonora, Trin, Sid, Handsome, Harry, Joe, Happy, Larkens — *miners*)

A Postilion   Tenor
Men of the Camp [1]

Immediately after this list is a "Preliminary Note" that introduces the listener
to the story in words reminiscent of a late-nineteenth-century dime novel:

> The action takes place in that period of Californian history which fol-
> lows immediately upon the discovery made by the miner Marshall of the
> first nugget of gold, at Coloma, in January, 1848. An unbridled greed, an
> upheaval of all social order, a restless anarchy followed upon the news
> of this discovery. . . . "In those strange days, people coming from God
> knows where, joined forces in that far western land, and, according to
> the rude custom of the camp, their very names were soon lost and un-
> recorded, and here they struggled, laughed, gambled, cursed, killed,
> loved, and worked out their strange destinies in a manner incredible
> to us of to-day. Of one thing only we are sure—they lived!" [2]

The note situates the opera's characters and adds an element of menace and
violence:

> around this mixed and lawless folk a conglomeration of thieving and
> murderous gangs has sprung up as a natural outcome of this same lust
> for gold, and infests the highways, . . . from the strenuous conflict
> between these two parties arises the application of a primitive justice
> of cruelty and rapacity.

After announcing the main themes of "love and moral redemption," the note
concludes by claiming for the story a degree of authenticity, referring to *The
Girl of the Golden West* as "an episode in this original period of American history" (ibid.).

Fanciulla's use of a specific historical moment, the California gold rush of
1849–50, as a backdrop for a love story recalls the historically "authentic"
grounding of dozens of earlier works, for instance, Hector Berlioz's and Giacomo Meyerbeer's grand operas. However, unlike *Les Huguenots* or *Les Troyens*,
whose historical models were hundreds of years in the past by the time of their
premieres, *Fanciulla*'s was a mere sixty years earlier, and its effects were still being felt by audiences in 1910. The Mexican-American War, which had ended

---

1. Guelfo Civinini and Carlo Zangarini, *La fanciulla del West* [libretto], English version by R. H. Elkin
(Milan: Ricordi, 1910), 4; hereafter referred to as "libretto, English version."
2. Ibid., 5.

in 1848, brought much of what is known today as the American West under U.S. jurisdiction after three hundred years of Spanish and then Mexican rule. United States armies encountered stiff opposition from the outnumbered and poorly armed Californios,[3] and bitterness lasted well after the war's end as vast land areas owned by Californios and Native Americans were taken over by U.S. settlers (often illegally, despite the peace settlement's promised protections).[4]

The war's violence and its aftermath created deep social, economic, and cultural divisions between the Spanish-speaking Californio population, Native American tribes, and the new U.S. migrants. Tensions were high at the time Belasco wrote *Girl of the Golden West*, and his play, especially its leading male character, Johnson/Ramerrez, reflects those tensions.[5] The many Californios who, like Johnson/Ramerrez, were forced to accept U.S. rule resented and resisted the takeover and posed a persistent threat to the American settlers and the U.S. army. Johnson/Ramerrez, a Californio impersonating a U.S. citizen in the years immediately following the 1848 Treaty of Guadalupe Hidalgo,[6] is an obvious representation of the uneasy union of American and Mexican cultures.

Belasco and Puccini shared a passion for the authenticity of their story and went to great lengths to create the illusion of reality in their productions (*Fanciulla*'s use of live horses on stage, for example, and the famous blood-dripping scene, which Belasco claimed was based on an actual event). In fact, the names of Belasco's characters are drawn from Californian history: Nina Micheltorena, the prostitute, shares her surname with Manuel Micheltorena, California's last Mexican governor, and the captured bandit, José Castro, bears the name of a defeated Mexican general. It is unlikely that Belasco chose these names unwittingly; indeed, as most writers on Belasco point out, the playwright prided himself on his historical knowledge and attention to "authentic" detail.[7] By giving the names of a past governor and a defeated general to a prostitute and a bandit, Belasco signals the extreme drop in socioeconomic status experienced by the Spanish-speaking population under the new U.S.

3. Spanish-speaking citizens of the California territory.

4. Ramon A. Gutiérrez and Richard J. Orsi, eds., *Contested Eden: California before the Gold Rush* (Berkeley and Los Angeles: University of California Press, 1998); Neal Harlow, *California Conquered: War and Peace on the Pacific, 1846–1850* (Berkeley and Los Angeles: University of California Press, 1982). Malcolm Rohrbough, *Days of Gold: The California Gold Rush and the American Nation* (Berkeley and Los Angeles: University of California Press, 1997).

5. Belasco's *Girl of the Golden West* was first performed in 1905.

6. The Treaty of Guadalupe Hidalgo, signed by the Mexican and U.S. governments on 2 February 1848, provided that Mexico cede its territories of New Mexico and Upper California to the United States.

7. Lise-Lone Marker, *David Belasco: Naturalism in the American Theater* (Princeton, N.J.: Princeton University Press, 1975).

government. Privileged status was, by contrast, enjoyed by the thousands of American settlers, many of them inexperienced miners, who flooded into California to partake in the Gold Rush. These miners fill the stage in the opening scenes of *La fanciulla del West.*

Prelude

Before the curtain rises on "a mining camp in the days of the gold fever—1849–1850,"[8] the orchestra, in its role as omniscient narrator, prepares the audience for the story by presenting the opera's main motifs in quick succession. The prelude's brevity and densely packed motivic content signal the exuberance of the Wild West but also its instability: the music lurches from whole-tone to diatonic scales, from major to minor, from energetic dotted rhythms to lilting eighth notes, all within the space of thirty-four bars. The unsettling sense that everything can change in an instant is conveyed not only by this discontinuity but also by the prelude's prominent whole-tone-oriented motif (ex. 2.1, mm. 1–2, 4–5, 13–14, 16–17).

Example 2.1. Prelude, mm. 1–34

8. Ibid., 4.

Example 2.1. *(continued)*

Continued on next page

Example 2.1. *(continued)*

Puccini labeled this motif simply "the motif of redemption,"[9] implying, somewhat misleadingly, a singularity of purpose in its deployment. Indeed, the motif appears when the word *redenzione* is sung in acts 1 and 3; however,

9. Puccini describes the motif in an interview with Arnaldo Fraccaroli printed in Milan's *Corriere della sera*, 10 October 1910. Chapter 7 contains an extended quotation from the article.

it also appears in other contexts, consistently serving a second function as a signifier of the presence of chance in the lives of the opera's characters.[10] The motif's dual function is most evident in the kiss scene of act 2 (see ex. 2.10), in which Puccini combines the descending whole-tone line with the rhythm of the prelude's love theme (ex. 2.1, mm. 6–12). By conflating the two themes, he marks the protagonists' love for one another as potentially redemptive but also destabilizing. The motif's mercurial character is conveyed by its disruptive and dissolving properties: it dissolves into the love theme but shortly thereafter reappears disruptively (ex. 2.1, mm. 13–14).[11] Both love and chance are swept aside in the last four bars of the prelude by a ragtime-inspired fragment (ex. 2.1, mm. 30–34) reflecting the quick pace, energy, and perpetual motion of the American West.

The cinematic jump-cut quality of the prelude and the arresting prominence of the whole-tone sequence announce the most significant departures in Puccini's style as it had developed in the years from *Manon Lescaut* (1893) to *Madama Butterfly* (1904). Carner comments on the *"fauve* sound" of *Fanciulla's* orchestra,[12] a result of the dark timbres of the extra woodwinds,[13] "explosive" use of low brass, and exclusively male chorus. The prelude, which occurs *before* the curtain rises (unlike in Puccini's previous works, with the exception of *Le villi* [1884]), establishes the orchestra as a force that operates independently of the characters and settings; it instigates stage action, rather than merely accompanying it, and displays Puccini's adaptation of Wagner's narrative use of the orchestra.[14]

10. Mosco Carner finds no unifying principle behind Puccini's multiple uses of the prelude's opening gesture: "with characteristic inconsistency he associated it with several other dramatic motives: the love between hero and heroine, moral redemption and homesickness." In *Puccini: A Critical Biography*, 3d ed. (New York: Holmes and Meier, 1992), 462–63. Michele Girardi, on the other hand, contends that "the broad sequence is intended to symbolize love as a redemptive force." In *Puccini: His International Art*, trans. Laura Basini (Chicago: University of Chicago Press, 2000), 286. Julian Budden describes the prelude's principal motifs as largely pictorial, "evoking a measureless landscape with branches of giant trees tossing in the wind" and goes on to say that "each carries an emotional charge which will be exploited to very different purpose elsewhere." *Puccini: His Life and Works* (Oxford and New York: Oxford University Press, 2002), 305.

11. For further discussion of Puccini's deployment of this motif, see chapter 7.

12. Mosco Carner, "Giacomo Puccini," in *The New Grove Dictionary of Music and Musicians*, ed. Stanley Sadie (London: Macmillan, 1980), 15:438.

13. Puccini adds oboe, clarinet, bassoon, and contrabassoon to *Butterfly's* instrumentation.

14. Girardi's analysis of *Fanciulla* is the most comprehensive discussion of the opera's music and takes into account recent European and American scholarship; Girardi, *His International Art*, 183–327. See also Budden's treatment in *Puccini*. These complement and in some cases correct Carner's still-useful analysis. Allan Atlas's illuminating *"'Lontano—tornare—redenzione':* Verbal Leitmotives and Their Musical Resonance in Puccini's *La fanciulla del West," Studi musicali* 21, no. 2 (1992): 359–98, is one of a handful of journal articles devoted to single aspects of Puccini's novel musical strategies in *Fanciulla*.

Act 1

All of act 1 takes place in the bar area of the Polka saloon.[15] Owned by Minnie, the admirable *fanciulla* of the opera's title, and with the words "A Real
Home for the Boys" painted on the wall above the bar, the Polka is the principal social and civic gathering place for the residents of the mining camp located at the foot of California's Cloudy Mountains. A secular space nestled in
a sacralized wilderness, the setting is used by the authors to present elements
of American life that are crucial to the story. These elements include nostalgia for a distant homeland; absence of a common culture; the prevalence of il-
literacy and violence; naive egalitarianism; a class system built on racial, ethnic, and gender differences; and an abiding faith in the general goodness of
material acquisition. It is the work of the first act to present these elements
and hold them in tension with the desires and beliefs of the characters. The
opera's several plot lines and subtexts develop as a result of this tension.

Distant locales mentioned in the libretto, such as Sacramento, San Francisco, Monterey, and Mexico, convey a sense of the camp's remoteness and establish the Polka as an oasis of relative civility in the midst of a threatening
and darkly forested outside. Other offstage areas include the Polka's dance
hall, adjacent to the bar area, and the Palmeto, a nearby brothel run by the "na-
tiva di Cachuca, una sirena" [a native of Cachuca, a siren],[16] Nina Micheltorena. Early in the act we learn that the saloon doubles as a schoolroom; thus
it is presented as a place of innocence in contrast to the morally suspect
brothel. The miners (pl. 3) patronize both places of business, not only to satisfy their social and sexual needs, but also to dull the pain of their homesickness and longing for loved ones.

Puccini accentuates the miners' longing by highlighting their emotional
fragility and loneliness in an ensemble number that involves the entire chorus
of miners.[17] "Che faranno i vecchi miei là lontano" [What are my folks doing back home, far away] (ex. 2.2) is in the tradition of Verdi's large-scale
choral numbers and serves to establish the emotional and class solidarity of
the singers: in this case, immigrant workers of European descent. The miners'
sense of alienation is embodied by Jake Wallace, an itinerant blackface min-

---

15. Most of the illustrations referred to in this chapter are from the December 1910 premier production
of *La fanciulla del West* at the Metropolitan Opera of New York and are included in the gallery.

16. Guelfo Civinini and Carlo Zangarini, *La fanciulla del West* [libretto] (Milan: Ricordi, 1910), 27; hereafter referred to as "Italian libretto." All translations are by the author unless otherwise noted.

17. All musical examples are taken from Ricordi's 1910 piano-vocal score, arranged by Carlo Carignani.

Example 2.2. Jake Wallace: "Che faranno i vecchi miei" (act 1, [20])

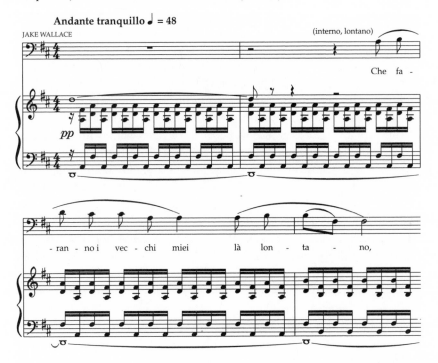

strel, who leads them in the nostalgic song.[18] The expulsion of two characters from the Polka's safe space is also important in establishing the saloon as an outpost of morality: the Australian, Sid, is expelled for cheating at cards, and Billy, a Native American, is thrown out because of his failure to marry Wowkle, the mother of his child.[19] Though the saloon's miners constitute the majority of the town's population, none is native to the region—they are all migrants or immigrants who have traded the security of their homes and

18. Though Wallace appeared in blackface for the premiere, the makeup was dropped in later performances. For a further discussion of Wallace's character, see chapters 6 and 8.

19. By the time of the Italian premiere in Rome on 12 June 1911, the scene in which Billy is expelled from the Polka had been cut. Girardi suggests that the reason for the cut was twofold: to remove a scene that impeded the narrative flow, and to assuage Toscanini's discomfort with the stereotypically negative portrayal of Native Americans. Girardi, *His International Art*, 299, n. 47. Leonard Slatkin's performances of 1991 and 1992 restored the scene (with Eva Marton and Alain Fondary [Munich] and Barbara Daniels and Placido Domingo [New York]). For more on Toscanini's changes, see Gabriele Dotto, "Opera, Four Hands: Collaborative Alterations in Puccini's *Fanciulla*," *Journal of the American Musicological Society* 42, no. 3 (Fall 1989): 604–624.

families for the promise of California gold. Only Billy and Wowkle are na-
tives, and while they too have been separated from their culture, they are not
miners, but servants, and as such are presented as peripheral to Cloudy Mountain's society.[20]

Minnie (pl. 4) is the central figure in the miners' lives, and her entrance, accompanied by her commanding signature theme, rivets the attention of all the
Polka's patrons. The music accompanying "Hello Minnie!" (ex. 2.3) is dominated by its descending-seventh interval (followed by the ascending third
and fifth of the chord), which is heard three times within the space of a
few seconds. The wide interval and the theme's rich orchestration of strings,
full brass, and timpani characterize Minnie as a grand, almost monumental, figure. However, for reasons that will be discussed in chapter 7, Minnie
never sings her own theme. Puccini links Minnie musically with the prelude's opening chord in its use of an augmented triad (C–E–G♯) in her signature gesture's second iteration. (Puccini's sketch of the first four notes of
Minnie's theme was included in an 11 December 1910 article in the *New York
Times*; see pl. 5.)

Example 2.3. Miners: "Hello Minnie!" (act 1, 42)

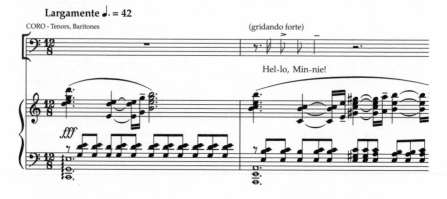

20. Puccini's "direct" knowledge of Native American habits and customs was limited to the staged
portrayals of Buffalo Bill's traveling Wild West shows, which the composer and other fascinated European
spectators believed reproduced "real scenes that went on at the frontier." Gara, *Carteggi pucciniani*, nos. 37, 38.
See Christian Feest, ed., *Indians and Europe: An Interdisciplinary Collection of Essays* (1998; reprint, Lincoln: University of Nebraska Press, 1999), for descriptions of the shows as performed in Italy and their reception by
local audiences; John Blair, "Blackface Minstrels and *Buffalo Bill's Wild West:* Nineteenth-Century Entertainment Forms as Cultural Exports," in *European Readings of American Popular Culture*, ed. John Dean and Jean-
Paul Gabillet (Westport, Conn.: Greenwood Press, 1996), 3–12.

Example 2.3. (continued)

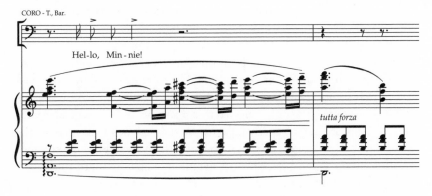

Minnie's maternal relationship with the miners is established in act 1's Bible scene, during which she leads "the boys"[21] in a discussion of Psalm 51. In "Lavami e sarò bianco come neve" [Wash me and I will be as white as snow] (ex. 2.4), Puccini for the first time in the opera links the prelude's descending whole-tone theme with the concept of redemption. In this scene, the miners are portrayed as childlike, homesick, dependent, and barely literate. Not only do they rely on Minnie for emotional succor and scraps of education, they also entrust their newly mined bags of gold to her for safekeeping. Minnie stores them in a barrel in the Polka, and the miners help her guard the hoard by taking turns sleeping next to the barrel each night. Though Minnie holds

Example 2.4. Minnie: "Lavami e sarò bianco" (act 1, 1 m. after 51)

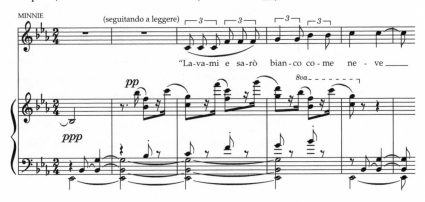

21. The words "A real home for the boys" appear on the wall behind the bar. Civinini and Zangarini, Italian libretto, 8.

no official civic or religious post, her authority exceeds that of any priest, teacher, or policeman. Not even the sheriff, Jack Rance, hovering malevolently on the fringes of the opera's early scenes, surpasses Minnie as a figure of local authority.

The first act's dramatic action is initiated by characters who enter the miners' safe refuge from the dangerous outside. The entrance of Ashby, a rumpled Wells Fargo security agent, is the first to advance the main plot: he brings troubling news of a gang of bandits led by a man who "robs like a real gentleman." [22] Ashby's entrance is accompanied by the prelude's final motif—the syncopated music that Puccini uses moments later to accompany the entrance of Dick Johnson. Clearly, Puccini does not mean to link this motif solely with Johnson. The composer uses it more broadly to mark an aspect of western American identity shared by Ashby and Johnson. The entrance of the well-spoken stranger from Sacramento sets in motion events that begin to rupture the Polka's cocoon of familial and social relationships (see pl. 6). Johnson is taken aback when, to his surprise, he recognizes Minnie as the woman he had met once before on the road to Monterey and to whom he had been deeply attracted.

Sensing a rival for Minnie's affections, Sheriff Rance (see pl. 7) reflexively displays a snarling animosity toward the outsider. Minnie's attraction for the stranger sparks an intense jealousy in the sheriff, who, despite having a wife in an unnamed, distant location, expresses his lust for Minnie openly. A limp three-note gesture $(E-D\sharp-C\sharp)$ is repeated throughout "Minnie, dalla mia casa son partito" [Minnie, I left my home] (ex. 2.5) and discloses a pitiful rather than rapacious aspect of Rance's character.[23] Minnie responds with a nostalgic monologue revealing her idealized view of romantic love. Important in establishing Minnie's innocent wish to find a man like her father, "Laggiù nel Soledad" [Down there in Soledad] (ex. 2.6) is less rewarding, both melodically and dramatically, than a soprano who must negotiate its sudden leap to a high C might justifiably expect.[24] Minnie's melodic plainness and unprepared leap indicates her naiveté, lack of education, and unworldliness.

22. Ibid., 20.

23. Many *Fanciulla* scholars accept Carner's description of Rance as little more than a Scarpia of the American West. However, the music of this arioso reveals character elements that have no parallel in Scarpia. For further discussion of Rance, see chapters 6 and 7.

24. Ricordi included this piece, Minnie's only freestanding aria in the opera, among the three that were printed in piano-vocal sheet music form shortly after the premiere. The other two were Wallace's "Che faranno i vecchi miei là lontano" and Johnson's "Ch'ella mi creda libero e lontano" (act 3) (see pl. 8). Minnie's aria was also the first musical excerpt from *Fanciulla* to appear in Ricordi's monthly periodical *Ars et labor*. Alessandro Peroni's "easy reduction" appears on pp. 907–8 of the November 1912 edition. Destinn

Example 2.5. Rance: "Minnie, dalla mia casa" (act 1, 67)

Example 2.6. Minnie: "Laggiù nel Soledad" (act 1, 5 mm. before 69)

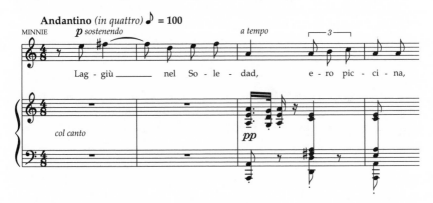

When Minnie and the stranger dance innocently to a tune hummed by the miners, Rance is consumed by envy and enraged by what he perceives to be Minnie's rejection. The music of "Mister Johnson, un valzer?" [Mister Johnson, a waltz?] (ex. 2.7), one of Puccini's stylistically characteristic *ballabile* melodies, recurs later to underscore Minnie and Johnson's increasingly intimate

---

commented publicly on the difficulty of her part in "Emmy Destinn Sang under a Handicap," *New York Times*, 12 December 1910.

Example 2.7. Miners: Waltz (act 1, [86])

(Tutti accompagnano il movimento: il primo quarto battendo leggermente il piede in terra,
e gli altri due quarti battendo lievemente le mani, seguendo così i due che danzano)

conversation; its use after the intervening scene (Castro's capture) both recalls
and forecasts their physical intimacy.

   After Minnie and Johnson's dance, the saloon's relative calm is shattered
by José Castro, a Mexican bandit, who is dragged violently into the Polka and
thrown to the floor by his captors. The audience learns, through a few urgently whispered lines of dialogue between Johnson and the captive, that
Johnson's true identity is that of the gentleman thief, Ramerrez, leader of the
feared Mexican gang described earlier by Ashby.[25] The audience also learns
that Johnson and his lieutenant, Castro, have come to the Polka with the sole
intent of robbing it. In a ruse devised by Castro and communicated covertly
to Johnson, the captured bandit lures the sheriff, Ashby, and all the miners out
of the Polka by promising to lead them to Ramerrez's hiding place. The ruse
succeeds, and Johnson is left alone with Minnie. According to the plan, Johnson is supposed to overpower Minnie and steal the gold during Castro's
diversion; however, he finds himself smitten and unable to carry out the plan.
It is at this point that the conflict between Johnson's two identities begins to
generate dramatic action. By the end of the opera, the consequences of his
warring identities will have wrought havoc in the lives of all the Polka's
denizens. The act ends with Minnie and Johnson alone together in the Polka,

----

25. Though the audience knows that Johnson's real name is Ramerrez, his true identity is revealed onstage only later in act 2. He is referred to throughout the opera as Johnson, and accordingly, most writers
refer to him as Johnson rather than Ramerrez. It is tempting to ignore convention and use his real name
in order to emphasize the dramatic import of the outlaw's imposture. However, to avoid cumbersome com-
posite names or abbreviations such as "Johnson/Ramerrez" or "J/R," we have decided to adhere to convention and use "Johnson" throughout.

both expressing wishes to prolong the intimacy of the moment. Minnie acts on her desire and, in "Se volete venirmi a salutare" [If you want to come by to say hello], invites Johnson to visit her at her mountain cabin that night (ex. 2.8). In addition to presenting the prelude's main themes of love and redemption here, Puccini uses Minnie's theme prominently in the duet as well. The act ends with Minnie's melodic imprint orchestrated as before with majestic strings and brass, suddenly followed by quiet, *divisi* violins along with an instrument specially created for the moment, a fonica (similar in sound to a vibraphone).[26] Simultaneously, fifteen offstage tenors hum Minnie's theme, thus contributing another unusual sonic effect to the painstakingly constructed atmosphere of love and foreboding. This ending both sums up the results of the first act's action and foreshadows that of the second. In Puccini's oeuvre it represents, in Girardi's words, "a completely new conception."[27]

Example 2.8. Minnie: "Se volete venirmi a salutare" (act 1, 5 mm. after 116)

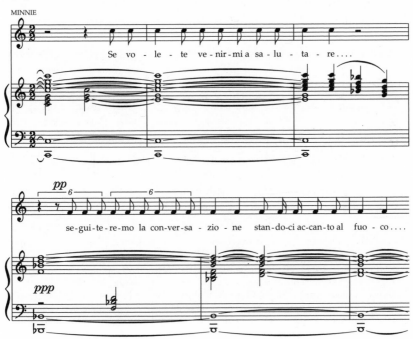

26. Spike Hughes describes the design of *Fanciulla*'s fonica in *Famous Puccini Operas: An Analytical Guide for the Opera-Goer and Armchair Listener*, 2d rev. ed. (New York: Dover, 1972), 155.

27. Girardi, *His International Art*, 307.

Act 2

The set for act 2 is Minnie's simple home, a rustic log cabin tucked away in the mountains and accessible only by way of a single path through the forest. All the action takes place either inside Minnie's cabin or outside her front door. The cabin, far removed from the Polka, is a representation of Minnie herself: unpretentious and warm, yet remote and isolated. At first only Minnie's servant Wowkle (see pl. 9), her boyfriend Billy, and their baby are present. In "Il mio bimbo è grande e piccino" [My baby is both tall and tiny] (ex. 2.9), Puccini uses "Indian" musical conventions that by 1910 had become standard (pentatonic scales, accompaniment by open fifths, low tessitura, narrow melodic range, and a *non vibrato*, monotone vocal style) and thus marks the Native American characters as culturally separate from the rest of the cast.[28] Upon Minnie's entrance, the atmosphere becomes highly charged in anticipation of Johnson's visit; Minnie, Wowkle, and Billy bustle about anxiously, tidying up the cabin. We learn that Minnie has never before entertained a visitor in her home; the fact of her virginity, hinted at in the first act, is thus underscored.[29]

Example 2.9. Wowkle: "Il mio bimbo" (act 2, [1])

28. Chapter 6 contextualizes issues concerning the opera's musical and dramaturgical uses of the racial Other. A thorough treatment of "Indianism" by Puccini's American contemporaries is Beth Levy, " 'In the Glory of the Sunset': Arthur Farwell, Charles Wakefield Cadman, and Indianism in American Music," *Repercussions* 5, nos. 1–2 (1996): 128–83. See also Michael Pisani, "Exotic Sounds in the Native Land: Portrayals of North American Indians in Western Music" (Ph.D. diss., Eastman School of Music, 1996).

29. Puccini's emphasis on Minnie's virginity and appealing rustic simplicity would seem to be related to his relationship with Doria Manfredi, a housemaid of similar physical description and social background who committed suicide after Puccini's wife accused her publicly of being the composer's mistress. The character Liù in *Turandot* may also have a link to this traumatic episode in Puccini's life. See chapter 3 for more information on this and related events, which interrupted work on *Fanciulla* for over a year.

If the Polka is understood to be, in part, symbolic of Minnie's public, nonsexual self, then the cabin symbolizes its opposite—her private, sexual self. This is evident during Minnie's last-minute preparations, in which she changes clothing and feminizes herself hurriedly by removing the pistol from her corset, adorning her hair with flowers, scenting her handkerchief with perfume, and squeezing her hands and feet into tight-fitting gloves and shoes. When all is ready, she dismisses the servants after chastising them for their premarital sexual activity. Wowkle's mature sexuality, represented by her baby, contrasts sharply with Minnie's incipient sexual awakening.

Johnson arrives. He and Minnie converse, and, inevitably, they kiss. "Un bacio, un bacio almen!" [A kiss! One kiss at least!] (ex. 2.10) is perhaps the most frenzied sexual moment in all Puccini and presents a virtual catalog of musical signifiers of desire: singers straining at the top of their ranges, timpani pounding, *agitato* strings, brass *senza sordini,* the whole-tone motif repeated over and over, louder and faster each time. Tension is suddenly released in the resolution of a C-sharp minor chord articulated by harp arpeggios, with

Example 2.10. Johnson: "Un bacio" (act 2, 9 mm. after 26)

Continued on next page

Example 2.10. *(continued)*

(si slancia nelle braccia di Johnson)

tuo!

(S'apre la porta, che sbatte violentemente a più riprese; tutto si agita dal vento che entra furioso e raffiche di neve penetrano nella stanza. Minnie e Johnson abbracciandosi si baciano con grande emozione, dimentichi di tutto e di tutti)

Largo vibratissimo

Ah!

Mosso

stringendo sempre

(La porta si chiude da sè...cessa il tumulto, tutto ritornando alla calma; dal di fuori si odono ancora raffiche di vento)

allargando

Example 2.10. *(continued)*

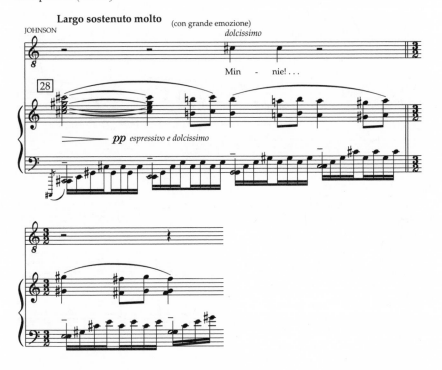

long-held notes in woodwinds and brass over lyrical strings playing the prelude's love theme. The sound of the wind machine reminds us of nature's
elemental and irresistible power. As if by sheer force of the kiss alone, Minnie's cabin door is blown open, and the pure whiteness of a gusting snowstorm obliterates the only barrier between Minnie's closely regulated life and
nature's unpredictable forces. Thus overtaken by gale-force passion, Minnie
is soon forced to confront other, darker forces of nature unleashed by her
relationship with Johnson. Rance, Ashby, and a search party of gun-carrying
miners burst in upon the lovers' idyllic moment, hot on the trail of the escaped bandit. With Johnson hiding in the background, Minnie pretends
that she is alone and listens to the sheriff's shocking revelation that the
Polka's mysterious visitor was, in reality, none other than the outlaw Ramerrez. The passage in which Rance exclaims "Il tuo damo alla danza. . .
era Ramerrez!" [Your dancing partner. . . was Ramerrez!] (ex. 2.11) is punctuated by an unexpected interjection of the prelude's syncopated music directly

Example 2.11. Rance: "Il tuo damo alla danza" (act 2, 4 mm. before 44)

after the word "Ramerrez." In disbelief, Minnie questions the sheriff's sources of information. Rance delights in telling her that the source is Johnson's lover, Nina Micheltorena, the infamous proprietress of the Palmeto brothel.

Devastated by the news of her lover's identity and furious to learn of Nina's role in his life, Minnie is barely able to maintain her composure. Her jealousy had been foreshadowed in the preceding scenes by her insistent, coy questions about the brothel owner; Rance's information only confirmed her worst fears.[30] Reeling from the revelations, yet still wanting to protect Johnson, she lies to the sheriff, telling him that she has neither seen nor heard anything of Johnson since leaving him in the Polka earlier that evening.

As soon as the search party leaves Minnie's cabin, she turns to Johnson and gives vent to her anger and jealousy, ordering him to come out from his hiding place and leave immediately. Minnie sings the command "Vieni fuori!" [Come out!] (ex. 2.12) three times, investing the final high B-flat with her full

30. Civinini and Zangarini, Italian libretto, 50, 57. Given the jealous rages of Puccini's wife, Elvira (with whom, according to Girardi, he shared a "sado-masochistic relationship" [Girardi, *His International Art*, 273]), it is fair to suggest that the composer may have drawn inspiration for Minnie's rage scene from his wife's frequent eruptions.

Example 2.12. Minnie: "Vieni fuori" (act 2, 2 mm. before 50)

fury. From this moment, according to Carner, the individual pathologies of the three leading characters are unleashed. Here Puccini joins his contemporary Richard Strauss in pushing psychological extremes to their musical limits on the opera stage.[31] Johnson complies, but only after trying, in vain, to convince Minnie of his love. First accompanied by orchestral variations of the syncopated theme, in "Una parola sola! Non mi difenderò" [Just one word! I won't defend myself] (ex. 2.13) Johnson recites his family's criminal history to explain his own criminality; the love theme then underscores his claims to sincerity and his shame about his past. A few moments after leaving Minnie's sanctuary, Johnson is spotted and shot by a member of the search party. Bleeding and unable to defend himself, having left behind his gun in the cabin, Johnson has no choice but to crawl back to Minnie for refuge. Minnie has heard the shots and knows instinctively what has happened. She opens the door and takes in her wounded beloved (see pl. 10).

Example 2.13. Johnson: "Una parola sola!" (act 2, 7 mm. before 52)

31. Strauss's operas *Salome* (1906) and *Elektra* (1909) both contain extended passages of uncontrolled emotional display, which Carner links to Puccini. Carner, *Critical Biography*, 466.

Knowing that the search party cannot be far off, Minnie exhorts Johnson to climb up into the loft and hide there until the searchers leave the area. After he is safely hidden, Minnie answers the sheriff's insistent knock upon her door. Though she feigns ignorance of Johnson's whereabouts, Rance is suspicious and lingers, looking for signs of Johnson. Suddenly, animalistically, the sheriff tries to force himself on Minnie. "Son pazzo di te! T'amo, ti voglio!" [I'm crazy about you! I love you, I want you!] (ex. 2.14). She fights him off, then dares him to find Johnson in her cabin. Musically, he and Minnie are evenly matched, with orchestral accompaniments of comparable intensity and sonic presence backing each character's position as they struggle.

Example 2.14. Rance: "Sono pazzo di te!" (act 2, 10 mm. after ⑥④)

Meanwhile, though Johnson remains hidden in the loft, he is unable to staunch the flow of blood from his bullet wound. The blood seeps through the loft's floorboards and onto the sheriff's hand, giving away Johnson's hiding place. Trombones signal Rance's sudden advantage moments before "Guarda... È la!" [Look... He's there!] (ex. 2.15) and dominate the orchestral texture to display the sheriff's newfound power over Minnie.[32] Now at the mercy of the sheriff, Minnie pleads for Johnson's life. In contrast to the arsenal of trombones that accompany Rance's discovery of Johnson, Minnie's "Ch'io v'offro quest'uomo e la mia vita! [I offer you this man and my life!] (ex. 2.16) is backed only by a foreboding, ominous woodwind complement. Orchestrally, she is now no match for Rance. In desperation, she strikes a bargain: if she beats Rance at a game of cards, then Johnson will go free; but if she

---

32. Belasco maintains that this was a true story, told to him by his father. See William Winter, *The Life of David Belasco*, vol. 2, bk. 2 (New York: Moffat, Yard, 1918), 203–5.

Example 2.15. Rance: "È là!" (act 2, 4 mm. before 67)

Example 2.16. Rance and Minnie: "Ch'io v'offro quest'uomo" (act 2, 7 mm. before 73)

loses, she must submit to the sheriff's desires and surrender her lover to him (see pl. 11). As Rance gloats over the terms of a game he feels sure of winning, Minnie distracts him long enough to take certain high cards from the deck and slip them into her stocking; she plans to cheat in order to win Johnson's freedom. The card game is underscored by a nervewracking pizzicato double-bass ostinato and woodwinds reminiscent of Minnie's plea. Snippets of the love theme punctuate the terse passages that pertain to Rance's intentions toward Minnie or Minnie's love for Johnson. Act 2 ends with a sudden resolution of the excruciatingly tense poker game: Minnie manages to pull out the hidden cards from her stocking and wins. Denied the spoils of victory, Rance leaves the cabin abruptly with neither Minnie nor Johnson to show for his evening's work. The orchestral advantage has shifted back to Minnie: now it is her triumphant laughter that is accompanied by trombones and timpani.

Act 3

In contrast to acts 1 and 2, in which almost all action is contained in indoor settings representative of varying levels of civility and decorum, act 3 takes place against the backdrop of the primordial, untamed forests of northern California. At the turn of the twentieth century such landscapes were strongly iconic of a distinctly American sense of freedom that was at once liberated from Old World social strictures, but also limited by lawlessness, physical danger, and societal chaos. The landscape's dense signification provides a complex subtext to all of act 3 (see pl. 12).[33]

According to the deal he has struck with Minnie, Rance cannot reveal Johnson's whereabouts, and the manhunt continues for several days after the card game episode, with miners uselessly combing the area for traces of the outlaw. The irony of the situation is clear: this state of affairs has been brought about by the momentous inversion of Minnie's and Rance's characters. The honest Minnie has, for the first time in her life, acted dishonestly, like Rance, while the corrupt Rance has, for once, acted honorably, like Minnie. The hapless miners absorb the costs of Minnie and Rance's deal.

Johnson is eventually spotted, pursued, and caught by the search party, which has, by this point, turned into an angry and violent mob. "A morte! A morte! Al laccio lo spagnuolo" [To death! Let's hang the Spaniard!] (ex. 2.17).

---

33. See Roderick Nash, *Wilderness and the American Mind* (New Haven: Yale University Press, 1967), and Patricia Nelson Limerick, "Disorientation and Reorientation: The American Landscape Discovered from the West," in *Discovering America: Essays on the Search for an Identity*, ed. David Thelen and Frederick E. Hoxie (Urbana: University of Illinois Press, 1994), 187–215. Chapter 8 contains further discussion of *Fanciulla*'s use of the western American landscape.

Example 2.17. Miners: "A morte!" (act 3, 15)

The miners mistakenly believe that Johnson and his gang are responsible for recent murders in the area. As the mob prepares to hang him from the nearest tree, Johnson denies a role in the murders, admits to the miners' accusations of thievery, and proclaims the sincerity of his love for Minnie. He asks them not to tell Minnie of his capture. "Ch'ella mi creda libero e lontano" [Let her think that I'm free and far away] (ex. 2.18) provided Caruso with his only solo aria of the opera.[34] As in Minnie's act 1 "Laggiù nel Soledad" and Rance's "Minnie, dalla mia casa," the opportunity for vocal display is very brief; Puccini did not want to interrupt the plot's forward motion for too long. However, it is the lyrical high point of *Fanciulla* in terms of a traditionally affective aria that is delivered conventionally by one of the leading characters.

Example 2.18. Johnson: "Ch'ella mi creda" (act 3, 26)

____

34. This song was popular among Italian soldiers in World War I (1914–18). Carner, *Critical Biography*, 463, n. 11.

Example 2.19. Minnie's entrance (act 3, 29)

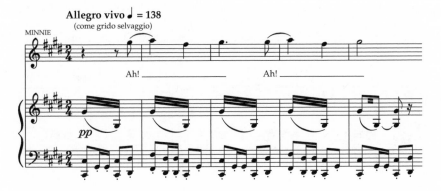

Example 2.20. Rance: "Impiccatelo!" (act 3, 30)

Just as the noose slips around his neck, the moment of musical repose is shattered violently as Minnie charges to the rescue on horseback with a pistol between her teeth. "Ah! Ah!" (ex. 2.19). Hurtling forward, her theme, now in a galloping variation, projects her commandingly into the scene. Minnie argues passionately for her lover's release, while Rance, with equal passion, demands his death. "Impiccatelo! [Hang him!] (ex. 2.20). Her theme returns with a sense of invincibility and near-maniacal urgency. This scene, completely fabricated by Puccini, Zangarini, and Civinini, reaches its climax as Minnie, after pleading shamelessly with the miners in "Non vi fu mai chi disse 'Basta!'" [No one ever said "Stop!"] (ex. 2.21), wins Johnson's release. Coming

Example 2.21. Minnie: "Non vi fu mai chi disse 'Basta'" (act 3, 8 mm. after 37)

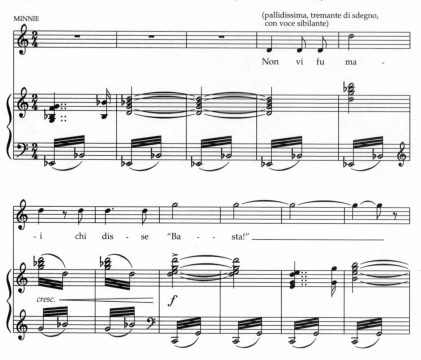

full circle musically and dramaturgically by echoing the Bible scene of act 1, Minnie reminds the miners of the sentiment of Psalm 51 sentiment in "Non v'è al mondo peccatore cui non s'apra una via di redenzione" [There's not a sinner in the world who cannot open himself to redemption] (ex. 2.22) and uses the same redemption theme to do so.[35]

At this moment, Minnie is at her most compelling; she is a charismatic, quasi-sacred figure who is able to persuade the mob to abandon its agenda of vengeance through a message of forgiveness, love, and the promise of redemption (see pl. 13). She presents herself not only as Johnson's divine intercessor, but also as the miners' idealized mother figure. Thus wrapped in the cloak of the universal mother, Minnie heals the first act's familial rupture, making it unthinkable for the miners to act against her or Johnson. "Le tue parole sono di Dio" [Your words are from God] (ex. 2.23). Only Rance insists

---

35. The Bible scene and redemption plot are discussed at length in chapter 7.

Example 2.22. Minnie and miners: "Non v'è al mondo peccatore cui non s'apra una via di redenzione" (act 3, 3 mm. before 44)

(Johnson s'inginocchia commosso, bacia il lembo della veste di Minnie mentre essa pone la mano sulla testa di lui quasi benedicendolo)

Example 2.23. Sonora: "Le tue parole sono di Dio" (act 3, 44)

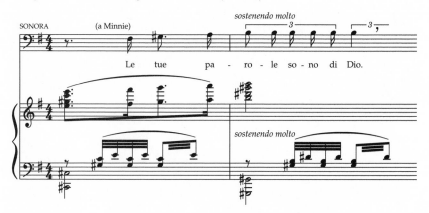

Example 2.24. Finale: "Addio mia California" (act 3, 11 mm. after 44)

on carrying out the hanging. The miners ignore the sheriff's commands, untie Johnson, and release him to Minnie. Minnie and Johnson depart the scene, riding into the vast and uncertain forested space. Rance and the boys of the Cloudy Mountain outpost bid goodbye as Minnie and Johnson are enveloped by the dense, cold, uncharted wilderness. We hear "Mai più ritornerai, mai più. . . Addio, mia California!" [You'll never come back, never . . . Farewell, my California] (ex. 2.24) as the lovers fade from view.

PART II

Creating the Opera

CHAPTER THREE

Puccini and La fanciulla, 1903–7

Most historical treatments of *La fanciulla del West* begin the year following *Madama Butterfly,* when Puccini began to search for a subject for his next opera. Stung by criticism that his operas had become formulaic, Puccini planned to strike out on a new musical path. He sought a libretto whose story line would represent a break from such earlier works as *Manon Lescaut, La Bohème, Tosca,* and *Madama Butterfly.* The well-known Puccini biographers Mosco Carner, Charles Osborne, William Weaver, and William Ashbrook, among others, describe the following stages leading to the creation of *La fanciulla del West:* Puccini's discovery in New York of the stage play *Girl of the Golden West;* his negotiations with its author, David Belasco, for rights to the play; and his three-year struggle to compose the opera in the face of a widely publicized scandal and creative differences with his librettists.[1] Concluding these narratives are accounts of the world premiere and surveys of the mixed reaction of critics to the opera. The present discussion of *Fanciulla* adds new information to the standard chronology in the form of newly available letters and other documents from Italian and American sources.

The addition of this material invites revision of the standard view of the opera's creation in four principal ways. First, the inclusion of the 1907–10

---

1. William Ashbrook, *The Operas of Puccini* (New York: Oxford University Press, 1968; reprint, with foreword by Roger Parker, Ithaca: Cornell University Press, 1985); Carner, *Critical Biography;* Charles Osborne, *The Complete Operas of Puccini: A Critical Guide* (New York: Da Capo Press, 1981); William Weaver, *Puccini: The Man and his Music* (New York: E. P. Dutton, 1977).

letters from Puccini to Carlo Zangarini reinstates Zangarini as the opera's main librettist, illuminates his working relationship with Puccini, and places him squarely in the narrative from beginning to end. Zangarini emerges from the shadows as a figure of considerable importance in Bologna and Milan's musical and literary circles—an image that contrasts sharply with the conventional portrayal of him as a journeyman writer. Second, access to Puccini's lucrative contract with the Metropolitan Opera and other important information from their archives allows us to consider the magnitude of the Metropolitan's financial risk in producing its first world premiere of an opera by a major composer. Negotiations preceding the contract and the terms of the contract itself generated much public discussion of the cultural value of *Fanciulla's* premiere and are important elements of its history. Third, a survey of newspaper accounts surrounding *Fanciulla's* premiere exposes the machinations of the New York press not only in shaping reaction to the opera, but in using the occasion of the premiere to establish itself as a new arbiter of international taste. Incorporating into the chronology the letters to Zangarini, the contract, and contemporaneous newspaper accounts, as well as new interpretations and primary sources, results in an expanded history of the creation, production, and reception of *La fanciulla del West*—a story that begins in 1907 with Puccini's choice of a subject and ends three years later with American and European reactions to the premiere.

The Search Begins

Puccini's first visit to New York in January 1907 was to oversee the staging of the first American performances of *Manon Lescaut* and *Madama Butterfly* at the Metropolitan Opera. The composer welcomed the opportunity to add these two operas to his *La Bohème* and *Tosca,* which were already staples of the Metropolitan's repertoire.[2] Through these activities Puccini established a solid, collegial relationship with the Metropolitan and laid the groundwork for his next opera, *La fanciulla del West,* to be produced there three years later.

Although reluctant to travel across the Atlantic, Puccini understood the financial gains to be made in the burgeoning American market: success at the Metropolitan meant increased fame worldwide and more demand for his work. Persuaded by the Metropolitan's generous offer of eight thousand dollars for a month's visit, Puccini made plans for the long ocean journey.[3] In a

2. Puccini had received the invitation to visit New York in late 1906 from the Metropolitan's impresario, Heinrich Conried, who met the composer in Paris during the French premiere of *Madama Butterfly.*

3. George R. Marek, *Puccini: A Biography* (New York: Simon and Schuster, 1951), 239.

letter from Paris to his sister Nitteti on 14 November 1906, Puccini wrote: "In January I am going to New York for *Manon, Butterfly, Tosca.* . . . But, first I shall return to Italy if only for a few days. I have to come, besides, for clothes. I must get a fur-lined coat because it is cold in New York. I ought not to have accepted the invitation to America, but now that I have, *il faut y aller."* [4] From Paris he also wrote to one of his most trusted and adored friends, Sybil Seligman (see pl. 14),[5] of his initial reluctance to venture to America: "I've had a letter from Heinrich Conried asking me to leave on December 15th!—I don't want to go!" [6]

After a brief trip to Italy to gather his personal effects for the long journey to America, Puccini and his wife Elvira (see pl. 15) set sail on the *Kaiserin Auguste Victoria* from Cherbourg, France, for a rough crossing of the Atlantic in early January 1907. Although the ship was comfortable, the journey was unpleasant. Elvira was seasick, and Puccini, ill humored, struggled with his diabetic diet. The ship was delayed for a few days off the coast due to heavy fog and finally docked at six o'clock in the evening on 18 January 1907, the evening of the Metropolitan Opera's premiere of *Manon Lescaut.*[7] The Puccinis were rushed from dockside to the theater, just in time for the eight o'clock curtain. The audience reaction to the opera was enthusiastic. Puccini was extremely pleased with the performance and praised the singers, particularly Enrico Caruso and Lina Cavalieri. In a letter to Seligman he called the evening "a really big success." [8]

The same exuberance did not hold for the Metropolitan's first performance of *Madama Butterfly.*[9] Puccini wrote Tito Ricordi, the son of his publisher,

---

4. Adami, *Letters,* 162–63.

5. Puccini's correspondence with Sybil Seligman spans the last twenty years of Puccini's life and includes some seven hundred letters. Seligman's son, Vincent, presents a detailed account of the friendship between the composer and his mother in *Puccini among Friends* (New York: Macmillan, 1938). Seligman believes that the earliest of Puccini's letters to his mother was the acceptance of a dinner invitation dated 22 October 1904 (65). They had first met after *Butterfly's* premiere at Brescia at the home of their mutual friend, Paolo Tosti, music master to the royal family and Sibyl Seligman's singing teacher. The daughter of the concert pianist Zilla Beddington and the wife of the London banker David Seligman, she was an aficionado of Italian opera and made frequent visits to Italy.

6. Seligman, *Puccini among Friends,* 93.

7. The lead roles were sung by Lina Cavalieri (1874–1944) as Manon, Enrico Caruso (1873–1921) as Des Grieux, and Antonio Scotti (1866–1936) as Lescaut.

8. Seligman, *Puccini among Friends,* 116.

9. In 1906 an English-language version of *Madama Butterfly* toured the United States, with Tito Ricordi supervising the premiere in Washington, D.C., and many of the opera's other coast-to-coast performances, which had been arranged by the impresario Henry Savage. *Butterfly* was performed more than two hundred times during the six-month tour. In mid-November the Savage Opera Company opened at the Garden Theatre in New York to an enthusiastic audience: "that the production was worthy, in the fullest sense,

Giulio Ricordi, that the press and public praised the production of the opera, "but not so as to please me. It was a performance without poetry. . . . Nobody knew anything."[10] He was unhappy with the soprano Geraldine Farrar, feeling that her voice was weak.[11] He believed that the conductor, Arturo Vigna, had not controlled the orchestra, and that Eugene Dufriche, the stage manager, had not adequately studied the mise-en-scène. Despite his disappointment, Puccini enjoyed New York for a few weeks following the production of *Butterfly* and became popular with chic society, accepting numerous invitations to parties and receptions.[12] In addition to sightseeing and shopping with Elvira, he spent time with the Metropolitan singers Cavalieri and Antonio Scotti attending the best of New York theater.[13]

Puccini saw numerous plays, including several by Belasco: *The Music Master, The Rose of the Rancho,* and *The Girl of the Golden West.*[14] Puccini had first heard about *The Girl* from the Italian nobleman Pietro Antinori[15] while the composer was still in Paris on his way to America. Antinori, who was just returning from New York, urged Puccini to see the new drama, which had been a great success for some months at the Belasco Theatre.[16] As Belasco's biographer William Winter wrote:

---

of the standards of grand opera, was as evident in the audience as it was on stage." "*Madam[a] Butterfly* Captivates New York Audience," *Musical America* 5, no. 1 (17 November 1906): 5.

10. Adami, *Letters,* 168.

11. The lead roles in *Madama Butterfly* were sung by Farrar (1882–1967) as Butterfly, Caruso as Pinkerton, and Scotti as Sharpless.

12. A much-repeated but illuminating anecdote about Puccini's activities during his first New York visit involves an admirer who frequented his hotel daily offering him $500 for a few lines of music. Each time, the composer refused. However, Puccini had found a spectacular motorboat he wanted to add to his growing collection for use on Lake Massaciuccoli at Torre del Lago. He quickly decided to give the autograph hunter a few bars of Musetta's waltz from *La Bohème* in exchange for the money to buy the vessel, which he immediately shipped to Italy.

13. William Ashbrook notes that Puccini and Cavalieri, renowned for her physical beauty, were romantically linked by "malicious gossip of the day . . . but, what basis there was for this is impossible to tell." Ashbrook, *Operas of Puccini,* 133.

14. *The Girl*'s premiere took place at the Belasco Theatre in Pittsburgh on 3 October 1905 and was produced in New York on 14 November 1905 at the Belasco Theatre on West Forty-second Street. During his fifty-year association with the New York theater, Belasco directed ninety-five plays and produced and/or directed seventy-two. He collaborated on nearly two hundred plays during his illustrious career. America's frontier was depicted in other Belasco productions, including *The Girl I Left behind Me* (1893), *The Warrens of Virginia* (1907), and *The Rose of the Rancho* (1906), "but none of these surpassed the picturesque realism hailed by critics and audiences in *The Girl of the Golden West.*" Marker, *David Belasco,* 6–139.

15. Antinori was a member of the well-known Tuscan winemaking family.

16. Belasco's *Girl* included selections of American music, including "Wait for the Wagon," "O Susanna," and "Old Dan Tucker," which may have helped to interest Puccini in the play. For further discussion see chapter 6.

During the season of 1906–07 Belasco's friend the Italian musical composer Puccini, who desired to write an opera on a characteristically
American subject, made a visit to our country for the purpose of select-
ing one. While in New York, in January, 1907, he attended performances
by Miss Frances Starr in *The Rose of the Rancho* and by Miss [Blanche]
Bates in *The Girl*.[17]

Winter was inaccurate: Puccini had not decided to write on a "characteristically American" subject, or on any subject, for that matter. He was still engaged in an exasperating search for his next libretto. In correspondence with
Tito Ricordi on 18 February 1907, Puccini agonized about his plight:

> The world is expecting an opera from me, and it is high time it were
> ready. We've had enough now of *Bohème, Butterfly* & Co.! Even I am
> sick of them! But I really am greatly worried! I am tormented not for
> myself alone, but for you, for Signor Giulio, and for the house of
> Ricordi to whom I wish to give and must give an opera that is sure to
> be good.
>
> Here too I have been on the lookout for subjects, but there is noth-
> ing possible, or rather, complete enough. I have found good ideas in
> Belasco, but nothing definite, solid, or complete.
>
> The "West" attracts me as a background, but in all the plays which
> I have seen I have found only some scenes here and there that are good.
> There is never a clear, simple line of development; just a hotch-potch
> and sometimes in very bad taste and very *vieux jeu*.
>
> . . . My dear fellow, I have been torturing my brains and my spirit. . . .
>
> In short, I assure you that my life is not all roses, and this state of
> mental excitement is making my existence nervous and my humor most
> melancholy.[18]

17. Winter, *Life of David Belasco*, 213. Dieter Schickling states that there is evidence that during Puccini's
1907 trip to the United States (18 January to 28 February), the composer may have visited California between 21 and 27 February. Schickling substantiates this hypothesis by noting that during work on the opera's third act, Puccini gave Zangarini a photograph of California's giant redwood trees, which the composer may have taken himself during this possible journey to the West Coast. Dieter Schickling, *Giacomo
Puccini: Biographie* (Stuttgart: Deutsche Verlags-Anstalt, 1989), 227. It seems highly unlikely that Puccini
would have made such a difficult trip to California given not only the short time period in which it could
have taken place, but also the limits of transcontinental transportation in 1907.

18. Adami, *Letters*, 169–70.

A Plethora of Subjects

Even before Puccini began seriously considering *The Girl*, he spent three long, tedious years looking at a number of other subjects. including Victor Hugo's book *Notre-Dame de Paris*, two Oscar Wilde plays (*The Duchess of Padua* and *A Florentine Tragedy*), several works (*La rosa di Cipro* and *Parisina*) by Gabriele D'Annunzio, the most flamboyant and fashionable Italian poet of the time, and a trilogy of one-act operas based on the short stories of Maxim Gorky.

For the first time since he completed *Madama Butterfly*, Puccini gave serious consideration to a new subject, the drama *Conchita*, based on the controversial novel *La femme et le pantin* (The Woman and the Puppet) by the French writer Pierre Loüys.[19] He was bolstered by the enthusiasm of his mentor, Ricordi, who believed the work could become another success along the lines of Bizet's *Carmen*.[20] In addition, the pressure his publisher put on the composer to make a decision and begin a new opera posthaste had a great influence on him. The subject matter was highly controversial at the time owing to the explicit nature of the sexual interaction between the characters. The story involves Conchita Perez, a Spanish prostitute who works in a cigar factory in Seville, and the wealthy Matteo, whom she mentally tortures by refusing him her sexual favors. With the intent of driving Matteo to suicide, Conchita attempts to humiliate him by simulating sexual intercourse in his presence with a young local boy. Instead, Matteo reaches a state of frenzied insanity and brutally beats her, awakening an erotic reaction in Conchita as she gives herself to him in sexual servitude.

At first Puccini was attracted by the psychological ambivalence of love and hate in this perverse relationship, a subject that some Puccini biographers believe reveals itself in his last opera, *Turandot*.[21] However, Puccini was bothered by the controversial nature of the drama about "the Spanish whore," as he called *Conchita*. He wrote to Seligman from Torre del Lago in the fall of 1906, "I'm rather preoccupied about *Conchita*—or rather, I am feeling weaker on the subject! What frightens me is her character, and the plot of the play— and then all the characters seem to me unlovable, and that is a very bad thing on the stage."[22] Puccini ultimately rejected *Conchita*; as he wrote to his friend

19. Puccini is thought to have first heard about the subject as early as fall 1903. Carner, *Critical Biography*, 165.

20. Ibid., 166.

21. Seligman, *Puccini among Friends*, 86.

22. Ibid., 88.

Carlo Clausetti,[23] "I am still in distress over the libretto. I am not doing *La femme et le pantin* anymore."[24]

Three years after the premiere of *Butterfly*, Puccini's search for an opera subject continued unabated. Even after seeing Belasco's *Girl*, he was not convinced it was the right subject for his next opera. He wrote Tito Ricordi that he was going to have an interview with Belasco before he left New York but did not "hope [expect] much from it."[25] His comments to Ricordi reflected his frustration with the ongoing search for the perfect libretto. Nevertheless, his thoughts kept returning to the play he had seen in New York; the exotic element of the American West in combination with an enormously successful Broadway play had been seared into the Italian composer's heart and mind. He would not and could not forget about it.

Prior to departing from America, Puccini gave a number of newspaper interviews, including one with the *New York Times* in which he outlined how he felt about Belasco's play:

> "I saw his [Belasco's] play *The Girl of the Golden West*, and found a heroine very naïve and refreshing. I find truth and sincerity in the American drama.
>
> "I haven't started a new score—at least, not on any definite idea. I have not found the subject, which appeals to me. I haven't even commenced to work on *La Femme et le pantin*. I have doubts if the American public would accept that after the treatment *Salome* recently received.
>
> "Shakespere [*sic*] I am afraid of. I have thought of *King Lear*, but who could ever act it among the singers?"
>
> "Why don't you take an Italian epic subject, as Wagner took German epic subjects?," he was asked [by the *New York Times* reporter]. [Puccini answered] "Curiously enough, Italian subjects don't interest me. *Benvenuto Cellini* I thought at one time would make an opera, but the love interest is too widely scattered!"[26]

On his way back to Italy, Puccini wrote the American playwright from the Hôtel de Londres in Paris on 7 March 1907:

---

23. Carlo Clausetti (1869–1943) was an Italian composer and businessman and one of Puccini's most faithful friends and supporters. He was the son of Pietro Clausetti, whose music-publishing firm was bought out by Ricordi in 1864. Clausetti became a director of Ricordi after the resignation of Tito Ricordi in 1920.

24. Gara, *Carteggi pucciniani*, no. 501, p. 341.

25. Ibid., no. 500, p. 339.

26. Marek, *Puccini*, 243. Taken from an interview in the *New York Times*, 28 February 1907.

Dear Mr. Belasco:

I was exceedingly sorry to have left New York without seeing you
once more. I have been thinking so much of your play, "The Girl of the
Golden West," and I cannot help thinking that with certain
modifications it might easily be adapted for the operatic stage. Would
you be good enough to send me a copy of the play, to Torre del Lago,
Pisa, Italia? I could then have it translated, study it more carefully, and
write to you my further impressions.

I cannot express to you all the admiration I feel for your great talent,
and how much impressed I was at the drama I saw at your theatre.

With kindest regards, and hoping to hear from you soon.

Yours sincerely,
Giacomo Puccini[27]

In April, after he returned to Torre del Lago, he told Seligman that Belasco
was sending him a copy of the play so that it could be translated into Italian.
Puccini's English was extremely poor, and up to this point he had only a general idea of the story. Nevertheless, he confided to Ricordi that he was still
struggling in his seemingly never-ending quest for a subject:

I receive story outlines and librettos daily, all second-hand junk . . . in
short, I'll frankly tell you that this inactive life is annoying to me. I have
so much energy . . . what can I do? Who is there that can give me the
one great idea? My God, what a wretched world the theater is, whether
Italian or foreign. But, I don't despair: when there is faith, one succeeds.[28]

This tortuous personal indecision drove Puccini to resurrect an old subject, the story of the French queen Marie Antoinette, which he had first considered while composing *Tosca.* He chose Luigi Illica as the librettist for his
version of the queen's well-known history.[29] The story of Puccini's relationship with Illica, while working on *Marie Antoinette,* is an excellent illustration of
how the composer dealt with his librettists during the creation of an opera and

27. Winter, *Life of David Belasco,* 214.

28. Gara, *Carteggi pucciniani,* no. 502, p. 342.

29. Luigi Illica (1857–1919) and Giuseppe Giacosa (1847–1906) were the librettists for Puccini's *La
Bohème, Tosca,* and *Madama Butterfly.* After Giacosa's death Illica was unable to write a libretto that met with
Puccini's approval. For a detailed account of the chronicle of "Marie Antoinette," which lasted from November 1897 to summer 1907, see Marcello Conati, "'Maria Antonietta' ovvero 'L'Austriaca': Un soggetto
abbandonato da Puccini," *Rivista italiana di musicologia* 33 (1998): 89–181.

illuminates the discourse and discord between Zangarini and Puccini reflected later in the 1907–10 letters. Marie Antoinette was a subject vigorously supported by Ricordi, who felt it was the type of material from which a serious opera could be created. Despite his publisher's advice, Puccini vacillated during this period between two dramatically different subjects: the renowned Queen of France was wrestling a spirited and tenacious heroine of the American West for Puccini's heart and for a place in the history of Italian opera. Puccini's correspondence with Seligman in early May 1907 indicates his interest in *Marie Antoinette.* He recounts to her that a story about the last days of the queen "seems to me a grand one!"[30] In this letter he continues by describing his view of the plot:

> A soul in torment—First act, prison; second act, the trial; third act, the execution—three short acts, stirring enough to take one's breath away. I'm absolutely taken up with this idea of mine—and I have found a title which seems to me fitting and appropriate because I couldn't call it *Marie Antoinette,* seeing that it only deals with the one episode of her tragic death. The title is: *The Austrian Woman*—what do you think of it?[31]

Although Marie Antoinette would never become the subject of a Puccini opera, Illica spent countless hours—in fact, years—creating a vast scenario that the composer kept cutting and refining until the libretto concluded with the three short acts Puccini described in his letter to Seligman. The composer was a difficult taskmaster, insisting on the right to make any changes he deemed necessary to produce a successful opera. Perhaps this iron-fisted approach originated in the young composer's relationship with Ferdinando Fontana, the librettist used for his first two operas, *Le villi* and *Edgar.*[32] Clearly, Puccini's interaction with Fontana shaped his future collaborations. Michele Girardi explains:

> *Edgar* was the only real failure of his career. Without suitable drama no musical talent can thrive; in this sense the lesson was very useful to Puccini, since it made him understand the necessity of choosing subjects

---

30. Seligman, *Puccini among Friends,* 125.

31. Ibid.

32. Fontana (1850–1919) was an Italian poet and dramatist. Amilcare Ponchielli, Puccini's teacher at the Milan conservatory from 1882 to 1883, introduced the two men.

himself, and defining the dramatic structures of the libretto in advance, before setting it to music. He would never again make a similar mistake.[33]

Puccini's difficulties with librettists continued to plague him throughout the remainder of his career, fueled by his obsession with "controlling every aspect of his creative output."[34] After the splendid success of his third opera, *Manon Lescaut*— cast and composer received more than thirty curtain calls at the premiere[35]—Puccini joined with Illica and Giacosa to write *La Bohème*. It is widely accepted that this exceptional duo wrote Puccini's three best librettos—*Bohème, Tosca,* and *Madama Butterfly*. But there was intense friction between Puccini and these two outstanding librettists. Giacosa threatened to quit several times and renounce all payment for his work on *Bohème*. Only after hearing excerpts from the finished work did Giacosa understand "the reason for his [Puccini's] tyranny over verses and accents."[36]

Later, when composing *Fanciulla*, Puccini had a number of disagreements with Zangarini, which resulted in his insistence that Zangarini work with a collaborator (see chapter 4). The following letters illustrate the explosive relationship between Illica and Puccini while the composer was still deciding whether to use *Marie Antoinette* or *Fanciulla* as the subject of his next opera. The trouble began when Puccini first wrote to Ricordi to vent his frustration:

> As for M[arie] A[ntoinette] I am not giving up on it, but have you read Illica's first act? Tell me how I ought to contain myself, please. Its extreme conciseness and form mean that we have to give [him] some rather strong criticism. Collaboration is a necessity. How should I tell him? I await some advice from you.[37]

Shortly after this missive to Ricordi, Puccini wasted no time in writing to Illica to convey his thoughts about *Marie Antoinette:*

33. Girardi, *His International Art*, 55.

34. Helen Greenwald, "Realism on the Opera Stage: Belasco, Puccini, and the California Sunset," in *Opera in Context: Essays on Historical Staging from the Late Renaissance to the Time of Puccini*, ed. Mark A. Radice (Portland, Ore.: Amadeus Press, 1998), 282.

35. Giacosa, Illica, Leoncavallo, Domenico Oliva, Marco Praga, Ricordi, and Puccini himself all contributed to *Manon's* libretto. It was agreed that no names would appear on the printed libretto. Ashbrook notes that "eventually there were eight. In November 1922 Puccini asked Adami to supply a line to replace one of the textual repetitions in *Manon's* Act 4 aria." Ashbrook, *Operas of Puccini*, 32, n. 47.

36. Carner, *Critical Biography*, 96.

37. Gara, *Carteggi pucciniani*, no. 522, pp. 353–54.

Having to write and rewrite is not a pleasant task; and since you yourself told me, on the day you decided to do the work that I proposed, that you would take on the collaborator I desired, I am telling you that it is now time to for you to choose someone, so as to share the labor as was done in the good old times with poor Giacosa. Do answer me.[38]

When Illica answered the composer he "was at the end of his tether. . . . He inveighed against art, against Marie Antoinette, and against Puccini with the passionate vehemence known to all his friends."[39] He wrote:

I have never spoken of collaborations, therefore you . . . are dreaming. . . . The first act of *Marie Antoinette* . . . was created the way you wanted it, almost as if you dictated it to me . . . and I still have the manuscript copy with your notes on it in your fountain-pen. So what you are writing now is a "new story." . . . But since no contract binds us, we are completely free. . . . For if I wanted to be impertinent, I could . . . answer you by advising you to take a good musician as a collaborator.[40]

Obviously Puccini disliked the harsh criticism that he, a world-renowned composer, should take on a musical collaborator. He answered with sarcasm: "Regarding what you write and advise me about getting a musical collaborator . . . I ask you, which are the operas that bring you the most profit and are most in demand around the world? The ones with a libretto by Illica and Giacosa and music by just one Puccini.[41] After the bitter exchange in these letters, even Ricordi finally acknowledged that the composer had all but guillotined *Marie Antoinette*. Although Puccini was still toying with the idea of an opera about the French queen throughout the spring and summer of 1907, the one recurring thought in his mind was Belasco's story of the American West. Seligman's opinion was the determining factor in his final decision, largely because he trusted and respected her judgment: she believed that Marie Antoinette, as a subject, would be "stale" and "hackneyed"[42] and unable to provide him with the proper inspiration for another great opera. In late May Puccini made a fateful trip to Britain, where, as Vincent Seligman describes,

38. Ibid., no. 523, p. 354.
39. Adami, *Letters*, 227.
40. Gara, *Carteggi pucciniani*, no. 524, p. 354.
41. Ibid., no. 525, p. 355.
42. Seligman, *Puccini among Friends*, 131.

"my mother undoubtedly took advantage of Puccini's visit to London to press the claims of *The Girl of the Golden West*. Before he had left, the battle was more than half won. It was she who commissioned the translator."[43] This move was critical in his final decision to choose *The Girl* and defer action on *Marie Antoinette*.

During the spring of 1907 Puccini began his three-year correspondence with Carlo Zangarini (1874–1943). These letters chronicle the long and arduous task of transforming *The Girl of the Golden West* into *La fanciulla del West*. Zangarini, the man Puccini chose for his first and main librettist, was an author, poet, and journalist from the city of Bologna, in the region of Emilia-Romagna in northern Italy. Tito Ricordi had suggested him for several reasons: he spoke English and was well respected in Italian literary and musical circles. Furthermore, his mother was an American, born in Colorado, and it was assumed that Zangarini would feel comfortable with an American topic. The composer's initial encounter with the poet was at the office of Casa Ricordi in Milan and was reported by the *Corriere della sera:*

> Puccini has recently had Carlo Zangarini as his guest at his favorite villa at Torre del Lago. . . . Puccini met Zangarini during a reading by Carlo of one of his works at Casa Ricordi. Now Carlo Zangarini, who had the task of adapting David Belasco's drama into a libretto, has delivered his work to the maestro, who hopes to have the music ready by the end of the coming year [1908]. The work will be in three acts, and, it appears that the last act will be different from the original English [play].
>
> The scene is California's famous El Dorado region during the gold fever in the year 1849.[44]

Another newspaper, *La sera*, printed an explanation of why Zangarini was chosen instead of Illica. The public wanted to know the reasons for the break-up of the successful partnership of librettist and composer:

> There has been much talk of the Puccini-Illica break-up, as the latter's name is associated (along with that of Giuseppe Giacosa) with the most recent works of the illustrious Maestro from Lucca. . . . It's all true.

43. Ibid.

44. *Corrierre della sera* (Milan), 7 November 1907. Appendix B contains the Italian texts of selected extracts; for this quote, see appendix B, no. 1.

Luigi Illica did not think it suitable to his own artistic dignity to collaborate with anyone else on the libretto of Puccini's new opera. As long
as it was with Giacosa, Illica did not object. Quite the contrary . . . but
once Giuseppe Giacosa was gone, Luigi Illica, who remains not only the
most prolific, but the best of our working librettists, thought a collaboration was unnecessary.

So that is why the librettist for Puccini's new opera is Carlo Zangarini; an important young poet of serious merit, who has no need of   .
being introduced to the public.[45]

Illica's break with Puccini was a tremendous boost for Zangarini's career. The
Italian press used the opportunity to write a number of articles about him
and his new association with the famous composer. Although it was a unique
chance for Zangarini to enhance his professional reputation, he was about to
embark upon one of the most difficult challenges of his life. As Vincent Seligman commented: "I do not know with what hopes, or with what fears, the
new poet approached his task; it was scarcely to be expected that he, a new-
comer, would be able to succeed, where his two illustrious predecessors had
so often failed, in completely satisfying his exacting task-master at the first
attempt."[46]

Puccini's Letters to Zangarini

The first letter to Zangarini in the Marvin Gray Collection (hereafter cited
as MGC) is dated 15 May 1907 and refers to the successful arrangements being made for Puccini to receive the original Italian translation of the play
from Seligman. Written from the Milan apartment the composer kept at Via
Verdi 4, close to the office of Ricordi and to La Scala, the letter precedes his
trip to London in late May of 1907, during which Seligman made her strong
case on behalf of *The Girl.* It appears to be the first letter indicating that Puccini
was serious about moving ahead with the Belasco play. He made arrangements
to meet with Zangarini to begin working on the libretto, even though a formal agreement with the poet would not be completed until the summer. The
correspondence is short, but its tone is urgent. Puccini was anxious to get
to work:

45. *La sera,* 2–3 December 1907; see appendix B, no. 2.
46. Seligman, *Puccini among Friends,* 143.

Via Verdi 4, Milan
15 May 1907

My dear Zangarini,
The expected word has come—when can I see you?
Greetings
G. Puccini (MGC 1)[47]

On his journey home to Torre del Lago, Puccini stopped in Milan, where he sent a poem to his English muse on 26 June indicating that he had not yet made a firm decision.[48]

Dearest Syb [Seligman],
I'm far from sorry
To leave at once for rural Torre,
There to bare my manly form
To the sun, the rain, the storm;
While my Maiden from the West
Lies uneasy on my chest,
And I study "Con amore"
France's Revolution story.[49]

However, days later, upon his return to Torre, he wrote Seligman, "I am waiting anxiously for *The Girl;* I've signed an agreement with the poet, who is awaiting it no less anxiously." In mid-July, he wrote her that he was "quite certain that *The Girl* is the opera I am going to do!"[50] During this decisive period, Seligman was important to him in many ways; not just as one of his most trusted friends, but also because, unlike Puccini, she spoke both Italian and English. In anticipation of launching into the new project, he asked her to help him locate American music of the 1850s as well as some Native American music. He wanted to understand better the workings of a vastly different culture, particularly the atmosphere of the Wild West and the California gold rush.

The first translations, which included acts 1 and 2 of the Belasco play, arrived at Torre on 8 July. The translations of the last two acts arrived shortly thereafter, and by 14 July Puccini had reorganized acts 3 and 4 of the play into a single

47. See appendix A for full Italian text. Puccini's letters contain highly idiosyncratic punctuation such as dashes, double dashes, and ellipses in place of periods. In most cases, we have replaced these with periods. Likewise, his underscored passages have been transcribed in italics.

48. Puccini often wrote letters in poetic form.

49. Seligman, *Puccini among Friends,* 136. Translation by David Seligman, Vincent's father.

50. Ibid., 138.

act. A man with astute theatrical instincts, he sensed that the two acts of the play needed more dramatic flair as well as shortening. Part of his initial reaction may have come from his still-bitter memory of the disastrous premiere of *Madama Butterfly* at La Scala in 1904, which some critics felt was too long (the first act was fifty-five minutes, the second, approximately ninety). As a result, Puccini had reworked the *Butterfly* score extensively. After reviewing the translations of *The Girl of the Golden West*, Puccini wrote to Giulio Ricordi on 15 July, informing him that he had written to the company's New York agent, George Maxwell, instructing him to negotiate an agreement with Belasco for this new opera. Puccini also stated that if Belasco's terms were "impossible" he "should go no further." [51] In the same letter, Puccini told Ricordi that much work needed to be done to make the play into a viable libretto, including rewriting acts 3 and 4 entirely. He also asked him to send the play to Zangarini immediately.

The composer wrote his next letter to Zangarini just after corresponding with Ricordi. In it Puccini underscores his desire to change the last two acts completely. He also mentions his dissatisfaction with the Italian translations sent to him from London. In addition, he requests that Seligman send him Belasco's original Broadway version of the play. He wishes to send it on to the poet, whose knowledge of English was initially of great comfort to Puccini:

> Torre del Lago, Toscana
> 22 July 1907
>
> Dear Zangarini:
>
> I think that Mr. Giulio sent you the badly translated version. I will send you the original as soon as I have received it.
>
> The 3rd and 4th [acts] are worth . . . very little, but it seems to me that there is substance to carry it well. I have ideas and we must get together. In August I am going to Abetone.[52]
>
> From Bologna to there (Abetone) is not a long way and if you wish we can have an appointment. I will have the car to send to pick you up at Pracchia.[53]
>
> Meanwhile read and see if it is possible to enlarge the outline successfully, especially [the number] of miners (trebling them) and make them the chorus—and try to have an outdoor scene. The last scene (i.e. 3rd act) but [the scene in the play] is winter; here is the stumbling block.

51. Adami, *Letters*, 175. A formal agreement with Belasco was finalized at the end of August 1907.

52. A mountainous resort area located in the Tuscan Apennines. The Abetone lies along the edge of a majestic forest and takes its name from one of the area's gigantic pines.

53. Pracchia is a Tuscan village between the city of Bologna and Pistoia.

Enough; read and ponder and invent and you will work it out for
certain.

Affectionate greetings

Yours,

Giacomo Puccini (MGC 2)

Puccini, who understood the value of theatrical effects, was moving ahead
quickly, reworking the play in his mind. He was already tripling the number
of miners in the original Belasco drama to form the opera's male chorus and
at the same time moving the final act from inside the Polka Saloon to the
foothills of California's Sierra Nevada mountains, with a backdrop of majestic
redwood trees. In a 14 July letter to Seligman, he outlined his initial thoughts
about revising the Belasco play:

> The third act doesn't appeal to me much! But, I think it would be pos-
> sible to rearrange it if one takes three things into account: the scene
> where he is brought on, bound. I should make the scene of his sentence
> and of the insults of the sheriff take place then—*no school episode*—then
> *she* arrives, surprised, and there is a big scene in which she pleads for his
> freedom—everybody being against her except Dick [Nick]. Finally the
> cow-boys are stirred to pity, and she bids a moving farewell to all—
> there is a great love duet as they move slowly away, and a scene of grief
> and desolation amongst the cow-boys, who remain on the stage in dif-
> ferent attitudes of depression, misery, etc., etc. But the scene must take
> place outside the Polka in a big wood, and in the background to the
> right there are paths leading to the mountains—the lovers go off and
> are lost from sight, then they are seen again in the distance embracing
> each other, and finally disappear—how does that strike you? In this way
> I mix the third and fourth acts together—tell me your opinion.[54]

Puccini was clearly attracted by the vast California wilderness and recognized
the challenges of recreating it on the opera stage. He expressed concern to
Zangarini about how to replicate the winter snow and howling winds of the
Sierra Nevada ("the last scene is winter; here is the stumbling block"), a dramatic element he and Belasco would later work out to perfection.[55]

54. Seligman, *Puccini among Friends*, 139. The content of this letter is discussed in chapter 7.

55. When Puccini saw Belasco's *Girl of the Golden West* during his 1907 visit to New York, he was impressed with the technical mastery used to create the snowstorm in act 2, which required thirty-two trained
stagehands to simulate the fury of a mountain blizzard. Belasco's intent "was to play upon the wild over-
whelming natural forces of the exterior environment to augment and reinforce the dramatic action." Be-

Puccini's correspondence with Zangarini continued on a regular basis, and by 25 July he sent the librettist the original manuscript and photos he had collected of California's forests, the grandeur of which inspired the composer's vision of the third act. In actuality, Puccini never visited California or the Sierra Nevada, either before or after the opera was finished. His entire conception came from picture books, some firsthand knowledge from colleagues such as Belasco, and a fantastic, fertile imagination. He was also inspired by the mountainous region of Abetone, which has an abundance of pine trees— none, however, as grand as the sequoias of the towering Sierra Nevada.

> Torre del Lago
> 25 July 1907
> Dear Zangarini,
> Today I am sending you the original [play] and the photographs— these latter *will help* and will make the drama more apparent—let me know, please, when you have received all this material and tell me your impression as soon as possible, because I'm anxious.
> Affectionate greetings
> G. Puccini (MGC 3)

The composer had finally chosen a new subject and was anxious to move ahead rapidly with the project with as little interference as possible.[56] His next letter, written nearly one week later, details how much thought he had already put into the work and some views on how to change the outline of the first two acts he had already received from Zangarini:

> Torre del Lago
> [1 August 1907][57]
> Dearest Zangarini,
> I have read two acts because the others haven't come.[58] I will send them now to Mr. G[iulio].
> Try to see him.
> The first act is a bit confused but it has substance. The second is very

---

lasco's vision of naturalism, combined with his feeling for theatrical intensity and realism, greatly attracted Puccini to the Broadway play. Marker, *David Belasco*, 151.

56. On 6 July 1907, Puccini wrote Seligman that he had signed an agreement with Zangarini, who was "anxiously awaiting" a copy of *The Girl*. Seligman, *Puccini among Friends*, 137.

57. In the case of a missing handwritten date, we have added the postmark date in square brackets.

58. This is a reference to the outline or treatment Zangarini had sent to Puccini. The outline is mentioned in MGC 2.

.

beautiful. However, I have ideas of other ways for enlarging it. . . . But, more on this after having finished reading. I think I have in hand what I need.

Cordial greetings,

G. Puccini (MGC 4)

In August Seligman and her family came to visit the Puccinis for the month. After a brief stay at Torre del Lago, the entire entourage moved up to Bosco-lungo, in the Abetone.[59] According to Vincent Seligman, Puccini could think and talk of nothing but *The Girl* during his family's stay in the mountains. In mid-August, Puccini wrote Zangarini from Abetone with his first thoughts about a title for his new opera, *Bella fanciulla dell'Ovest*. The title would later change, of course, to a combination of English and Italian, the suggestion coming again from Seligman. In the letter, Puccini implores Zangarini to visit him:

Boscolungo Abetone

[14 August 1907]

Dear Zangarini,

If you find yourself a few steps from Tito Ricordi and it is possible have him give you the original English text and the photographs of the *bella fanciulla dell'ovest*—*I should call it that.*

Then let me tell you that I have a car here. Pracchia is the stop for the train.

Come together with Tito [Ricordi] or alone. I *need* to make definite these things, which *have taken hold* of me. I have *ideas.* Belasco or not it *must* be done.

Affectionate greetings

G. Puccini (MGC 5)

This reference to David Belasco relates to the contractual negotiations between Puccini and Belasco, which were not resolved until the end of August.

Puccini's correspondence refers continually to his conception of the "grandiose" third act, which captivated his musical imagination and theatrical passion (see the 14 July letter to Seligman). The next two letters show how Puccini created the idea of moving the final act outdoors into the great California forest, combining the third and fourth acts of Belasco's play into one.

---

59. When the lowlands of Torre del Lago became too warm in the summer, Puccini would move up to the picturesque Abetone.

These letters also bring to light his personal excitement and enthusiasm for *La fanciulla:*

Abetone

[27 August 1907]

Dear Zangarini,

Increasingly the California-disease takes hold of me. I have copied several photographs of the most beautiful part of the forest where the highest and largest trees are, all for the scene in the third act. I am *determined* that it must be in the open air in a large clearing of a forest with colossal trees and with ten or more horses and sixty men. It will be a magnificent third act! Courage!

Greetings

G. Puccini (MGC 6)

Boscolungo

29 August 1907

Dear Zangarini,

I knew that our men were not cowboys. But I liked calling them that because it struck my fancy. Let us think about the third act. I see it as grandiose — in a great forest. You mentioned the manhunt to me. I have an idea. In the clearing or on the veranda which will barely be showing on the stage, why not make the headquarters (so to speak) where at the beginning (while the dialogue between the sheriff and Nick is occurring, and the second sheriff can be there too, awaiting the results of the manhunt) groups of men on horseback and on foot come together from time to time, bringing contradictory reports about the bandit's tracks, and finally a group of horsemen arrives dragging a man tied up — *it is he.* From here on do as the play indicates [but] with our changes, or rather, with yours.

It's an idea I've jotted down — questionable — cancelable — discardable. This is to say, I am not writing the gospel. You be the filter.

Affectionate greetings

G. Puccini (MGC 7)

This last letter clearly shows how early in the opera's creation Puccini conceived the major changes needed in the play to create the third act. It is interesting to note that the reference in the beginning of this letter refers to the correction Zangarini made when Puccini referred to the chorus of miners as "cowboys." The composer acknowledged that it was only "per simpatia"—because it struck his fancy. He noted also with seeming enthusiasm the librettist's thoughts in his outline of the extensive manhunt in act 3. At this point in their relationship, Puccini was exchanging many ideas with Zangarini, asking him for suggestions on his bold theatrical changes. Father Dante del Fiorentino, a close family friend and counselor, said of the relationship, "Composer and librettist became close friends, and they were inseparable."[60]

With the warm Italian summer waning, Puccini wanted to meet with Zangarini as soon as possible at Torre del Lago, and recommended that the poet take particular note to "simplify" the first act.

> (Write to me always at Torre del Lago)
> [12 September 1907]
> Dear Zangarini,
> I am going for five or six days to a little villa in the hills at Chiatri. Then I will return to Torre del Lago—brood and consider well. I recommend most especially simplifying the first act and think about the *grandeur* of the third. For the second [act] there is nothing new to be done.
> Yours always—I hope we can see each other soon here in Torre
>
> Affectionate Greetings
> G. Puccini (MGC 8)[61]

During the same week, Puccini also sent a letter to Giulio Ricordi assuring him that the work on the opera was progressing. The letter was in response to concerns that Puccini begin composing as soon as possible:

> Zangarini is in constant touch with me, and in a few days is coming to me with material. I have not gone to sleep nor am I letting myself grow cold on the subject of the West—far from it! I am thinking of it constantly and I am certain that it will prove to be a second *Bohème*, unless my brain and energy fail me.[62]

60. Dante del Fiorentino, *Immortal Bohemian: An Intimate Memoir of Giacomo Puccini* (New York: Prentice-Hall, 1952), 128.

61. After his summer guests had left and the weather began to cool in the lowlands, Puccini, as was his habit, moved from the Abetone to his villa in the tiny hamlet of Chiatri, in the hills above Torre del Lago. At Chiatri he could overlook Lake Massaciuccoli and beyond to the sea and was able to find the solitude he needed to work.

62. Adami, *Letters*, 175.

Around this same time Puccini wrote another letter to his publisher reiterating how he expected *Fanciulla* to be another success like his popular third opera, *La Bohème*, "but more vigorous, more daring and on an altogether larger scale."[63] He explained his lofty ideas for the final act in the great California forest and his hope that Zangarini would soon produce a text. Responding to Puccini's entreaties, the poet did make a brief visit in September to exchange and discuss ideas with him at his villa, Chiatri, just above Torre del Lago.

After the visit, Puccini renewed his intense correspondence with Zangarini, who was working hard, moving between his apartment on the Piazza Duomo, near the Milan cathedral, and his permanent home in Bologna. Puccini put a note at the top of his letter of 28 September 1907 stating that "it will be necessary to get together soon." It seems the reason for the request is really twofold: first, because Ricordi was pressing the composer to produce an opera; and second, because there were several important issues surrounding the rough draft of the libretto Puccini needed to discuss (see pl. 16). Important elements of the third act were unresolved, which, as the following letter suggests, still included two entrances for Minnie.

> Torre del Lago
> [28 September 1907]
>
> Dear Z,
>
> I've received the two acts. The first is going fairly well. The *end* seems cold to me. In the third Minnie's first entrance doesn't convince me. It seems to me that it is not worth the effort to have her enter and exit for the *cardsharp-ace* scene, only to return at the *critical* moment. In that case it would be better (if there were not a plethora of duets) to have her enter to sing a duet with the tenor. Doesn't it seem so to you?
>
> Regarding the *cardsharp-ace* scene, couldn't it be done at the high point, that is, when she has arrived to defend *him?*
>
> Affectionate greetings
> G. Puccini (MGC 9)[64]

---

63. Ibid., 176.

64. Puccini was probably referring to an early formulation of the opera's third act when Minnie recalls the card-game scene that occurred in act 1. In that particular scene, the Australian miner, Sid, is referred to as a *cardsharp*, who found "an extra *ace*." For further discussion of the 28 September 1907 letter, see chapter 7. The verso of Puccini's 28 September 1907 letter contained a short note, written, most likely, by a Zangarini family member named Katie in Bologna. Presumably, Zangarini had instructed Katie to open letters from Puccini to see if there was information regarding the opera, which needed to be communicated immediately. Katie's note reads, "I opened the letter because I figured it was from Puccini and thought it might

Clearly, Puccini was also formulating ideas for the opera's climatic rescue scene. The correspondence confirms that the relationship between the composer and Zangarini was warm and friendly for a while, particularly during the long hours the two men spent together at Torre del Lago in the fall and early winter of 1907. Zangarini's memoir describes their creative process during this period. While walking near Lake Massaciuccoli the two men improvised dialogue from act 1. In this way, the first ideas for the redemption plot were born.[65] The poet was learning to cope with Puccini's idiosyncrasies, but like his predecessor, Illica, Zangarini encountered constant challenges.

Puccini's Impatience

During the first few weeks of October 1907, Puccini's correspondence with Seligman indicated his annoyance with both the weather and his idle hands. He complained about being bored and that his senses were being "dulled" waiting for Zangarini, who finally arrived on 12 October. Though Puccini wanted the poet to stay with him until *Fanciulla* was finished, Zangarini lodged himself at the Hotel Florence in the nearby seaside town of Viareggio. In a lighthearted tone, Puccini acknowledges Zangarini's need to keep his distance while at the same time expressing his frustration and impatience to move forward.

Torre del Lago
[13 October 1907]

I will not bother or annoy you
Only spur you, if I do not die.
With the *Girl* you rob me of peace.
If I think of it! But the hours waiting
Are gay with expectation.
(We are almost at month's end.)
Think, my friend, that they all have
Threatening, stern and ugly looks
Waiting for our opera.
But on the carousel let it soon

---

perhaps be necessary to send a telegram. But seeing that there is no need, I'll forward it on to you." She addresses Carlo Zangarini by his English nickname, Charlie.

65. Zangarini, "Vigilia pucciniana," *Il resto del carlino* (Bologna), 20 September 1910. See chapter 7 for further discussion of Zangarini's memoir and the idea for act 1's Bible scene.

Turn, revolve, mow down and kill
Him who has the ears of King Midas.
Pray to the Tuscan sea for strength
To be able to work well.
Commend yourself to Malfatti,
That it give you hares, not cats.

I greet you, O Zangarini,
Yours,
Giacomo Puccini (MGC 10)

Zangarini had completed the first act but would not let Puccini read anything until he had finished. In the verse, Puccini reminds Zangarini that the
world (including Giulio and Tito Ricordi) is waiting for this new opera with
"threatening, stern and ugly looks." He also hopes that working near the sea
will give his librettist the inspiration to work fast like a hare and not sleep and
lounge like a cat.

By late October Puccini realized he could do nothing more until he had at
least part of the libretto to review. Rather than increase his anxiety and bore-
dom by waiting at Torre del Lago in bad weather, he made a brief visit to Vienna to supervise the production of *Madama Butterfly* there. Before leaving Italy
for the Austrian capital, Puccini wrote Zangarini, who had moved from Viareggio to Torre. The impatient composer gave the librettist one last reminder
to keep working on the libretto. He penned the correspondence from his
Milan apartment:

Milan, Via Verdi 4
23 October 1907

Dear Z.

I leave at 11:20 tonight. Today I spoke so much and so well of you
with Mr. Giulio, Tito, Toscanini, Gatti-Casazza, and Simoni.[66] No *Tosca*
at the Scala, Mr. Giulio unmovable![67] You cannot believe how much this
pains me! It would have been such a beautiful revival and have come off
so well! Patience. Squeeze your mighty brain for the *Girl!* I ask you to

66. The names refer to Giulio Ricordi; Tito Ricordi; Arturo Toscanini, the famous Italian conductor;
Giulio Gatti-Casazza, general manager of the Metropolitan Opera in New York (1908–35) and the director
of La Scala in Milan (1898–1908); and Renato Simoni, the Italian playwright who collaborated with
Giuseppe Adami on the libretto of Puccini's last opera, *Turandot*.

67. Shortly thereafter, Giulio Ricordi did agree to a performance of *Tosca* at La Scala. Toscanini conducted the new production on 29 December 1907.

talk to my hunter Amanzio, and let him know that I have sent him some
birds for the enclosure.[68]

Affectionate greetings from

G. Puccini (MGC 11)

Puccini spent the last week of October and the beginning of November in Vienna. His undated letter from the Hotel Bristol reveals his continued frustration regarding the libretto for *The Girl*. His sharp theatrical instincts told him
an important element was lacking.

Hotel Bristol, Vienna

(Oct. / Nov. 1907)[69]

Dear Zeta,

I wrote you in Bologna, because Tito told me about the *Suonatore
di flauto* which you had to finish![70] and you worry me at the thought
that you had to cut short your work. Now I know that you are at Torre
and I'm very pleased. I hope that this letter of mine will reach you there.
Butterfly goes on stage Thursday. The dress rehearsal went very well.
Huge emotion in everyone. Great poetry in the mise-en-scène. It looks
good then. Now to our concerns. Don't forget our *Girl*. The more I
think about her the more I fall in love with her. Think seriously about
the third act. I don't find that one good yet. There's material to make
something beautiful of it. But it still lacks something special, something
unexpected, something not heard before. . . . It's lacking a "gimmick"
and it needs it. What will it be? Who knows? We really need to put our
brains through the *wringer* and search and search and search.

> Here the second-act finale will have
> a great effect because it is expressed
> with such special poetry.

I have put this in a box because it is the "gimmick" of *Butterfly*. In
a different way, with a different order of ideas, we need the *Butterfly*
second-act finale in *Girl* as well. Not a humming chorus, not that—

68. Puccini is asking Zangarini to follow through with his caretaker regarding the addition of some
new birds to his aviary.

69. Michele Girardi believes the letter was written between 25 and 29 October 1907 (private
communication).

70. The reference is to Zangarini's translation of the libretto of *Hans il suonatore di flauto*. See
appendix C.

you understand—but a *something* that makes people say from sheer
amazement: bravo, by God! Think about it then, and take courage, dear
Zangarini.

Most affectionate greetings,

G. Puccini (MGC 12)

In this letter (see pl. 17) Puccini refers specifically to the end of the second
act of *Madama Butterfly*, which, through a brilliant combination of technical
staging and evocative choral and orchestral music, creates an aura of a painful,
unrequited love that foreshadows the tragedy in the third act. Helen Greenwald describes this musical and theatrical tour de force:

> Puccini translated this scene into an extended and uniquely tinted win-
> dow in which Butterfly's vigil is underscored by sound—a humming
> chorus as ethereal as the lighting—and sight. Thus even though Puccini
> suspended both action and dialogue insofar as they are traditionally
> understood in opera, he did *not* stop them. Rather, he abstracted them
> by substituting visual time for action, unfolding it through the gradual
> changes in light adopted from Belasco, and substituting an unseen hum-
> ming chorus for dialogue.[71]

In the same letter from Vienna, Puccini mentions the dress rehearsal for
Butterfly—"Huge emotion in everyone. Great poetry in the *mise-en-scène*. It
looks good then." He points out to Zangarini that the production of this
opera is extremely successful in Italy as well as abroad. It is the composer's
way of trying to push the poet to work not only more creatively but also more
quickly so that his libretto will have as powerful an impact as the now well-
received *Madama Butterfly* and will be finished in a timely fashion.

In stark contrast, his letter to Seligman that same week complains that rehearsals for *Butterfly* are only going "so-so" and characterizes the singers as
"unsympathetic." He also shares with her how sad and alone he feels and how
often he thinks of her and wishes she were near him. In giving two different
accounts of the same events, we see how Puccini attempted to manipulate
both Zangarini and Seligman in order to accomplish his professional and personal agenda.

By the end of the first week in November, Puccini was in Milan, on his way
back to Torre del Lago. From there he wrote to Seligman that he was pleased
with *Fanciulla*, since the first act was already finished and the second was near-

71. Greenwald, "Realism," 284.

ing completion. In typical fashion, however, his next letter to her, on 8 November, shows his dissatisfaction with his librettist and predicts what was to
become reality in the early spring.

> I am entirely taken up by Minnie. The poet hasn't quite finished, but
> I shall soon have the libretto complete. I think the third act is going to
> be simply marvelous—if only the poet will understand me; but I am go-
> ing to make every conceivable effort so as to be certain of getting what
> I want.[72]

Arriving at Torre once again, the composer immediately writes to Zangarini:

> Torre del Lago
> 17 November 1907
> I bought a dog called Nick! Thanks for the fruit that you could
> have sent to Torre since you were there already. And Minnie? I entreat
> you as one with all the insistence and anxiety he can. Think of the great
> Third [act].
> Ciao
>
> Affectionately
> G. Puccini (MGC 13)

The dog he refers to bears the same name as the bartender/waiter at the Polka
Saloon in *Fanciulla*. After scolding Zangarini for sending a gift of fruit to Milan instead of Torre, Puccini states the real reason for the correspondence—
the composer's desire to have the libretto finished, especially the third act. He
expresses desire for the completed opera again at the end of the month in another letter written late in the evening from his lakeside villa:

> Torre del Lago
> 10 P.M.—22 November 1907
> Dear Zanga,
> While the wind roars and the nocturnal gunshots resound on the
> Lake, I improvise on Minnie. And you should be at work. I cannot tell
> you how happy I am that the libretto is taking a turn for the good. But,
> my friend, you need to make haste. Time is passing, and remember that

---

72. Seligman, *Puccini among Friends*, 150.

we have promised the opera for next year! Squeeze, mangle your brain, and let the day be soon when you tell me that the West is finished. Ciao

Yours

G. Puccini (MGC 15)

When Puccini began a detailed reading of Zangarini's work, he realized that the librettist's grasp of English was not as thorough as he had hoped. In addition, he thought the poet had taken too many linguistic liberties with the original play in its portrayal of Minnie and the miners. However, as Vincent Seligman points out,

> Zangarini's task was, in many respects, more arduous than that of his predecessors. Both the atmosphere and the dialogue of this story of the wild and wooly West were extremely difficult to transpose into Italian; the names themselves—Billy, Wowkle, Johnson, Wells Fargo and the rest have an air of incongruity in their Latin settings. . . . Also, owing to the shortcomings of the "traitor-translator," it was left to the librettist not only to adapt, but to re-translate, the play;[73] and although Zangarini's mother came from Colorado, his grasp of our idiom does not seem to have been quite perfect—if I may judge from the following ode indited to my mother from Torre del Lago in the intervals of libretto-making, which I found amongst her papers. True, it is signed *Charlie* Zangarini; but its inspiration seems to derive at least as much from the paternal, as from the distaff, side.

> Torre del Lago
> 18 October 1907
> With a mile of Minnie
> and a wish of mine,
> With the voice of waters
> From the lake divine,
> let, good Muse, my verse
> everywhere you go,

73. In a letter to Seligman on 8 July 1907, Puccini criticizes the translation he received from London: "That poor translator (who is a bit of a traitor too)—only 200 francs! It's terribly little; I'll tell them to give him another 100—would you mind handing it over to him when he has finished the translation, and I'll pay you back after?" Seligman, *Puccini among Friends,* 137. The reference to "traitor" is a play on words: the Italian for translator is *traduttore,* and for traitor, *traditore.* Ibid., 131.

bring salutes and kindness
English So and so!
Charlie Zangarini[74]

As 1907 drew to a close, Puccini's mood seesawed between "feeling well" and feeling despondent about being "kept waiting" by Zangarini. In the last letter of 1907 the composer vented his frustrations:

> Torre del Lago
> 5 December 1907
>
> Dear Z,
>   It's agreed. Monday I expect you and with what anxiety! But do not fail me. I hope that you will come finally with all of it. I am in fine form and ready—I can't get Minnie and her companions out of my mind.
>
> Affectionately yours
> G. Puccini (MGC 16)

Puccini busied himself for the next three weeks with family, holiday obligations, and his favorite sport, hunting. However, a few days before Christmas his feelings about the poet's work exploded again in a letter to Seligman in which he exclaimed, "I feel like blowing my brains out. Zangarini is keeping me waiting. Still, he has already worked well—and I think that it will be a chic libretto."[75] Ironically, the *Corriere della sera* was simultaneously reporting in their "Theatre News" column that Zangarini had already written two full acts and part of the third, and that Puccini had made only small modifications to the libretto. The article also described the composer's affinity for the subject:

> The opera will have three main parts, for soprano, tenor and baritone, as well as about fifteen secondary characters. The protagonist will be the only woman on the stage, since there won't even be a female chorus. There will be a male chorus only in the last act. Puccini is more infatu-

---

74. Ibid., 145. Seligman footnoted the Zangarini verse: "The exact meaning of the Address is not altogether clear; but lest there should be any misunderstanding about the poet's flattering intentions, I hasten to add that the expression 'You so-and-so' as a term of disparagement was as yet unknown to Hollywood—or to Colorado."

75. Ibid., 151.

ated than ever with his chosen subject, which corresponds splendidly to his artistic temperament. He hoped that *La fanciulla del West* could go on stage by the end of 1908 but, at this point, we believe it will not be finished until the spring of 1909. Naturally, now is not the time to wonder about the theatre where it will have its premiere. Puccini has not hidden from us the fact that he would like the opera to have its premiere outside of Italy, for example in New York . . . or in London . . . we are still hoping . . . that Puccini's new creation will meet its stage debut in one of our most important Italian theatres.[76]

With the holiday festivities at an end, Puccini began anew his crusade for a completed libretto. He wrote to Seligman that he had given Zangarini an ultimatum: if he couldn't have the work by 15 January 1908 he would find another librettist. Three days later he called the beleaguered poet "that pig of a Zangarini."[77] At the end of January, most of the work from Zangarini finally arrived. Puccini seemed delighted but was still plagued with reservations. He told Seligman that the poet had produced "a really beautiful libretto—it is not fully built but the foundations have been laid."[78] He expressed the same viewpoint in a letter to Giulio Ricordi, commenting that although it was "done well," there would have to be numerous corrections. He continually said that he was "savoring the moment in advance when I shall finally set to work! Never have I had such fever for it as now!"[79] Ricordi never ceased to remind the composer that after four years his publishing house was still waiting for the next Puccini opera.

Before the composer began putting pen to paper, however, he took another trip abroad, this time to Egypt, with his wife, Elvira. His rationale for the two-week sojourn was to attend a performance of *Butterfly* in Alexandria, but, in fact, the trip was purely for pleasure—a respite before he began composing his new opera in earnest. He sailed from Naples on 2 February 1908 aboard the Egyptian Mail Steamship Company's SS *Heliopolis,* a ship he called "magnificent." He stopped in Naples not only to pick up the steamer but also to hear Richard Strauss conduct his controversial opera *Salome.* Puccini's mood at the time was one of lightheartedness; he was soon to begin work on his opera and was embarking on a visit to an exotic new destination. His next letter to

76. *Corriere della sera* (Milan), 30 December 1907; see appendix B, no. 3.

77. Seligman, *Puccini among Friends,* 152.

78. Ibid.

79. Adami, *Letters,* 177.

Zangarini, a poem with numerous clever metaphors and puzzling allusions, was written aboard ship (see pl. 18):

SS *Heliopolis*
3 February 1908

I am on the sea
dancing a lot,
and what are you up to?
Do you think of *The Girl?*

You have finished the third [act]
With Tito nearby
Mind that a glove
Should appear—

I read the two acts
With an eye in Crusca[80]
I put Etruscan words
here and there—

Tomorrow evening
In the thick darkness
I will be in Egypt,
As God wills—

I am here lodged
As an elderly prince,
The friend dances
The vile polka.[81]

Rainy season,
Wind from the east,
All the people here
Speak badly—

They are all English,
German, and French,
Women with hips,
Women bamboo.

80. The dictionary.
81. The name of the saloon in *La fanciulla.*

Elvira is dead,
Laid out on the bed.[82]
Cautiously,
I study the work.[83]

I smoke Egyptians [cigarettes]
Drink mineral [water],
But this evening
I'll take cognac—

O Bolognese[84]
Lecturer,
Every evening
I will read you—

Many greetings
From the high seas—
If you want to play,
Cover up well
Ciao

Yours
G. Puccini (MGC 17)

After his return from Egypt, Puccini began chastising Zangarini for not working faster, openly criticizing the "lengthiness," unrealistic "language," and
overall form in what the poet had already written:

Torre del Lago
10 March 1908

Dear Zanga,
    Instead of giving me news of the third act, you rhapsodize with
a merry spirit on the usual Cremonese theatrical rigamarole!
    Think, my dear friend, of our work! I have in front of me the first
and second. The more I read the more I find that they need *attention*—
not so much for the dramatic *continuity*, as that's all right—except for
a certain lengthiness—but to my ear the *language* is not what is needed.

---

82. A reference to Elvira's propensity for seasickness.
83. He was studying the completed libretto material sent to him by Zangarini.
84. Refers to Zangarini, who resided in Bologna.

The form also needs some reworking. Therefore don't let yourself wander off into complacency. You must still sweat over it.

Ciao, write. I leave for Rome on the fourteenth—
I'm going to the Grand Hotel.

Yours affectionately,

G. Puccini (MGC 18)

It was at this point in their working relationship that, according to Michele Girardi, Puccini began to feel that he was "dealing with an incompetent," making it necessary for the composer to "shoulder all responsibility for dramatic decisions." On 12 March Puccini complained, "I'm doing the hunt [scene] and the prelude, but Zanga is being lazy. Will the famous third act ever arrive? I'm beginning to doubt it." [85] As Zangarini's revisions dragged on into April, Puccini was finally forced to take action. He demanded an immediate meeting with the librettist:

Torre del Lago

[4 April 1908]

Dear Zangarini,

Monday I will be in Milan. I must speak to you urgently and am staying solely for this.

Therefore let me find a note from you in my entry-way telling me when I can see you and where and whether I should come to you or you to me—whichever you think better. It's *urgent* that I *see* you. Ciao

Yours affectionately,

G. Puccini (MGC 19)

The intent of the "urgent" meeting was to discuss the addition of a collaborator, which Zangarini resisted. He felt strongly that there was no need for another librettist, since he was so close to completing *Fanciulla*. This response so enraged Puccini that he told friends and associates he was at "open war" with the poet. Ricordi stepped in to settle the squabbles between the two men. In the end Puccini won the battle by threatening legal action.

On 11 April Zangarini was forced to accept as collaborator Guelfo Civinini (1873–1954),[86] an Italian journalist, poet and novelist from Livorno (see

---

85. Letter to Luigi Pieri, a longtime friend from Lucca. Gara, *Carteggi pucciniani*, no. 543, p. 366.

86. Civinini wrote no libretti apart from his collaboration on *Fanciulla*. By the time he was asked to work on *La fanciulla*, he had already established a reputation as a journalist, popular novelist, and playwright. He later served in World War I as a war correspondent. He wrote for many Italian publications, including *Il giornale di'Italia, La riforma, La patria*, and the *Corriere della sera*.

pl. 19). The speed and quality of Zangarini's work became major sources of irritation for the composer. Though Zangarini spent hours analyzing the changes Puccini requested, the poet's reworked verses could not satisfy the impatient composer.[87] Another source of Puccini's discontent was the librettist's lack of a "sense of theatre," which he communicated indignantly to Ricordi on 29 April 1908:

> Yesterday Zangarini was with me, here, all words, but nothing concrete. He brought me part of the plan for act 3—made according to my instructions, but nothing well thought out, or theatrical in expression— and I told him bluntly that it was no good because he had not felt it— and I'm convinced that this man has no sense of theater—not one good idea, not even the most simple, well-delineated scene.[88]

Puccini wrote to the poet one more time in mid-April, after the collaboration was settled.

> Torre del Lago
> [15 April 1908]
>
> Dear Zangarini,
>   Received your letter. Up to now you had nothing new. Again, I'm expecting the prose outline of the third [act]. And now that so many storms have passed you *must* do it and show your sense of theatre with a practical and well-balanced vision, not forgetting to keep an eye on the idea of redemption, which must linger above the whole work. Show us this sense in all its fullness.
>   Ciao
>
> Yours always
> G. Puccini (MGC 20)

Puccini encouraged him to complete the third act from an existing outline: "Now that so many storms have passed, you *must* do it."[89] The idea of

---

87. Geminino Zangarini, the last surviving relative to know Carlo personally, confirmed that the poet's working style was slow and deliberate and that he sometimes allowed himself to be distracted. Conversation with Rosalind Gray Davis, Bologna, September 1997. It was during this research trip to Italy that Gray Davis located Zangarini's descendants and found boxes of untouched material on "my famous relative," as Geminino Zangarini liked to refer to his uncle. This documentation yielded much of the information on the librettist's life and his connection with the Puccini-Zangarini letters.

88. Girardi, *His International Art*, 278.

89. This is a reference to the legal entanglements and arguments regarding the addition of a collaborator.

redemption again surfaces in Puccini's vision of the final act; it is a theme that is of paramount importance to the composer as he continues his struggle to produce what he hopes will be his finest opera to date. This is the last letter to Zangarini of 1908; the gap in correspondence from 15 April 1908 to 7 August 1909 indicates the temporary split between the two men.

During this period, Puccini was already corresponding with Civinini, asking him to begin studying the libretto with a "view to an economical reduction of Act I, which I think is too long."[90] The idea of cutting the text surfaces in Puccini's early correspondence with Civinini. It appears Puccini wanted the new librettist to act as editor and reviser for *La fanciulla*, since Zangarini had already written most of the libretto.[91] But in the composer's eyes, neither man was ideal. Puccini expressed misgivings about both in a letter to Seligman on 2 May 1908.

> I should have liked to come for a short time to London, but I don't think it is going to be possible, as I have work to do. The second librettist [Civinini] is due on Tuesday; the other has been discharged on account of incompetence—what a lot of time wasted! The first one was a present from *Savoia* [Tito Ricordi]! The second one too, for that matter—all the same I hope this one will be better.[92]

A few months later, on 11 July 1908, after realizing Civinini's inadequacies, he wrote a similar letter to Ricordi:

> You are right, we are in the hands of unconscionable people! These librettists are a disaster. One has disappeared and the other doesn't even reply to my letters! . . . This first act is long, full of details of little interest! I really need someone here with me to follow my instructions properly, how can it be done? I am discouraged, because I would like to make

90. Adami, *Letters*, 178. The earliest sketches for the opera bear the date 24 May 1908. Budden, *Puccini*, 296.

91. Although Puccini and Zangarini did not communicate for a time during the late spring and early summer of 1908, the composer wrote Seligman two letters that indicate that some interchange took place between the two men. The first one was sent on 30 August, the other on 3 September 1908. Both letters describe traveling to Bologna to consult with Zangarini: "I shall go to Bologna on Sunday with my poet [Zangarini]. . . . [If I go] don't know where to stay in Bologna—because I hear it is very difficult indeed to find anywhere to spend the night. . . . I shouldn't come to Venice because the poet [Zangarini] has to go to Milan and I must come back here [Torre del Lago] to work." Seligman, *Puccini among Friends*, 157.

92. Ibid., 153.

cuts, but they must be made systematically, with the necessary connections, and I cannot do it alone.[93]

Although Puccini was unhappy with the work of both librettists, the tone of his letters indicates that, on a personal level at least, Zangarini was more suited to work with the demanding composer than Civinini, who was more outspoken. Vincent Seligman recalled his first meeting with Zangarini: "I remember meeting the kindly poet at Abetone, and I feel confident that he like Adami, preserves nothing but feelings of admiration for the terrible Doge [Puccini] whose vassal he had become."[94]

"Progress Is Slow"

As the summer heat invaded the lowlands, Puccini moved from Torre del Lago to Chiatri, where he sought refuge and quiet in order to continue work on *La fanciulla*. Within a span of three weeks he wrote four separate letters to Seligman concerning the difficulty he was experiencing:

Undoubtedly *The Girl* is more difficult than I thought—it's on account of the distinctive and characteristic feature with which I want to endow the opera, [that] for the time being I've lost my way and don't go straight ahead as I should like. (22 June 1908)

I've felt less unhappy, but how difficult it is to write an opera at the present day! I hope to do something, which you will like—I am most anxious that it should please you, who are my dearest and most beloved friend, loyal and sincere. (26 June 1908)

I'm working, sometimes well, sometimes not so well—but progress is slow—and I feel worn out. I should like to see this work, which is most difficult, go forward more quickly. (5 July 1908)

Those two librettists are a perfect plague—one of them has hurt himself and the other takes not the slightest notice [Zangarini], and

93. Gara, *Carteggi pucciniani*, no. 547, p. 368. Also in Girardi, *His International Art*, 279. In another letter written to Ricordi on 13 July 1908, Puccini commented on the word *fanciulla*. He told Ricordi he would never use it in the title because the last two syllables can be taken to mean stupid or childish in Italian, and he was afraid that people might use it to refer to him. Adami, *Letters*, 180.

94. Seligman, *Puccini among Friends*, 144.

I need them to correct the first act by shortening and re-writing it.
(12 July 1908)[95]

Zangarini was already at work on several other librettos during the first
part of the summer and was ignoring Puccini's entreaties, in retaliation for
having been forced to collaborate with Civinini. In August, as Chiatri became
too hot, Puccini moved higher still into the Abetone, where he received the
revisions from Civinini. Though much of this work was good, he needed still
more revisions. But after only two weeks at Boscolungo, the composer was
restless and uncomfortable and wanted to return to Torre:

                                                      Boscolungo Pistoiese
          Dear Civinini,
              Did I tell you? It is raining continually here, and we are leaving for
          Torre del Lago on Wednesday. You should therefore come soon, and we
          shall fix up Act III, to my joy and yours, not to speak of our dear Uncle
          Giulio, who writes me that he is wasting away like a burning candle.
                                                      Yours sincerely,[96]
                                                      [no signature]

Once back at Torre, Puccini was not in the mood for composing because of
a chronic throat problem that had started the previous spring.[97] Though he
wrote to Civinini and Seligman on the same day (21 September 1908), telling
them that he was "seriously getting to work" on *Fanciulla*, his desire after so
many frustrating years to produce a new opera of epic proportions collided
with a devastating personal tragedy.

The "Affaire Doria"

The fall of 1908 began a torturous and chaotic time for the entire Puccini family (see pl. 20). The calm of the small village of Torre del Lago and Puccini's
working environment was shattered in late September by Elvira Puccini's violent jealousy. She began to suspect her husband of having an affair with the

---

95. Ibid., 154–56.

96. Adami, *Letters*, 182. The reference to Uncle Giulio wasting away refers to Giulio Ricordi being
anxious for *The Girl* to be completed.

97. A heavy smoker, Puccini's persistent throat infections were thought to be the first sign of the
throat cancer that eventually killed him sixteen years later.

housemaid, Doria Manfredi (see pl. 21).[98] Her fierce campaign of harassment
and persecution of the young woman began in earnest in late September, dis-
rupting the entire household as well as Puccini's work on *Fanciulla*. By 4 October Puccini found himself completely embroiled in this destructive situation
and wrote to Seligman about his misery: "My life goes on in the midst of sadness and the greatest unhappiness! . . . I should like to leave my home—but
the opportunity never occurs because I lack the moral strength to do it. . . . As
a result *The Girl* has completely dried up—and God knows when I shall have
the courage to take up my work again!"[99]

Puccini did escape from Torre and took refuge at the Hotel Bellevue in
Paris. But Elvira was unrelenting in her war against the housemaid. She sum-
marily dismissed Doria and informed as many villagers as possible that the
reason for the dismissal was the alleged affair between her husband and the
maid. Puccini was still in Paris when he wrote Seligman about the firing,
which, he insisted, occurred without any proof of wrongdoing between himself and Doria. In the same letter he related that his life had been virtually
destroyed by his wife's jealousy and that he was so unhappy he had "often lovingly fingered my revolver!"[100] After his brief escape to France, Puccini returned to Italy; from Milan he wrote again to Seligman about neglecting
his work on the opera: "I'm very much concerned about my poor beloved
Minnie. I'm neglecting her too much; but the day will come when I will give
myself over entirely to her even if it means sacrificing my night's rest for her
sake."[101] Finally the composer returned to Torre del Lago, where the situation deteriorated even further as Elvira continued her attempt to ruin Doria's
reputation and drive her out of the small village. His wife's behavior and its
toll on Doria's health and mental state appalled Puccini. As Christmas approached he wrote Seligman, who, throughout the drama, acted as Puccini's
personal confidante:

> My work goes on, but so slowly as to make me wonder if it will ever
> be finished—perhaps I shall be finished first! As for the "Affaire Doria,"

98. Doria Manfredi's relationship with the Puccini family began in 1903, when she was sixteen years
old. Elvira hired her to care for her husband while he recovered from injuries sustained in a serious automobile accident. His convalescence took nearly a year, and during this time Doria became part of the
Puccini household.

99. Seligman, *Puccini among Friends*, 166. During this period Zangarini was working on other original
librettos, translations, and adaptations, which included *Jaufré Rudel*, with music by Adolfo Gandino; *Medea*,
music by Luigi Maria Cherubini; and *Saltarello*, by Amleto Zecchi. See appendix C.

100. Ibid., 167.

101. Ibid., 168.

Elvira's persecution continues unabated; . . . I've seen the poor girl se-
cretly once or twice—and the sight is enough to make one cry; in addition to everything else she's in a very poor state of health.[102]

On 23 January 1909 Doria tried to escape Elvira's relentless attacks by swal-
lowing a lethal amount of sublimate, a corrosive poison used as a disinfec-
tant. Residing at the Hotel del Quirinale in Rome, Puccini received word
of Doria's suicide attempt. The young woman did not die immediately but
suffered excruciating pain for five days as the poison ate its way through her
system.[103] Immediately following her daughter's death, Doria's mother and
brother had the local physician, Rodolfo Giacchi, examine the girl. Although
his post-mortem determined her to be a virgin (virgo intacta), the report was
suspect because of Puccini's friendship with the doctor.[104] Armed with Giacchi's information, her relatives threatened to file suit against Elvira Puccini.
The village of Torre was up in arms against Elvira, but she had already escaped
to Milan to distance herself from the anger of the local residents. Still in
Rome, Puccini was devastated when the word of Doria's death reached him.
He made it clear in the weeks following Doria's suicide that he wanted nothing more to do with Elvira and asked Giulio Ricordi to initiate a formal separation between the couple.

On 1 February 1909 Emilia Manfredi, Doria's mother, filed a formal lawsuit charging Elvira Puccini with causing her daughter's suicide by continual
and blatant defamation of character. The magistrate proclaimed the case was
to be heard in the court at Lucca on 6 July 1909. In the meantime Puccini, unable to concentrate on Fanciulla, traveled from Rome to Capalbio,[105] then back
to Torre del Lago, then to Milan and Paris in a vain attempt to cope with his
grief over the dead girl and his worry about his wife's impending trial. Despite
all the interruptions, Puccini still talked about getting to work again on the
opera. However, even after returning to his home in April, he wrote to Seligman, "The Girl languishes—my spirit is too broken to allow me to work. I'm
here with a sister and two nephews—I shoot a little, and I'm unhappy and

---

102. Ibid., 168. Puccini used the term "Affaire Doria" to describe the tragic events of fall and winter
1908. Seligman, Puccini among Friends, 168.

103. On 31 January 1909, the Corriere della sera printed an account of the suicide, which appears to have
been told by an unidentified family member or close friend of the Manfredi family. The article quoted
Doria as saying that she poisoned herself because of "rumors," and that she was "innocent" of the accusations made by Elvira.

104. Giacchi had been best man at the wedding of Giacomo and Elvira in January 1904.

105. Capalbio is a hunting preserve in the Tuscan Maremma.

bored." [106] To keep his mind occupied Puccini traveled, overseeing performances of his operas or planning future productions. In May 1909 he journeyed to London for performances of *Tosca*, spending time with Seligman and her family. His next stop was Paris, where he talked with representatives of the New York Metropolitan Opera about mounting a production of *Manon Lescaut* the following summer in the French capital. [107] A few days later, he decided to return to Italy to begin work again on *Fanciulla* and to face Elvira in person before the trial.

On 6 July 1909 the well-publicized trial began in Lucca. Elvira was charged and found guilty on three counts: defamation of character, libel, and menace to life and limb. Against the advice of Puccini and his attorneys, she decided not to make a court appearance. Her own attorneys had advised her not to attend the trial; instead, she stayed in Milan, feigning illness and offered no defense against the accusations. Court records include the deposition of Doria's mother, taken on 1 February 1909, in which she described her daughter's care of Puccini following his auto accident. She claimed that her daughter's actions were completely misunderstood by "the wife of the composer, who used the occasion as a pretext to start a war against Doria made up of abuses." [108] In conclusion, Signora Manfredi charged "persecution and defamation of character" as the cause of her daughter's suicide. Based on this testimony, the judges decided on a penalty much harsher than either Elvira or Puccini expected: "The Court does hereby declare Elvira Bonturi Puccini guilty of the crimes ascribed to her and sentences her therefore to the overall punishment of five months and five days of confinement, [and] to a fine of 700 lira. . . . She is also responsible for all court expenses." [109] In the meantime Puccini, without Elvira's knowledge, was negotiating with the Manfredis to drop the charges in exchange for a large cash payment. Arrangements were finally concluded with the family, who agreed upon a settlement of 12,000 lire. The case was not officially closed until 2 October, when the Court of Appeal "declared the action extinct." The Puccini family had previously reunited at Bagni di Lucca in late July. From there Giacomo wrote Seligman: "[It] seems as if life is going to be less unpleasant. Elvira seems to me to have changed a great deal

---

106. Seligman, *Puccini among Friends*, 176.

107. Schickling reports that Puccini was in London (at Claridge's Hotel) from 20 May to about 3 June and stayed in Paris (at the Hotel Westminister) until 8 June, where he attended performances at the Théâtre du Châtelet.

108. A detailed account of the court testimony appears in Aldo Valleroni, *Puccini minimo* (Torino: Priuli e Verlucca Editori, 1983), 156–60.

109. Ibid., 160.

as the result of the hardships of the separation, which she has endured—and so I hope to have a little peace and to be able to get on with my work." [110]

The period from October 1908 to July 1909 was a difficult and at times even shattering personal experience for Puccini; nevertheless, he remained passionate about *Fanciulla*. Some began to question the long delay of his newest opera. The composer gave them this explanation in response:

> They accused me of laziness . . . because I stayed silent for a few years. Among the innumerable proposals that I had from librettists, even well-known ones, and not just from Italy, but also from Europe and America, not one matched up to that ideal of passion which my musical spirit needs: and I rejected them all. But this *Fanciulla del West* immediately caused me to love her; she took possession of me, seduced me; I will not have any peace until I can write the words, "the end" on the last scene of the opera. [111]

The tragedy continued to have an effect on Giacomo and Elvira's relationship. They had exchanged too many ugly words and personal accusations for their life to resume as it had been before the incident. Puccini's infidelities had sown the seeds of mistrust between the couple many years before the tragedy. Perhaps Elvira created the incident with the servant to vent years of pent-up anger over her husband's indiscretions with women who were, artistically and culturally, her superiors. Michele Girardi believes the "principal trigger" was respectability:

> Unlike Puccini's other women, Doria belonged to the same background, albeit not to the same social class, as Elvira; furthermore, she had lived for some years in their house. Perhaps she was viewed as a rival because she was the sole person capable of usurping the only role left to Elvira, that of attending the material needs of the man with whom she lived, but who had not loved her for many years. [112]

Because of Puccini's reputation with women, historians have questioned the official version of the suicide and its aftermath. Girardi states that "we do not

---

110. Seligman, *Puccini among Friends*, 181.

111. *Corriere della sera* (Milan), 13 February 1909; see appendix B, no. 4.

112. Girardi, *His International Art*, 272. Budden observed sadly that Elvira included even Seligman as one of her enemies during this period, returning a present to her "together with a cutting note about false friendships. . . . Elvira continued to insist that the blame was entirely his; nothing but an admission of guilt would satisfy her." Budden, *Puccini*, 299.

know for certain the extent of Puccini's relations with Doria and despite everything, we cannot exclude the possibility that there was intimacy of some kind." [113] If there had been any proof of Elvira's accusation the international scandal that would have ensued might have seriously damaged the composer's career. One can only imagine how Puccini's enemies would have used the story of an unsophisticated housemaid's suicide, triggered by the sexual dalliances of an Italian national hero and the unrestrained actions of his jealous wife. Although the bitterness and suspicion lingered for years after the couple's reconciliation, the tragedy that stopped Puccini's work on *La fanciulla* and nearly destroyed two families finally was officially over. The postscript to Elvira's letter to Puccini, sent the day of the verdict, reads:

> Have you read the *Corriere* [*della sera*, a Milan newspaper]? Today the news will be all over the other newspapers as well. And they wanted to avoid scandals! But, it would have been less scandalous if it were known to everybody that you had an affair with the servant rather than this [the outcome of the trial]. Are you persuaded now that Giacchi and Giulia [Doria's relative] have been the most disgusting in all of this? I am still right! And you still love this town [Torre del Lago]? How I detest it. [114]

Although she "hated it" Elvira returned in September to the quiet Tuscan village and tried to resume her life. Her husband went back to his piano and finally "a purgatory of ten months had come to an end." [115]

113. Ibid., 271. See also Girardi, *His International Art*, 37 and n. 27.

114. Postscript to letter from the Museo Casa Natale Giacomo Puccini, Lucca. Giulia Manfredi's testimony was instrumental in the trial against Elvira and was used to prove persecution and defamation of character. See also Girardi, *His International Art*, 271, n. 19.

115. Budden, *Puccini*, 300.

CHAPTER FOUR

Minnie Returns

After a tumultuous ten months that included Elvira's jealous accusations, the suicide of Doria Manfredi, and the trial that followed, it was time for Puccini to concentrate on finishing *La fanciulla del West*. In August 1909 the composer resumed work in earnest, as he explained to Seligman in a letter dated the twenty-second: "I am a little quieter now and I am working. . . . [The opera] is beginning to take on life and strength! Forward and courage."[1] Also in the beginning of August, Puccini contacted Zangarini once again. The composer had not severed his working relationship with the poet; instead, after their legal quarrels in April of 1908, the two men parted company for about a year, during which Puccini's energies were consumed by the suicide and lawsuit and Zangarini fulfilled other musical commitments. As soon as Puccini felt able to continue work on the opera, he immediately contacted the librettist, summoning him to Bagni di Lucca:

Bagni di Lucca
[7 August 1909]

Dear Z,

Can you come here for a few days to work on the libretto, to make certain corrections needed for musical reasons? It's a question of just a little work, but you will be very useful to me, even a necessity. Of course

---

1. Seligman, *Puccini among Friends*, 184. Puccini was still at Bagni di Lucca when he wrote this letter.

you shall have the fee for rewriting! I await your reply immediately, in order to schedule my [thermal] baths as well.

> Affectionate greetings,
> G. Puccini (MGC 21)

Recognizing the importance of his position as librettist for one of the most popular living operatic composers in the world, and having already given so much of his time, effort, and creative ability to the project, Zangarini agreed to work again with Puccini until the opera was complete. He was joined in Bagni di Lucca by Carlo Carignani, Puccini's arranger of vocal scores. Civinini, on the other hand, had done most of his work with the composer in the spring and early fall of 1908, spending much of his time using his editing skills to tailor the poetry to Puccini's musical needs. Civinini explained:

> I was by his [Puccini's] side for about twenty days last May and for another twenty days this past September, during the most intense period of his work, and thus I had the good fortune to be immersed in "Minnie's" first spark of life. . . . I will never forget those days when she [Minnie] was born . . . last spring [1908], in the cerulean calm of Torre del Lago. After he had already completed most of the libretto, Carlo Zangarini (who is becoming the most fashionable librettist) was called away due to other commitments, and had to interrupt his work, and travel to Italy and Germany to sketch out scenes and search for the perfect rhymes for his innumerable composers. I was left alone with the maestro [Puccini], and we worked together.[2]

Work Progresses

At the end of September 1909, Puccini wrote Seligman that he was working diligently on *Fanciulla* and had nearly completed the second act in short score, "where there's a love duet, which seems to me to have come out well."[3] Elvira, who was now in Torre del Lago along with Tonio, seemed to have come to terms with the conditions of their marriage, and an uneasy peace was established between them. In October Puccini was interrupted again by another trip to oversee a production of *Butterfly* in Brussels, where he wrote Seligman, "I'm working confidently, and I'm longing to be back at Torre so as to return to my

2. *Corriere della sera* (Milan), 28 October 1908; see appendix B, no. 5.
3. Seligman, *Puccini among Friends*, 185.

Minnie. I've nearly got to the third act—a good step forward, in fact."[4] By early November he was back at Torre and working on the third act, which was more problematic than he had imagined. He told Seligman, "Let's hope that it will soon be finished. I've got to the third act, which is a bit heavy to do. But it will come out all right—at least we must hope so."[5] Arnaldo Fraccaroli, an Italian journalist and biographer and a longtime friend of Puccini, described the composer's work habits during this period as concentrated and intense:

> In the evening from about 10 P.M. to about 1 or 2 after midnight, he would sit down at his piano with an enormous supply of coffee and cigarettes beside him, a big pencil and numerous sheets of lined paper before him nervously tormenting the keyboard, drawing from it thrills of happiness, sighs of sadness, spasms of love, flames of rebellion, and tired notes that seem dropped from weeping eyes. He would pound on the keyboard until he was able to produce something which satisfied him.[6]

Puccini favored working at night, choosing to spend his daytime hours out shooting waterfowl with his hunting companions from Torre.

By late December the composer had moved to his apartment in Milan, where he spent Christmas and the first weeks of the New Year working. Feeling lonely and without familial support, he wrote to Seligman questioning whether he was "alive" and told her, "For the time being I have Minnie—the rest is emptiness."[7] From January to July 1910, while Puccini continued scoring the opera, Zangarini maintained his apartment in Milan on the Piazza Duomo just around the corner from Puccini's apartment on the Via Verdi, making working together convenient. On 2 January Puccini contacted Zangarini by letter in the form of an obtuse poem, thanking the librettist for his new year's greetings and expressing the hope that this difficult period of work would be rewarded in the future:

> Milan, Via Verdi 4
> 2 January 1910
>
> Dear Zanga,
> Thanks for your [new year's] greetings,
> which arrived very clearly

4. Ibid., 186–87.
5. Ibid., 187.
6. Arnaldo Fraccaroli, "Puccini e *La fanciulla del West*," *Corriere della sera* (Milan), 15 October 1910. An English translation of the entire article is also in the archives of the Metropolitan Opera.
7. Seligman, *Puccini among Friends*, 188.

even following uncorked bottles
with corks flying into the walls.

I'm passing dark days
writing real torpedoes
in kangaroo form
for days not far in the future.

Let's hope they won't be hard,
that they're clear, not dark
that the ears of filthy listeners
won't be clogged.

And continually it ripens
to the sound of drums.

Ciao
G. Puccini (MGC 22)

Zangarini left Milan to return home to Bologna for Christmas. After the holiday he traveled to Venice for the 11 January premiere of *Jaufré Rudel,* for which he had written the libretto. Meanwhile Puccini, who was eager to finish his opera, anxiously awaited the librettist's return to Milan, scheduled for a week after the Venice premiere. They were finally reunited in Milan, and the scoring of the first act of *La fanciulla* was completed by the third week of January. On the twenty-fourth, the composer, still concerned about the "majestic" third act, sent a quick note to "Z"—again in rhyme:

Milan, Via Verdi 4
24 January 1910

Dear Z.,
The first verses of Act 3 are bereft!
Zanga needs to come back to Via Verdi—And scrawl
some doodles on the sheet that is before me
chosen words
with subtle hand
(and to write well remove your gloves).
Jot down on paper with a quick hand
(paper from Fabriano's).
    Come in the afternoon
    here "at home."

G.P. (MGC 23)

In another letter dated 30 January, Puccini asks Zangarini if he understood the changes he had requested and exhorts Zangarini to add them to the libretto (see pl. 22):

Milan, Via Verdi 4
30 January 1910

Dear Z,
A line occurs to me which says:*
(Page 1 of the 3rd act)

Rance (in a dark voice):
maledetto cane
*parea ferito a morte!
E pensar che da allora
è stato lì curato (priore)
scaldato dal respiro di Minnie, etc.[8]

(He's cured then)
Do you understand?
The verse parea ferito a morte must be uttered
It's necessary. Are you leaving?
Ciao

Yours
GP (MGC 24)

Although Puccini wanted the librettist to stay in Milan, Zangarini left for Bologna to oversee a production of Saltarello, another opera for which he had supplied an original libretto. Puccini decided to leave Milan and return to Torre del Lago, where he concentrated on finishing La fanciulla. By April he had orchestrated two hundred pages, including the entire second act. He wrote Seligman, "I'm living like a hermit without emotions and without anything else—I've still got the whole of the third act to do, and I'm beginning to be a little fed up with Minnie and her friends. Let's hope the third act will satisfy me as much as the other two—if only it were finished soon!"[9]

In May, Puccini went back to his apartment in Milan, where he wrote Zangarini in Bologna, imploring him to send a copy of the closing lines of act 3:

8. Damned dog! He seemed to be mortally wounded! And to think that since then he has been taken care of, warmed by Minnie's breath, etc. [Puccini plays on the double sense of curato (cured/curate), adding the parenthetical "prior."]

9. Seligman, Puccini among Friends, 189.

Milan, Via Verdi 4

[28 May 1910]

Dear Z,

I lost the last pages of the libretto where you gave me the lines. They were close to these—but 2 stanzas—

Addio, mia dolce terra!
Addio, mia California!
Bei monti della Sierra,
nevi, addio![10]

And another stanza in the same meter—do you remember it?
I ask you to write it out again for me and send it to me immediately.
I leave Monday for Paris, Hotel Westminster, rue de la Paix.
Ciao

Affectionately yours,
G. Puccini (MGC 25)

Important Interlude

Taking a brief hiatus, Puccini traveled to Paris with Tonio and Elvira for two weeks in June to oversee the production of *Manon Lescaut*. The Metropolitan Opera Company of New York was presenting the work as part of the Théâtre du Châtelet's Italian opera season. During this visit, the managing director of the New York company, Giulio Gatti-Casazza, made the final contractual arrangements with Puccini for the world premiere of *La fanciulla*, to open in December at the Metropolitan. There may have been some underlying political and economic reasons that the *Fanciulla* contract was signed in Paris during the French premiere of *Manon Lescaut*, seventeen years after that opera was first produced.[11] Max Smith, a critic and reporter from the *New York Press*, speculated that the agreement was linked politically to the current premiere:

Why was this peculiar time chosen for the signing of the "Girl of the Golden West" contract? . . . Is it unreasonable to suspect that the performance of "Manon Lescaut" in Paris was a condition imposed by the Ricordis and Puccini before giving to the Metropolitan Opera Company

10. Goodbye, my sweet country! Goodbye, my California! Lovely Sierra peaks, snows, goodbye!

11. The premiere of *Manon Lescaut* took place at the Teatro Regio, Turin, 1 February 1893. Revised Teatro San Carlos, Naples, 21 January 1894; definitive version, Teatro alla Scala, Milan 26 December 1922. Budden, *Puccini*, 494; Girardi, *His International Art*, 490.

the valuable privilege of producing the Italian composer's latest operatic creation? The Ricordis, and Puccini as well, were more than anxious to have the work introduced to Parisians all the more so because every effort had been made to prevent this Italian setting of the story, which Massenet [12] also has put to music, from being presented in France. That "Manon Lescaut" written years ago, was not produced in the French capital until last night, when all of Puccini's other important works have been frequently sung here, is in itself a peculiar circumstance. That the first production finally was effected by a visiting operatic troupe from America is also remarkable. As a matter of fact the publishers of Massenet's "Manon" the most influential publishers of music in France, have been fighting for years against the admission of Puccini's setting of the same subject, and by threatening to withhold rights of performance of other important works put out by them from time to time, succeeded in shutting the doors of local lyric theatres against the Ricordi opera. [13]

Max Smith's assumption was not without some historical basis. Ricordi's method of linking the performance of successful, established works, such as Verdi's *Falstaff*, to a newer opera was seemingly common practice during that period. Puccini's *Manon Lescaut* was well received by the French public but less so by critics, who ascribed the work's success to the work's conductor rather than to its creator. Arthur Coquard, critic for the *Echo de Paris*, described Toscanini as "the real hero of the evening. His was the intelligence and the will, his the creating spirit which infused life—and what life—into the work." [14] Attitudes such as Coquard's did not bother Puccini, who "was used to such treatment by the French press and could afford to ignore it." [15]

Despite the six-year interval since his last premiere, Puccini's fame was then at its height, and the Metropolitan's astute managing director understood the financial and cultural benefit the opera house would derive by launching the newest Puccini work in America. Toscanini, Tito Ricordi, George Maxwell (Ricordi's New York representative), and Alfred Seligsburg (attorney for the Metropolitan Opera) were present for the historic occasion. As an indication

12. Jules Massenet's *Manon* premiered in Paris on 19 January 1884. Both Massenet's and Puccini's operas were based on the novel by François-Antoine Prevost, *L'histoire du Chevalier Des Grieux et de Manon Lescaut*, written in 1731.

13. "Songs and Singers," *New York Press*, 20 June 1910.

14. *New York Press*, 20 June 1910.

15. Budden, *Puccini*, 301.

of the importance of the forthcoming world premiere, newspapers reported, the contract was signed with a special gold pen. The following is a translation of the contract, which brought to the United States the first world premiere of an opera by a major European composer. It was signed by the Metropolitan's managing director and the composer.[16]

Paris, 9 June 1910

The following have been agreed upon today by the Metropolitan Opera Company of New York and Maestro Giacomo Puccini, resident in Torre del Lago:

1. Maestro Giacomo Puccini agrees to come to New York in the months of November and December 1910 and remain there for four consecutive weeks. It is understood that, excepting the case of *force majeure*, the premiere of *La fanciulla del West* will take place on 6 December 1910, and the composer must be present in New York two weeks before the first performance.

2. In these four weeks Maestro Giacomo Puccini will assist with the performances of his operas, and he will oversee of the staging of *La fanciulla del West.*

3. The Metropolitan Opera Company agrees to remit to Maestro Puccini the amount of 20,000 lire, that is, Twenty-Thousand Lire, plus round-trip fares from Milan for said composer and his wife, as well as full room and board for those four weeks in New York.

4. The amount of 20,000 lire will be remitted to the composer in installments of 5,000 lire[17] each at the end of each week.

5. By *room and board* it is meant: 1 living room, 1 bedroom, 1 bathroom, and meals, *as well as automobiles.*[18]

6. During those four weeks Maestro G. Puccini agrees to put himself entirely at the disposal of the Metropolitan Opera Company for the above-mentioned duties, and without the consent of the Metropolitan

16. The original contract is located in the archives of the Metropolitan Opera and has been translated and reprinted with the permission of the Metropolitan Opera archives.

17. The exchange rate circa 1910 was approximately 5.26 lire to $1.00. Hence, the sums of 20,000 lire and 5,000 lire mentioned in items three and four would be the approximate equivalent of $71,760 and $17,940 in today's dollars (2002). John J. McCusker, "Comparing the Purchasing Power of Money in the United States (or Colonies) from 1665 to Any Other Year Including the Present," Economic History Services, 2001, URL: http://www.eh.net/hmit/ppowerusd/.

18. The phrase regarding automobiles was added by hand to satisfy Puccini, who loved motorized vehicles of any kind.

Opera Company he may not assist with any other performances of his works, either in concert form or in the theatre.

7. All these conditions have been accepted by mutual agreement and are in force from the time both parties affix their signatures to the present document.[19]

Puccini agreed to the New York contract for a number of reasons, not the least of which were a special signing bonus and his close friendship with Gatti-Casazza, the former La Scala impresario. But perhaps the composer explained his rationale best in a newspaper interview. The reporter asked Puccini why he had chosen New York as the place for the first production of the new opera.

> "There are many reasons," replied the composer, "any one of which would have been sufficient. In the first place, you have in New York the greatest operatic institution in the world. The Metropolitan is absolutely unique. In Mr. Toscanini as its conductor, in its splendid corps of singers, its magnificent orchestra, it is unrivaled. Besides, it was America that furnished the inspiration for the opera. Here its characters, its spirit, will be understood as nowhere else."[20]

Another reason for the decision was the composer's recollection of the disastrous premiere of his last opera, *Madama Butterfly*, at La Scala in 1904, after which he declared he would never agree to open another opera in Italy.

Reports of the signing were wired immediately to newspapers in New York and Europe. The *New York Times* correspondent sent a special cable to his paper stating:

> New York's Metropolitan Opera Company goes from triumph to triumph. In Paris tonight was witnessed the production [in France] of Puccini's *Manon Lescaut*. Tonight's performance was made the occasion for the signature to contracts by which Puccini's "Girl of the Golden West" will be given for the first time at the Metropolitan Opera House on Dec. 6, and Puccini told me he hoped to be present. Gatti-Casazza announced that Caruso and Emmy Destinn would sing the chief roles.[21]

19. See appendix B, no. 6.

20. "Puccini Would Rather Talk Duck Shooting than Grand Opera," *New York Evening World*, December 1910.

21. "Our Opera again Triumphs in Paris," *New York Times*, 9 June 1910.

Another New York newspaper, the *Sun,* reported:

> At the end of the opera [*Manon Lescaut*], the audience called for Gatti-
> Casazza, who declined to present himself. Gatti-Casazza announces
> officially that an agreement for the production of "The Girl of the
> Golden West" in America was signed tonight. The opera will be pro-
> duced for the first time at the Metropolitan Opera House on Decem-
> ber 6. Emmy Destinn, Caruso and Amato will sing the principal parts.[22]

During this same time, acts 1 and 2 of *Fanciulla* were sent to the composer-
conductor Ettore Panizza in London. His assignment was to work on a reduced orchestration of the opera for smaller stages and orchestra pits. Smaller
theatres could not accommodate *Fanciulla*'s large score and unique staging demands, for which the Metropolitan Opera House was, however, well suited.[23]

Finishing *La fanciulla*

Contract in hand, Puccini returned to Torre del Lago in mid-June to complete
his opera. With the premiere's deadline fast approaching, he wrote a short,
impatient postcard to Zangarini on 2 July asking him if he remembered "the
stanza of the opposing chorus, page 13, third act—for which I indictated the
meter to you? Mind that you find it for me, I need it—what a nuisance to
lose pages." [24] In the next letter, sent on 13 July (see pl. 23), Puccini requested
as a "great favor" from Zangarini more lines for some of the miners who, during a crucial section at the end of the third act, are persuaded by Minnie to
spare her lover's life.

Torre del Lago
13 July 1910

Dear Zanga,
    I beg a great favor of you. Quickly, quickly, please send me other
verses for page *14b*, where Minnie's recitative is:

> "*E anche tu lo vorrai,*
> *Joe,*" etc.

---

22. "Enthusiasm for *Manon*," *Sun*, 9 June 1910.

23. In August 1911 a reduced version of the score was finally published to guarantee more exposure for
the opera.

24. MGC 26.

It's not a question here of Minnie but of the scene alongside Sonora:

"*È necessario*
Troppo le dobbiamo—
dediti anche tu," etc.[25]

from these [verses sung] aside I would like to make something more
important, and therefore I request that you let me have some interrupted
lines, divided between *Sonora, Joe, Happy, Harry,* and *Bello*—with some
of them, who have already gone over to Minnie's side, urging the whole
group [of miners] and their companions more strongly to obtain the
pardon [of Johnson] for Minnie. Thanks. Send them to me right away,
I implore you. 7 or 8 or 10 little verses are *urgently needed* in addition to
those that are printed, placed either in the middle or at the end.

Yours affectionately,
G. Puccini (MGC 27)

Racing to finish the opera, Puccini wrote his librettist a second letter the same
day with requests for more changes and additions to the same section of the
last act.

Torre del Lago
13 July 1910

Dear Zanga,

After the word *redenzione* ("redemption") on page 14b, Minnie remains ecstatic and Johnson kneels in front of her, and she puts her hand
on his head as though blessing him, etc. We could have Sonora and the
other boys say: Look, if you have the heart, take away from Minnie the
man who will make her happy; come on, hurry up, you decide Harry
(who perhaps is reluctant) or else Joe (as you wish); do it for her, for
me, join together in granting them life and happiness, etc., etc.—Since
after *Minnie's* word *redemption* there is a long orchestral postlude, during
it I would have Sonora fire his last rounds, etc. Do you understand very
well? I hope so.
Ciao and thanks

Yours,
GP (MGC 28)

25. Minnie: "And you too will want it, Joe"; Sonora: "We must; We owe her too much. You make up
your mind too."

On 31 July 1910 Puccini wrote Zangarini a final letter proudly announcing the completion of *La fanciulla:*[26]

> Torre del Lago
> 31 July 1910
>
> Dear Zanga,
>
> Minnie is up in the mountains together with her man, whom she has won, and so she will remain until December. I have cut and reduced the finale a great deal—it was too long-winded. You can well understand that at midnight one cannot get lost in chatter, no matter how pleasant. And the end has turned out well, and I hope that audiences will not be worrying about their overcoats while the doings of my boys are drawing to a close.
>
> I am reading the *Corriere*. Oh why didn't you tell them something fantastic, for instance, that I wrote the opera on music paper with no less than 5-line staves and blue-black ink, and that the clarinetists are playing on gas pump nozzles? . . .
> Ciao
>
> > Yours affectionately
> > G. Puccini (MGC 29)

Puccini explains how he had cut the finale because it had been, in his opinion, overwritten by Zangarini, a complaint of the composer at various junctures during the creation of *La fanciulla*.[27] It is likely that during the last year of the opera's creation, the librettist grew to understand and accept Puccini's revisions, believing in his flair for dramatic staging as well as his musical ability.[28] In fact, as the premiere's date came closer, Zangarini spoke out consistently, commending the composer and his working style. Puccini's letter refers to a 31 July interview with the librettist published in the *Corriere della sera*. In the article Zangarini, "who had been working closely with the composer on making

26. The letter of 31 July 1910 is Puccini's last to Zangarini.

27. In Puccini's 5 November 1907 letter to Seligman, he states: "The first act is finished now, but it will be necessary to return to it later, as it needs to be made clearer and to be smartened up." Seligman, *Puccini among Friends*, 50.

28. Zangarini lauded Puccini in "Vigilia pucciniana," *Il resto del carlino* (Bologna), 20 September 1910. In addition, Vincent Seligman quotes Giuseppe Adami, librettist for the composer's later works, as saying: "I understood then that Puccini was always right, and that the alterations which he was constantly demanding and on which he insisted so obstinately were based upon something, which one could not hope to fathom, in his soul and in his creative mind." Ibid., 143.

last minute changes on the final version of the opera," was asked to describe the work. He said:

> In general terms, the chief characteristic of Puccini's music in his new score is the perfect and most impressive union of word and music, so as to make *Fanciulla* a work of art that unfolds, as it fills out and reinforces it. . . . Among Puccini's scores it is the one that most bears the mark of his fundamentally theatrical conception." [29]

Zangarini's praise for Puccini and his new opera stands in stark contrast to an article written by Civinini just prior to *Fanciulla*'s premiere. Printed first as an open letter in *Il giornale d'Italia* in early December 1910, the piece was reprinted in the *Corriere della sera* on 4 December 1910.[30] Civinini protested that Puccini had reworked the opera's verses without following elementary metrical rules. Perhaps Civinini felt that he should have been consulted about changes made to his portions of the libretto during the composer's final months of work. It is also possible that Civinini may not have been aware that Puccini retained Zangarini for a second time to help him finish the opera's libretto.

Before Puccini wrote Zangarini on 31 July, he corresponded with his publisher to inform him of the opera's completion. In this letter, Puccini makes a clear reference to his last-minute abbreviation of the librettist's work:

> Torre del Lago
> 28 July 1910
>
> Dear Signor Giulio,
>   The opera is finished!
>   I have done a little cutting and left out some rather nice but useless things from the libretto. This was done at midnight. I assure you, that as it now stands, it is emotionally, as well as scenically and in its fine conclusion, a work that will matter. It was last night, with me as judge and Carignani[31] as counsel, that the case of Minnie and her friends was concluded.
>   God be praised![32]

---

29. *Corriere della sera* (Milan), 31 July 1910; see appendix B, no. 7.

30. "Il libretto della *Fanciulla del West*, una lettera di Guelfo Civinini," *Corriere della sera* (Milan), 4 December 1910.

31. Carlo Carignani, a musician and longtime friend of Puccini's, assisted in arranging some of the composer's vocal scores.

32. Adami, *Letters*, 185.

After the work was finished, the composer visited the nearby seaside resort of Viareggio, where he wrote to Seligman about his accomplishment:

> Viareggio
> 15 August 1910
>
> So the Girl is finished at last!
> Now I'm leading a peaceful existence; whenever I feel like it, I go and have a dip in the sea. I'm waiting for my new car to go to Spain or to the north—I haven't yet decided which.
> The Girl has come out, in my opinion, the best opera I have written.[33]

Puccini had great confidence in his new opera. He had survived seemingly insurmountable personal and professional challenges and produced what he believed to be an innovative work with a dynamic, modern musical expression and mise-en-scène. To celebrate the occasion, the composer took his family on a driving tour of Switzerland for two weeks in September. The vacation was a much-needed rest for Puccini before his upcoming trip to New York, but it was also a means of reestablishing ties with both his wife and his son after the horrendous ordeal of the past year and a half.

---

33. Seligman, *Puccini among Friends*, 192. Puccini completed the orchestration of *Fanciulla* on 6 August 1910.

CHAPTER FIVE

Puccini, Publicity, and the 1910 Premiere

With the opera completed and the contract signed, *Fanciulla* moved toward its New York premiere guided by a new set of imperatives, which were determined by material concerns. Simply put, the Metropolitan could not afford for this event to be anything less than a sensation: the financial investment was huge and the cultural risk even greater. As the narrative of events presented in this chapter will show, *Fanciulla*'s debut was also New York's debut on the world stage. By presenting the first-ever American premiere of an opera by a major European composer, the Metropolitan organization hoped to win legitimacy for New York as one of the world's great opera cities. The unprecedented amount of advance publicity, both in New York and abroad, shows that no expense was spared to guarantee the opera's success and to advance the Metropolitan's broader agenda.

The Metropolitan publicists succeeded in shaping pre-premiere opinion in a number of ways. They gave the press great access to Puccini, Belasco, Toscanini (see pl. 24), and the principal singers, resulting in a flurry of interview articles, and managed to make the premiere into a bona fide society event, guaranteeing that New York's wealthiest residents and most famous celebrities would attend the opera and that society newspaper writers would cover the event. A number of common threads run through the advance newspaper articles. One of the Metropolitan's favorite publicity angles was to claim that the opera blended together two different worlds—that *Fanciulla* represented a synergy of old and new, European and American. The publicity also stressed the Italian nationality of its authors and performers. Implicit in this coverage was the selling point that *Fanciulla* was not just a European opera, but an unassailably authentic *Italian* opera, composed and conducted by Italians. It was, therefore, judged to be among the most valuable of operatic commodities.

At the same time the advance publicity was propagating the idea of the opera's quintessential Italianness, it highlighted the distinctly American features of the story and the producers' efforts to portray them realistically on the opera stage. Newspaper articles contained proud descriptions of uniquely American ways of walking, gesturing, and even kissing that the European singers found impossible to imitate. While the novelty of a western theme accounts in part for the press's preoccupation with the opera's American features, it is likely that publicists emphasized this dimension of Puccini's new work in the hope of exploiting the audience's familiarity with Belasco's stage play. The constant references to these features seemed designed to assure Belasco loyalists that the Americanness of the original play had not been overtaken by the Italianness of the opera.

Another common theme in *Fanciulla*'s publicity was the portrayal of European capitals as envious of New York's premiere. New York critics appeared to relish the fact that they were displacing their European counterparts by being the first to review the opera and judge its merits. Newspaper writers repeatedly informed their readers of the historic nature of the event and lost few opportunities to assume the tone of the opera world's new standard-bearers. Reporters seemed to share the Metropolitan's financial and cultural objectives and printed stories that helped to sell tickets and echoed the organization's view of the opera's value.

The content of reviews proved more difficult to control than the tone and subject matter of advance publicity. It is clear that reviewers became obsessed with the "inauthentic" American qualities of the opera and gave only cursory attention to the remarkable experimental qualities of Puccini's work. This attitude was perhaps predictable, considering the hyperbole that *Fanciulla* was "the perfect blend of two worlds": it was only natural that the press would critique the opera on this point, having been led in that direction for months.

For better or worse, the content of premiere reviews long outlives the normally short life span of newspaper ephemera. *Fanciulla*'s first critics' superficial and often pedestrian observations continue to resonate, and their notions of the opera's failings form the core of the work's interpretive history. While its American qualities are certainly important elements (this topic is treated at length in chapter 6), the critics' narrow preoccupation with it can be seen as an unintended result of the Met's massive publicity campaign. In other words, advance notices raised expectations of an operatic Americanness that Puccini never intended to create. Consequently, the 1910 New York reviews have distorted the opera's critical discourse by focusing on *Fanciulla*'s American aspects and failing to examine its more substantial features.

"Great Success" Predicted

The American publicity machine for *Fanciulla* was in full swing by the summer of 1910. Stories appeared announcing the agreement between Puccini and the Metropolitan Opera to perform the work in New York, in addition to numerous articles about subjects relating to the premiere. When asked by the *Chicago Record-Herald* in August whether the new Puccini opera was finished, Caruso replied: "I think so, but I don't know a word of it. I hope to have the part soon, which I shall first create at the Metropolitan in New York. I hope it will suit me well, like the other tenor parts in former operas by Puccini, all of which I have sung with great pleasure from '*Manon*' to '*La Bohème*'; from '*Tosca*' to '*Butterfly*.'" [1] Two months later the tenor was singing in Berlin when he prophesied "great success" for *La fanciulla:* [2] "[the score] is an advance over anything that the creator of *La Bohème* and *Madama Butterfly* has ever done. . . . The entire score has caught the local American color admirably, and the rough atmosphere of the mining camp has not interfered in the slightest respect with the truly artistic scenario." [3]

American newspapers lauded the opera company for using Belasco, an "American dramatist," and for hiring local artisans to make the scenery, properties, and costumes in New York. There were stories about such behind-the-scenes participants as Edward Siedle, the Metropolitan's technical director, and James Fox, its well-known scenic artist, both of whom created an astonishing mise-en-scène for the opera's first performance. In a lengthy story, the *New York Times* reported:

> The American composer may or may not be receiving his just due but
> at any rate the Metropolitan Opera Company will this year do honor
> to the American dramatist, scene painter, and costumer in an opera,
> which has an American subject. When Puccini's "Girl of the Golden
> West" receives its first production on any stage at the Metropolitan on

---

1. Special dispatch to the *Chicago Record-Herald*, 1 August 1910.

2. Puccini wrote the tenor role of Dick Johnson for Caruso, "and the tessitura, above all that of the brief solo 'Ch'ella mi creda,' seems consciously designed to emphasize his gifts. After his return to Italy following the triumphant premiere, in January 1911 Puccini sent the tenor some poetic lines of gratitude, highlighting the roles in which Caruso excelled (*Manon, La Bohème, Tosca, Fanciulla*)." It was the first time the composer had written a part expressly for Caruso. Girardi, *His International Art*, 281, n. 27.

3. "Rush in Berlin to Hear Caruso," *New York Herald*, 24 October 1910.

December 6—or later—there will be enough elements of local interest
to make the opening notable on that account, even if people were not
going to cross oceans to hear the first performance of a new work by the
most popular of Italian composers.[4]

In late September newspapers reported that Toscanini and Puccini had met at
Torre del Lago to study and work together on the score, preparing for the re-
hearsals that were scheduled to begin in October.[5] The journalist Charles
Henry Meltzer of the *New York American* interviewed Toscanini:

> The maestro has assimilated every note, every shading, every suggestion
> in the score. He could play "La fanciulla" in the dark.
> "The opera," said Toscanini, "is flooded with melody. And the mel-
> ody is of the kind with which Puccini has already won us. But there are
> new things above all, exquisite new timbres, tones and colors in the in-
> strumentation. It has more vigor, more variety, and more masculinity,
> than the orchestration of the composer's earlier operas. It is more com-
> plex. In one word, it is more modern."[6]

Full orchestral score in hand, Toscanini sailed for New York in October with
other members of the Metropolitan's company, including the assistant conductors Richard Hagermann and Francesco Romei and the chorus master,
Giulio Setti. On 15 October Giulio Gatti-Casazza, the Metropolitan's director, met the conductor at the pier and told reporters covering Toscanini's arrival that he was looking forward with confidence to the premiere of the new
opera.[7] By the end of October Toscanini had sent a telegram to the anxious
composer saying that the first reading of his score at the Metropolitan had
gone extremely well. Reports detailing Puccini's anxiety about the opera
abounded in the New York press before his trip to America:

> Giacomo Puccini, always nervous, is more than ever so, now that the
> time for his visit to New York to produce "The Girl of the Golden
> West" is drawing near.
> He has learned with pleasure that Madame Destinn, Caruso and

4. "Puccini's New Opera to Be Seen First in New York," *New York Times*, 25 September 1910.

5. Toscanini became artistic director of the New York Metropolitan Opera in 1908 and retained the
position until 1915.

6. "Toscanini Discusses Operas New and Old," *New York American*, 18 October 1910.

7. "Toscanini Brings Score of New Puccini Opera," *New York Herald*, 16 October 1910.

Amato are to interpret the leading characters of his new opera, but he is as much agitated over the details of presentation as ever. Friends who have visited him at his villa at Bagni di Lucca, on the Tuscan hills, say that his nervousness is almost distressing, and they are trying to dissuade him from encountering the worries of rehearsals in New York.

The composer is taking the matter so much to heart that he is showing his age and New Yorkers will see a very much older looking man than he was when he visited that city in 1906 [i.e., 1907].[8]

Puccini Sails for New York

Owing largely to Puccini's proprietary feelings about his work and his need for personal privacy, little information was released to the general public about the opera's music prior to rehearsals. However, he did send Seligman a copy of *La fanciulla* on 8 October, prior to its official publication, and asked her not to let any journalists see it. A few weeks later he set sail for New York with his son, Tonio, and Tito Ricordi (see pl. 25).[9] Ricordi was assuming more and more of his father's duties and was to be the official producer of the new opera.

The Metropolitan's management had booked the best suite aboard the new luxury liner *George Washington* for the composer. Elvira did not accompany her husband, probably to prevent any publicity that would detract from the opera, and public reports explained her absence by saying she had had enough of New York during her 1907 visit.[10] Puccini seemed to have a grand time aboard the *George Washington*, as evidenced in the letter he wrote to Ricordi:

> November 10, 1910
>
> My dear Signor Giulio,
>
> Here we are, actually at sea. We have what is called the Imperial
> Suite. A princely bath, a room with two gilt bedsteads with various
> sorts of opaline-tinted lamps; a drawing-room with luxurious divans
> and mikado mirrors; dining-room with furniture in the best English
> taste, ingenious cupboards which are even lighted inside, everything

8. "Puccini Very Nervous over His New Opera," *New York American*, 24 September 1910.

9. According to Schickling, Puccini was in Paris from 6 to 9 November 1910 and, from there, he traveled to London, where he boarded the ship to New York. Schickling, *Giacomo Puccini*, 426.

10. Howard Greenfield, *Puccini: A Biography* (New York: G. P. Putnam's Sons, 1980), 205.

comfortable, large and spacious as in the most modern of hotels. Price
320 (pounds) for passage alone. Large windows with sumptuous silk cur-
tains. In short, a stupendous suite! Praise be to the Metropolitan! . . .
Enough for the present. Take care of yourself; I hope to find you on my
return completely restored to health, and that the success of the *Girl* will
have given you cause for rejoicing.[11]

Puccini and his entourage landed in New York on 16 November to much public fanfare. Not wasting a minute, he promptly began a whirlwind of social
and promotional activities (see pl. 26). Elvira, on the other hand, was miser-
able waiting for news at Torre. She wrote Puccini several letters expressing her
unhappiness. The following excerpts confirm that he had forbidden Elvira to
join him:

> November 29
> You ask me what I am doing. What should I do? I am bored and al-
> ways alone. Then I go out simply to escape solitude and sadness.

> November 30
> The fact that you did not allow me to go with you, and the way in
> which you expressed that prohibition, hurt me deeply. I shall not get
> over it. Remember this. You deprived me of a great satisfaction, that of
> participating in your triumph. . . .
> Now you are a great man, and compared to you I am nothing but
> a pygmy. Therefore be happy and forgive me if I have annoyed you with
> my lamentations.[12]

Puccini himself was attending grand parties, sightseeing, shopping, and overseeing rehearsals. He wrote to his sister Ramelde shortly after his arrival, describing the scene: "We are staying at this immense hotel [the Knickerbocker]
with fifteen or more floors and live like royalty. We have four rooms and two
bathrooms with lots of light and magnificently refined meals, everything paid
for. Rehearsals are going very well."[13] Although Puccini reveled in all the delights New York had to offer, he spent the majority of his time at the Metropolitan observing rehearsals from the back of the house, soft hat pulled down

11. Adami, *Letters,* 185.
12. Marek, *Puccini,* 259.
13. A. Marchetti, *Puccini com'era,* no. 385, p. 389.

over his eyes, "watching the child of his musical brain spring to life—but slowly." He made notes to share with Toscanini and Belasco and when necessary jumped up with a protest or suggestion.[14]

Belasco's Contribution

Belasco's contributions to the staging of *La fanciulla* were numerous and important. Considered one of the first significant directors in the history of American theater, he played a major part in helping to establish the principles of stage naturalism in the United States around the late nineteenth and early twentieth centuries.[15] Lise-Lone Marker characterizes the movement as "a complete rebirth of the theatre, replacing stagnation and rigidity with something vital and alive. . . . Naturalism sought to present the facts of man's life and environment with a fresh, new, and rich explicitness."[16] Belasco's description of his genre was poetic and concise: "My chief concern is neither with 'old' art nor 'new' art—but true art. If it not be true art to reflect, depict and interpret Nature—then, indeed, I know not what art is."[17] In addition to Belasco in the United States and André Antoine with the Théâtre Libre in France, other prominent directorial figures in this movement were Otto Brahm with the Freie Bühne, founded in 1889 in Germany, and Konstantin Stanislavski with the Moscow Art Theatre, founded in 1898 in Russia. This revolutionary movement was itself spawned by a political and technological revolution that, as Helen Greenwald says, reflected "not only the social problems arising out of the rapid industrialization of Europe (especially France), but also the rapid 'industrialization' of the theater itself."[18] It was within this context that Belasco and Puccini forged their collaborations, bringing together their own independently developed "art forms," each "from a similar point of view."[19] In relation to *The Girl of the Golden West*, the strange dichotomy of the Wild West setting and the overpowering beauty of the western land-

14. *New York American*, 5 December 1910.

15. Naturalism in drama stressed naturalistic detail in scene design, costume, and acting technique. It attempted to abolish the artificial theatricality prominent earlier in the nineteenth century. The movement was most closely associated with Théâtre Libre, founded in Paris in 1887 by Andre Antoiné. The Théâtre Libre became a model for experimental theaters throughout Europe and the United States. *The Columbia Encyclopedia*, 6th ed. (New York: Columbia University Press, 2002). www.bartleby.com/65/.11 March 2002.

16. Marker, *David Belasco*, 8–10.

17. David Belasco correspondence, draft of article for 4 June 1921. Billy Rose Theatre Collection New York Public Library for the Performing Arts, series I, box I.

18. Greenwald, "Realism," 279.

19. Ibid., 283.

scape clearly seduced both Belasco and Puccini, each in his own way. In one of Belasco's many articles, he described how he integrated these two seemingly dissimilar atmospheres into a unified whole, a vision that clearly attracted Puccini enough to create an opera: *"The Girl of the Golden West* had the sordid setting of a saloon and a gambler's den on the frontier. I knew I must give it something of beauty, so I introduced a California landscape. Drenched in sunshine it lay blue, half tropical, an undulation of cerulean hills and green valleys that called forth the heroine's reverent exclamation: 'My California!'"[20]

As seemingly parallel as their viewpoints were, Belasco was faced with some unique production and interpersonal challenges in helping Puccini transform *The Girl of the Golden West* into an opera. As he recounted in his book, *The Theatre through Its Stage Door,*

> It was necessary to harmonize this incongruous collection of nationalities and make them appear as Western gold-miners——to create through them an atmosphere of the wild Californian days of 1849. I was much in doubt whether grand opera singers who commanded princely salaries and were accustomed to special prerogatives unknown in the dramatic profession would be willing to submit to my dictation. I soon discovered my doubts had been without foundation. . . . Never before had I dealt with a more tractable and willing company of stage people.[21]

Wearing his customary clerical collar and black suit, the "Bishop of Broadway," as he was fondly known, took charge of many intricate details of the opera's staging. He attempted to inform singers who knew little if anything about the Wild West or matters of American speech and deportment during the rough and violent days of the California gold rush. There was only one American in the opera; the rest of the main cast included ten Italians, a Bohemian, a Pole, a Spaniard, a Frenchman, and two Germans. The *New York Times* reporter attending the rehearsals described the scene inside the opera house:

> Somewhere in the darkened hall sits the man who is really responsible for every movement, every situation in the play. He is the stage director

20. "Beauty as I See It," *Arts and Decoration* (July 1923), 60. Theatre Collection, New York Public Library for the Performing Arts.

21. David Belasco, *The Theatre through Its Stage Door* (New York: Benjamin Blom, 1969), 102.

to whom everybody comes—Toscanini, Speck, Caruso, Amato, Destinn, even Puccini. This man dressed in black with flowing white hair has given up every other duty for the time being. You may find David Belasco only at the Metropolitan Opera House these days. Mr. Puccini speaks in Italian and so does Mr. Toscanini. Mr. Belasco speaks in English, and yet there very seldom is any need for an interpreter. They understand each other, these men. Composer Puccini and conductor Toscanini lean forward to catch every word, which falls from the lips of the "Wizard of the Theatre."[22]

Belasco worked tirelessly with all the main singers. This included instructing Caruso on the fine art of western kissing: "No, he doesn't grab hold of her roughly. He comes forward this way, see? With his arms out-stretched. Just a little one [kiss]."[23] As one rehearsal observer put it, "People will pay $10 a seat and $120 for grand tier boxes next Saturday night but they won't see Belasco show Caruso how to kiss a young lady saloonkeeper. Money can't buy everything. I saw it, and it didn't cost me a cent."[24]

Belasco was pleased with Emmy Destinn's interpretation of Minnie.[25] She reportedly loved the opera:

> The music is exquisite. I think Puccini has never reached this level of inspiration before and such perfection in the way he suited the music to what happens in the drama.
>
> The comments of certain critics who said that he wasn't able to capture the spirit of America are wrong. On the contrary, I strongly believe he knew how to interpret the American soul in a very splendid way. The part of Minnie, which I sing, is not as difficult as that of *Butterfly;* but it is certainly the most beautiful of all the principal female parts created by Puccini. When I sing Minnie's part, it feels as though I am reliving my

22. "Teaching the West to Singers of Italian," *New York Times,* 5 December 1910.

23. "Puccini's Girl of the Golden West," *New York Times,* 5 December 1910.

24. *New York Times,* 5 December 1910.

25. Destinn and the baritone Dinh Gilly, who sang Sonora in the premiere of *La fanciulla,* were involved in a long-term romance. Throughout the liaison Gilly was married to a Frenchwoman who apparently complained that he returned home only to father another child. The romance came to an end during World War I "while they were interned on her estate outside Prague. When a young air captain crashed on the grounds, Destinn nursed him back to health—and married him." Gilly was interned for the duration of the war and never returned to the Metropolitan. See Robert Tuggle, *The Golden Age of Opera* (New York: Holt, Rinehart, and Winston, 1983).

early childhood. My father was the owner of a mine in Bohemia . . . so
when I sing Minnie it seems as if I am singing the happy songs of my
youth.[26]

"Rehearsals Are Excellent"

By the beginning of December the house of Ricordi had published the libretto
and a piano-vocal score.[27] As for Puccini, he was delighted at the pace and the
progress of the rehearsals, yet was still making last-minute changes to the vocal numbers and orchestration (see fig. 5.1). He described the process to Elvira:

                                        New York, 7 December 1910
Dearest Elvira,
        . . . The rehearsals are excellent. I think it will be a success and let's
hope it will be a big one. Tomorrow we have the dress rehearsal . . . after the premiere there will be a dinner and reception at the Vanderbilt's
place and maybe others. What happiness! . . . Tonio is well; I think he
has a crush on a ballerina. Whenever he has a chance he takes off and
I am left all alone. But this is good for him and we need to let him live
his life. Fosca has written me a charming letter; I wish she had always
been like this with me.[28] How are you doing? I hope you are feeling better. . . . The opera is turning out splendidly. The first act is a bit long
but the second is magnificent and the third is majestic. Belasco has been
at all the rehearsals with great interest and love. Caruso is magnificent
in his part, Destinn isn't bad, but it will require more energy from her.
Toscanini is perfection, kind, good, accessible. In other words, I have
faith in my work and am hoping the best for it. But it is tremendously
difficult as far as music and staging. The staging is very different in the
details from what I imagined. I even made some changes in the instrumentation, some reinforcement, and a small cut in the first act, primarily
because Destinn doesn't sing it the way I would like.
        The staging is magnificent; you'll see it in Rome in June. I can't wait
to see my little nuisance of a wife (I am too) don't get offended. Can we

26. *Corriere della sera,* 28 December 1910; see appendix B, no. 8.

27. Giacomo Puccini, *La fanciulla del West: opera completa per canto e pianoforte,* reduction by Carlo Carignani
(Milano: Casa Ricordi, 1910).

28. Puccini believed that Fosca, Elvira's daughter by her first husband, was partially to blame for
inflaming her mother's jealous feelings toward Doria. Fosca, like Tonio, sided with her mother during the
scandal.

Figure 5.1. During rehearsals for the premiere of *Fanciulla*, the tenor Enrico Caruso created this detailed caricature of the opera's principal participants. (Metropolitan Opera Archives, New York)

go to Torre for a couple of days? I would like to go. Now I need to eat a
bit [his diabetes had been bothering him in New York]. Think seriously
about a good cook, really, look for one, find her and take her with you.
Bye, kiss you.

Your Giacomo

Tonio also wrote a short postscript to his mother:

> Dear Mamma, I send you my best regards. I am giving this letter to
> a gentleman who is leaving tomorrow so it will get to you sooner.[29]

Italian newspapers reported details of the rehearsals and praised the orchestra
under the energetic direction of Toscanini, who was referred to by cast members as "Napoleon" because of his commanding demeanor and short stature.
As the day of the premiere neared, it seemed that every aspect of advance publicity had been exploited for maximum effect (see pl. 27). Robert Tuggle, the
current Metropolitan Opera archivist, notes that not until the opening of their
new opera house fifty-six years later did such extraordinary worldwide publicity surround an operatic event.

More than a thousand people attended the 9 December dress rehearsal.
The *New York Telegraph* reported that it was "perfect" in every detail and added
that the audience read like a who's who of the operatic, theatrical, and social
worlds—the directors and singers of the Metropolitan Opera and their families, New York's high society, and Broadway's best all clamored to watch this
unusual musical and theatrical feat.[30] Blanche Bates, the actress who had played
Minnie in the original Broadway play, attended and was overcome with emotion. "Tears were running down her cheeks, and when her companion said,
'why Blanche, you can't go out into Broadway with a face like that,' she simply mopped her eyes some more."[31] The usual subdued rehearsal etiquette
was replaced with joyous enthusiasm, and the audience walked out of the opera house ecstatic. Following the performance Puccini hosted an impromptu
lunch at his hotel, the Knickerbocker, with Gatti-Casazza, Belasco, Tito Ricordi, George Maxwell, and Tonio.

29. We are grateful to Gabriella Biagi Ravenni, a founder of the Centro Studi Giacomo Puccini in
Lucca, for making the letter available to us; see appendix B, no. 9. The letter is preserved at the Museo Casa
Natale Giacomo Puccini in Lucca, and is the property of the Fondazione Giacomo Puccini.

30. "Last Dress Rehearsal of *The Girl of the Golden West* Held in the Metropolitan," *New York Telegraph*,
9 December 1910.

31. Ibid.

Golden Tickets

Tickets for the premiere were sold out in advance, and the management of the Metropolitan tried to prevent speculation by devising an elaborate system of signing and countersigning for tickets. The buyer signed for the ticket at the time it was purchased, but it was not delivered until just before the performance, whereupon the ticket holder signed for it again before being allowed to enter the theater. It was impossible, however, to foil the speculators, who sold them for as much as thirty times the box office price. Indeed, tickets were already marked up by the Metropolitan to double the usual price. One speculator claimed there were "no tickets left at any price. . . . I have been offered $100 for a single seat for the 'Girl' at least a dozen times a day. . . . But, we're sold out, clean as a whistle. We could sell ten times as many seats as the house holds if we had 'em. And we could dispose of them at double and triple prices, too."[32]

Numerous reports and anecdotes circulated in the New York papers about the demand for tickets:

> Speculators who have been fortunate enough to secure subscription tickets for Saturday's premiere expect to obtain fabulous prices for them. One sidewalk operator yesterday said he expected to obtain $200 for a pair of orchestra chairs.[33]
>
> A few seats for Saturday night have fallen into the hands of speculators, and these are being offered to would-be purchasers at prices ranging from $75 and up. It is not probable that the announcement of a second performance will lower these rates, as many people who desire to hear the first performance have been unable to obtain seats.[34]
>
> A speculator said yesterday that probably not more than a score of tickets have fallen into the hands of scalpers.
>
> "I have six—a number greater than that of any man on Broadway," said this speculator. "I secured these by a personal canvass of a number of subscribers. I paid an average of $25 for each of these seats. I was offered $75 apiece for two of them today. I refused to sell, as I am confident I can get at least $100 apiece for them on Saturday."[35]

32. "$100 Offered for Seat to *Girl of the Golden West*," *New York Press*, 9 December 1910.
33. "Speculators Expect to Get Rich at New Opera's Premiere," *New York Herald*, 9 December 1910.
34. "$75 for Opera Seats," *New York Times*, 9 December 1910.
35. *New York Evening World*, 9 December 1910.

Even Otto H. Kahn, chairman of the Metropolitan Opera board of directors, found it difficult to enter the theater the evening of the performance without a valid ticket:

> One of the most amusing incidents of the evening was the refusal of a doorkeeper to admit Otto Kahn, the head of the Metropolitan executives. Mr. Kahn declined to be ruffled by the action of his subordinate.
> "He did rightly," said Mr. Kahn. "It was quite proper for him to refuse me admission if he did not know me. I think his salary should be raised." [36]

A Magnificent Spectacle

The long-awaited evening of 10 December 1910 finally arrived, and the premiere of *Fanciulla* was reported to have been spectacular in every way. Massive traffic jams, created partly by the necessity of verifying signatures, clogged the streets, and a tremendous crowd of onlookers waited in freezing weather for a glimpse of New York's affluent, which included the Guggenheim and Vanderbilt families, J. Pierpont Morgan, John Jacob Astor, and a host of musicians, composers, high-ranking military officials, and foreign diplomats. The New York society columnist Cholly Knickerbocker wrote enthusiastically in her column about the splendid showing of the elite, who, resplendent in glorious gowns and dazzling jewels, took their usual places in the great golden horseshoe of boxes.

> J. Pierpont Morgan entertained his sister, Mrs. Walter Burns, of London, Lady Johnstone, wife of Sir Allen Johnstone, and his daughter Miss Anne Morgan. Mrs. Burns was dressed in heliotrope chiffon velvet with diamond ornaments. Lady Johnstone wore black velvet with diamonds, and Miss Morgan was in black velvet with netted lace.
> . . . Mrs. Otto H. Kahn was in pale gray satin and silver and wore diamonds. Mrs. Morris Kellogg wore silver satin with embroideries of dull silver, and ornaments of diamonds and pearls. [37]

36. "Incidents of the Night," *New York Sunday American*, 11 December 1910.
37. "Society Flock to Greatest Opera Opening City Ever Saw," *New York Sunday American*, 11 December 1910.

Other newspaper accounts reported in pages of detail on the opulent costumes of the affluent:

> Beautifully as the women of New York dress for the opera on regular
> nights, they seemed last night to have surpassed their previous efforts.
> Those in the "golden horseshoe" were radiant, but they had rivals in
> other parts of the house.
>   Mrs. Vanderbilt wore a costume of white satin with a necklace of
> large diamonds.
>   . . . Mrs. Stuyvesant Fish—Gray satin draped with black Chantilly
> lace, diamond tiara.
>   . . . Mrs. Oliver Harriman—Black velvet, the corsage bordered with
> silver lace.
>   . . . Mme. Nordica—Elegant costume of cloth of gold embel-
> lished with gold net and filet lace, necklace and tiara of emeralds and
> diamonds.[38]

The Italian press also reported on the spectacle:

> As we got closer to the starting hour of the opera, the crowd increased
> until the theater seemed practically a beehive of activity. The curious
> people wanted to see the *grandes dames* arrive in their fancy automobiles at
> the theater door completely wrapped in cloaks and furs. But, it was hard
> to see anything because they were bundled up and all you could really
> see was the sparkle of diamonds, or the tip of a nose sticking out of a
> mass of feathers and reddened by the stiff wind. . . . The city is covered
> in snow and ice.[39]

Looking at the premiere from another, more serious, viewpoint, John C.
Freund of *Musical America* saw the evening as epoch-making:

> There is a subconscious feeling that this night marks an epoch in Ameri-
> can life, for this night will give New York, and through her, the United
> States, a place by the side of Paris, London, Berlin, Vienna and Milan as
> a center of music and art, and, perhaps, in the not distant future lead the
> way so that the great composers will learn to make their first appeal for

---

38. "Society in Great Array Attends the Premiere; Women Wearing Gorgeous Gowns and Jewels,"
New York Sunday Herald, 11 December 1910.

39. *Corriere della sera* (Milan), 12 December 1910; see appendix B, no. 10 ("American Enthusiasm").

a verdict here, and so show the world that we have taken the lead in presenting the works of the masters, as other great cities of the old world
have done hitherto.[40]

The curtain was announced for 8:00 P.M., but Toscanini delayed the start until 8:20 P.M. to give the latecomers a chance to find their seats in the hall, which
had been lavishly decorated with Italian and American flags. Despite the confusion and cold outside, the opera was warmly received inside the theater. The
audience's reaction seemed inevitable according to this account:

> Applause. The whole night was a hurricane of applause. Who can de-
> scribe that wondrous tumult as celebrity after celebrity, familiar or new,
> made his bow before the majestic curtain of old gold.
>   Success. This opera was a popular success before it was written. It
> was never intended that it should be anything else.[41]

There were no fewer than fifty-five curtain calls throughout the premiere performance. During the first act, the audience interrupted the singing twice and
erupted in a spontaneous burst of applause at the curtain. Fourteen curtain
calls followed. At the close of the second act, there were nineteen more and
"the singers, Mr. Toscanini, Mr. Puccini and Mr. Belasco were brought out
repeatedly before the curtain, and were completely buried in the mass of floral
tributes that were passed over the footlights."[42] As the audience quieted,
Gatti-Casazza presented Puccini with a huge solid silver wreath designed by
the jewelry firm of Tiffany & Co., a gift from the directors of the Metropolitan Opera. Toscanini and Belasco also received large wreaths from the directors, and Puccini was again called to accept another floral tribute, this one in
the shape of a horseshoe with his photograph in the center.

The third act opened after the intermission fanfare, and it was reported
that at its end the house applauded for more than fifteen minutes. Feeling
jubilant during the final curtain calls, Caruso amused the audience by drawing
his revolver out of his holster and rubbing his neck where the lynching rope
had passed around it. Observers said he appeared to love being a cowboy and
looked quite dashing in his costume, "Mr. Caruso was indeed at his best . . .

40. "First Production of Puccini's Opera," *Musical America* 13, no. 6 (17 December 1910): 1.

41. Tuggle, *Golden Age*, 71.

42. "Curtain Calls Frequent, Belasco and Puccini Respond to Brilliant Audience," *New York Tribune*,
11 December 1910.

playing the part with the dignity of the old-time Westerner, who expects to die with his boots on."[43]

Behind the scenes, Puccini told the cast and conductor, "My heart is going like a contra-bass, but I am unutterably happy. The performance has been perfect. I have no doubt now of its success."[44] Gatti-Casazza called it a great historical event for the Metropolitan, lauding the efforts of all the singers and of Maestro Toscanini: "It is a great success. The acting of Miss Destinn, of Mr. Caruso, of Mr. Amato, of Mr. Gilly is a revelation."[45] Belasco was "divinely happy."[46] Before the performance, George Maxwell presented Belasco with a lavish vellum-bound copy of the opera's score. A gift from Tito Ricordi and Puccini, it was autographed by Puccini, Toscanini, Ricordi, and every member of the cast. The next day in the *Sunday American* the Bishop of Broadway wrote:

> I may be pardoned if I confess that I was proud and happy as I watched "The Girl of the Golden West" last night. It was the child of my brain—a child begotten of a thousand memories, of tales heard at the fireside and born of the years of experience amid the scenes and the people depicted in the drama. For I myself am a Californian and my own father was a forty-niner. My earliest recollections are the stories my father and mother told me of those perilous days. As a boy I had been a member of a strolling company of players, and I had played in the barrooms that were exactly like that in which Caruso and Emmy Destinn and Amato sang so gloriously last night. The scenes I loved so well, all the dear old memories, the pain and passion of long forgotten years, were glorified by the art of the greatest living composer, Giacomo Puccini.[47]

Following the opera, a large formal reception provided an opportunity for New York society, leaders of American industry, and well-known artists and musicians to meet the celebrated composer.

> An interesting feature of the night was the reception for Mr. Puccini given by the Metropolitan's Board of Directors following the performance, in the foyer, which was specially decorated for the occasion.

43. "Dramatic Singing in Dramatic Scenes," *Sunday New York Times*, 11 December 1910.
44. *New York Sunday Tribune*, 11 December 1910.
45. Ibid.
46. Ibid.
47. "Operatic Performance Described for the *Sunday American* by David Belasco," *New York Sunday American*, 11 December 1910.

Palms and plants in bloom were in the corners and the walls were hung with vines of Southern smilax. It was in a measure informal, refreshments being served by Sherry from a buffet.

It brought together those who were in every way representative of New York Society, art, the drama and music were all included in the hundreds who went to congratulate the composer and those who were concerned in the presentation of this grand opera founded on an American theme.

Mr. Puccini lingered back of the scene after the last note was heard, conversing with some of the singers. Meanwhile the foyer was being filled. Mr. Puccini speaks no English, and French and German were the medium of the rapid words of congratulations and praise.

Compared with many operas which have their place in classic repertory, "The Girl of the Golden West" has a cheerful ending, and the guests were in a joyous mood as they discussed it with the composer. He conversed with social leaders of this and other cities, singers, actors, critics, longhaired and bald, painters and sculptors and theatrical managers.[48]

The Critics Comment

On Sunday morning, in the daily newspapers, words like "brilliant," "sensational," and "a triumph"[49] heralded the success of the new opera (see pl. 28); however, the critical reviews that followed were mixed. The reviewers of the *Tribune*, the *Sun*, and the *World* appear to agree in their assessment of the opera: "Signor Puccini has achieved surprising, let us say even amazing effects with his harmonies and his orchestration; he has failed utterly to suggest the feeling which is native to Mr. Belasco's play" (*Tribune*); "The opera is lacking in what the painters call 'quality.' The Puccini quality is there, but it is restrained" (*Sun*); "The music, generally speaking, strikes one as constrained, too elaborate and too modern in harmonic structure to suggest the primitive elemental types whose thought and action it is intended to illustrate" (*World*);[50] "The whole opera is musically far inferior to 'La Bohème,' 'Tosca' and 'Madama Butterfly.' What the public has always wanted, wants now, and always will want in any opera, above all things is melody. . . . There is surprisingly little of this in 'The Girl of the Golden West.'"[51]

48. "Reception Given for Mr. Puccini," *New York Herald*, 11 December 1910.

49. *New York Evening Post, New York Tribune, New York Telegraph*, 11 December 1910.

50. "Puccini's Operas as Heard by Critics," *New York Herald*, 12 December 1910.

51. "What the Critics Said About It [*Fanciulla*]," *Musical America* 13, no. 6 (17 December 1910): 5.

Richard Aldrich, author and respected music critic of the *New York Times*, was more judicious in his approach, complimenting the cast as the "perfect ensemble," the Metropolitan Opera for providing its finest talent even in the opera's minor parts, and the orchestra's performance as superb. He believed the immediate success of the work was due in large part to the dramatic significance of the libretto: "The play has been skillfully arranged for the use of the musician—the librettists' names are C. Zangarini and G. Civinini. They have kept the really essential features that distinguish Mr. Belasco's work and have made them count as far as they could in its operatic form."

As for the music, Aldrich recognized that the opera was a logical next step in the composer's development:

> In *Madama Butterfly* it was observed that he had ventured far into a region of new and adventurous harmonies. He has now gone still further into this field of augmented intervals and chords of higher dissonance. He has made much use of the "whole tone" scale and the harmonies that associate themselves with it. In a word, there is a marked predilection for the idiom that is coupled particularly with the name of Debussy. Mr. Puccini has himself avowed it—it was one of the first things he said to the reporters when he reached these shores.
>
> He seemed then to be forestalling criticism; but why should there be criticism of such a course on the part of a modern composer? It has often been said that Debussy has added a new form of harmony and of melodic outline, a new idiom, to the available means of musical expression, as other composers have done before him as far back as the dim twilight of the beginnings of art. . . . Mr. Puccini has but taken rightfully what is his to take, if it suits him to take and use it. But he has used it in his own way and filled it with the contents of his own ideas. There is plenty of the personal note in what he has written, and nobody would suspect it of being Debussy's. Yet it may be doubted whether any who knew the composer only through *La Bohème* would recognize him in this, so far has he traveled in thirteen years.[52]

The Italian press reported on the premiere's great success in New York; but critics such as the well-known Primo Levi had harsh words for the opera, call-

---

52. Richard Aldrich, review of *La fanciulla del West*, *New York Times*, 11 December 1910. The review is also in his book *Concert Life in New York, 1902–1923*, ed. Harold Johnson (1941; reprint, New York: Books for Libraries Press, 1941).

ing it an exaggeration of voices and instruments.[53] Others were more positive, noting the score's modern approach coupled with the characteristic Puccini sound:

> The music of *La fanciulla* is profoundly Puccinian. Someone hearing it without knowing anything more about it would not have difficulty identifying the composer. The frequent use of certain characteristic chords, which almost seem to be discords, now and then remind one of *Butterfly* and *Tosca.* . . . However, *La fanciulla* represents a new stage in Puccini's music, characterized by a refined harmony and a boldness of orchestration that make performing and conducting it very difficult.[54]

In the Roman music publication *Musica,* the critic Enrico Begni called Minnie the "little sister of Madame Butterfly" and predicted the opera would be well received in Italy.[55] But, as Girardi observes, "No one noticed . . . that *La fanciulla* represented an important turning point in Puccini's oeuvre, a move away from his previous style toward new, unexplored paths." [56]

The opera had its second performance at the Metropolitan the following Saturday and the ticket prices were again double the published rate for the premiere. The rush for seats did not compare with that of opening night, and speculators were forced to sell seats at regular box office prices. Critics found the second performance to be more "eloquent" than the first, attributing this to the cast's improved disposition once the tension of the world premiere had passed. Belasco was not present for the performance, but Puccini and Toscanini were acknowledged once again with fierce applause during the opera's many curtain calls.[57]

Italy Beckons

Finally, on 28 December 1910, after all the acclaim, Puccini announced that he would return to Italy accompanied by his son. Tito Ricordi remained behind

---

53. Gara, *Carteggi pucciniani*, 391. The Primo Levi referenced in this text was a well-known critic who wrote about *Fanciulla*, most notably in his *Paesaggi e figure musicali* (Milan: Fratelli Treves, 1913), 468–83. He is not to be confused with the respected Italian novelist, essayist, and scientist Primo Levi (1919–1987), whose works were influenced by his imprisonment at the Nazi concentration camp Auschwitz during World War II.

54. *Corriere della sera* (Milan), 12 December 1910; see appendix B, no. 11 ("The Music").

55. "*La fanciulla del West* a New York," *Musica* (Rome), 18 December 1910.

56. Girardi, *His International Art*, 282.

57. For a history of Metropolitan Opera performances of *Fanciulla*, see appendix D.

to attend additional performances in other American cities and to follow up on company business. The composer spent New Year's Eve on board the *Lusitania*,[58] fresh from his professional, personal, and financial triumph in New York. The worldwide coverage of the event created a larger market for Puccini's work at opera houses around the globe, delighting his publisher. During the voyage, the composer wrote to several friends and associates, including Clausetti and Carla Toscanini.[59] To Signora Toscanini he expressed gratitude for the conductor's brilliant work and for the family's kindness toward him:

> I'm thinking and rethinking of those days [in New York], about the rehearsals, the premiere. . . . Everything is over now, but what is left is very strong and good feelings for all of you, and this will remain with me forever. You were so good and kind to me, so sweetly thoughtful. Toscanini is such a patient and affectionate friend.

The remainder of the letter expresses Puccini's melancholy and pensiveness about his life and his future:

> I keep thinking of you both, and I envy you. I would like to be like you, with your family bond so strong, with your children who love you so much, and surrounded by friends who support you. I, unfortunately, feel so lonely in this world and it really saddens me. Yet I've always tried to be loving, but I have never been understood, or rather, I have always been misunderstood. . . . Please preserve our friendship so I will have some nice, intelligent friends who tolerate and understand me. Thank you for everything you have done for me, and believe in my eternal affection for you.[60]

Although Puccini was one of the most celebrated composers in the world, he missed the warmth and closeness of family life and still felt alienated from his wife as a consequence of the Doria Manfredi tragedy. His letter to Clausetti, written on 1 January 1911, had a decidedly different tone:

58. The *Lusitania* was immortalized five years later during World War I when it was torpedoed off the coast of Ireland by a German submarine. The surprise attack sank the ship in less than twenty minutes, causing more than one thousand casualties.

59. On board the *Lusitania*, Puccini wrote a letter to Elvira stating that the Toscaninis had been gracious hosts to him in New York, and that Carla Toscanini had helped him pack for the voyage home. Marek, *Puccini*, 265.

60. Gara, *Carteggi pucciniani*, no. 572, p. 383.

Figure 5.2. Enrico Caruso created this self-portrait, which includes Puccini and Toscanini, in 1911. Puccini appears to be holding the puppet figure of a cowboy under his arm. (Cavallari, *L'avant-scène opéra*, Paris: Editions Premières Loges, 1995)

I am coming back. Tomorrow evening I will be in London, where I will stay for two days, and then straight to Milan.

... The whole opera turned out well. ... The first act is a little long ... and there is no way to interrupt it with applause. ... It lasts for an hour and five minutes. The second and third acts speed along like automobiles at eighty [km] per hour. The musical execution is magnificent and the *mise-en-scène* is astonishing. Caruso great. Destinn, very good. Amato, excellent. Toscanini, immensely good, a true angel.

The third evening more than a thousand people were turned away. During four performances (including the third in Philadelphia) the opera made 340,000 lire.[61]

La fanciulla del West was performed nine times at the Met during the winter season, with the last performance on 27 March 1911 (see fig. 5.2). Caruso's final season appearance was during a matinee on 4 February, although he returned to sing the role of Johnson again in the autumn. Amedeo Bassi, who replaced Caruso, made his debut in March and did three more performances during the 1910–11 season, including one on 18 March at the Brooklyn Academy of Music with the complete cast and Toscanini conducting. *Fanciulla* was played as

61. Ibid., no. 573, p. 383.

part of the Met's repertory through the 1914 season and was not revived there until 1929 with the great Moravian soprano Maria Jeritza (Minnie), Giovanni Martinelli (Johnson), and Lawrence Tibbett (Rance), Vincenzo Bellezza conducting (see pl. 29).

Fanciulla was well received in other U.S. cities, giving American audiences in various sections of the country a chance to hear the work before it premiered in Europe, an unusual occurrence at that time. Performances in Philadelphia, Boston, and Chicago were especially notable; the Philadelphia production, on 20 December 1910, featured the complete Met cast with Toscanini conducting, and in Boston *Musical America* reported that the performance "was a great event. . . . Puccini has caught his public, and is holding them in an iron grasp. . . . Carmen Melis, as Minnie, seems to have added an unforgettable portrait to her already extensive gallery."[62] On 27 December in Chicago, the soprano Carolina White made headlines singing the role of Minnie; the *New York Times* reported that "Miss White's pleasing personality won favor with her audience even before her full and fresh soprano voice had awakened the interest of the critics. . . . Miss White's interpretation was a distinct success, and she sang with such expression and power that the audience greeted her with enthusiasm."[63] Bassi sang Johnson, and Maurice Renaud sang Rance; Cleofonti Campanini conducted the Chicago-Philadelphia Opera Company.[64]

La fanciulla Performed in Europe

The first European production opened at London's Covent Garden on 29 May 1911 and Puccini, who dedicated the score to England's Queen Alexandra,[65] was present to supervise the rehearsals. Some members of the London press had already praised the music and singing from the Metropolitan's production, but apparently there was a mild undercurrent of resentment in Europe at New York's growing importance in the musical world.[66] A report in

---

62. "Boston Stirred by *The Girl*," *Musical America* 13, no. 12 (28 January 1911): 5.

63. "Carolina White as Minnie," *New York Times*, 28 December 1910.

64. During the fall of 1911 Henry Savage opened an English-language version of *Fanciulla* at the Park Theatre in Waterbury, Connecticut. Savage's Company visited 117 cities in the United States and Canada with three conductors and five sets of principals. The announcement in *Musical America* called it "Grand Opera in English with a gloriously beautiful and impressive production, greater even than his memorable special ones of *Parsifal, Die Walkure, Aida* and *Madam[a] Butterfly*," *Musical America* 14, no. 23 (14 October 1911): 126, 133.

65. Queen Alexandra and her husband, King Edward VII, were devotees of opera. One of the queen's favorites was *La Bohème*.

66. "Press Is Almost Unanimous in Its Praise for *The Girl of the Golden West*," *New York Herald*, 12 December 1910.

Musical America expressed this viewpoint on its front page: "The London press prints glowing accounts, sent from New York, of Puccini's new opera, 'The Girl of the Golden West.' An undercurrent of resentment is displayed, however, in the fact that both Puccini and [Engelbert] Humperdinck are giving New York the first productions of their new works.[67] Some of the writers seem to think that New York is becoming altogether too important as a musical center."[68] The reviews following the Covent Garden performances were mixed, with most of the critics predicting the opera would have limited popularity.

The *London Times* reviewer recognized Puccini's "extraordinary gift of creating an atmosphere," calling the new work "a very exciting melodrama—in fact, the game of poker under the oil lamp in the mountain cabin, with Rance gloating over Minnie and Johnson lying fainting on the table between them, is one of the most exciting scenes of its sort in any opera, and most of the action is very rapid."[69] In addition to applauding the composer's theatrical ability, the critic also praised the singing of Emmy Destinn (Minnie), Amedeo Bassi (Johnson), and Dingh Gilly (Rance). Puccini, staying at the Hotel Savory for most of May, oversaw the Covent Garden rehearsals along with conductor Cleofonte Campanini (Toscanini was already in Rome preparing for the Italian premiere). But the London critic, like so many of his American counterparts, disliked what he called

> the absence of the lyrical element. . . . The melody is kept mainly to the orchestra and is confined to fragmentary themes repeated with changing tonality. . . . In the second act the lyrical element is subordinate rather than predominant, and in numerous places, where Puccini in old days would have written a swinging melody, we are now given declamation over a shifting, delicately-coloured background. The two methods are not properly fused.[70]

The London reviews began setting a tone for the European premieres that followed, like dominos falling one after another. In essence, reviewers failed to recognize the change in Puccini's style, expecting instead the lyrical music and

---

67. The world premiere of Engelbert Humperdinck's *Königskinder* was held at the Metropolitan Opera on 28 December 1910.

68. "London a Bit Resentful of New York's Operatic Prominence," *Musical America* 13, no. 6 (17 December 1910): 1.

69. "Puccini's New Opera," *The Times* [London], 30 May 1911.

70. Ibid.

arias that were such a hallmark of his earlier operas. Reporting on the performance from an American perspective, the *New York Times* called the opera *The Girl of the Golden West* rather than *La fanciulla del West*, saying that the London audience "testified to its enjoyment of this melodrama set to music by repeated calls for the composer, the conductor, Campanini, and . . . Emmy Destinn, who repeated her New York triumph."[71]

Months before the London event, Puccini expressed his concern about *Fanciulla*'s first Italian performance. In correspondence to Toscanini on 23 March 1911, he outlined fears that his favorite tenor for the role of Johnson, Caruso, would not be able to perform at the crucial Roman premiere due to an illness.[72] Ultimately, the event took place on 12 June 1911 at the Teatro Costanzi without Caruso, who was replaced as Johnson by Amedeo Bassi (who had sung the role in the London premiere); Eugenia Burzio sang Minnie, and Pasquale Amato, from the New York cast, sang Rance, with Toscanini as conductor. During this period, Puccini also wrote to Toscanini consulting him about revisions—or, as Budden suggests, "refinements"—to the opera.[73] The Italian premiere was well received by the audience, and King Victor Emmanuel III and Queen Helena invited Puccini into their box to offer their congratulations for a magnificent opera.[74] Although the Italian critics were, on the whole, complimentary about the composer's newest work, their comments were at times cautious, and many were perplexed by the opera's music. Giovanni Pozza of the *Corriere della sera* commented:

> It was a triumph. We can say this with joy and without restraint. . . .
> And, Italy, from Rome has decreed it a triumph at the Costanzi [Theatre] tonight. *La fanciulla del West* won a magnificent victory: a victory which established itself little by little, act by act in a continuous crescendo of emotion and enthusiasm and to which this magnificent theatre, that welcomed the most elite portion of the public, not only from Rome, but all of Italy, has given this [opera performance] a character of true solemnity.

71. "London Sees Puccini Opera," *New York Times*, 30 May 1911.

72. New York Public Library for the Performing Arts, Music Division, the Toscanini Legacy, Puccini Letter: Torre del Lago to Toscanini, New York, 23 March 1911, series L, part 1: correspondence (folder L30, subfolder A-1).

73. New York Public Library for the Performing Arts, Music Division, Puccini Letter: Torre del Lago to Toscanini, N.Y., 2 February 1911, series L, part 1 (folder L30, subfolder A-1); Puccini Letter, n.p., to Toscanini, n.p., 1 June 1911. See Gabriele Dotto, "Opera, Four Hands: Collaborative Alterations in Puccini's *Fanciulla*," *Journal of the American Musicological Society* 42, no. 3 (Fall 1989): 604–24.

74. "King Praises Puccini," *New York Times*, 13 June 1911.

I don't know if in *Fanciulla* one should actually recognize a new style in the composer. Many have said so; I don't believe it. But of one thing I am sure, that never as in this opera has Puccini demonstrated a more confident mastery over his genius and his art.

. . . The new opera is without a doubt the most perfect that contemporary Italian music has given us.[75]

Gaetano Cesari, from *Il secolo*, noted the composer's increased mastery of the orchestra, while Nicola d'Arri, critic of the *Giornale d'Italia*, remarked that Puccini's rich instrumentation made *La fanciulla* among the most exquisite and robust of his scores. Alberto Gaseo, of the *Tribuna*, complimented the librettists for creating a workable text from such unusual material and added: "The opera has every element necessary for a lasting and popular success; it was written for the public at large . . . who will understand and love it, just as they loved *Tosca* and *Butterfly*. Once again, Giacomo Puccini was able to reach the zenith of his artistic talent."[76] On the other hand, critics such as Levi and the reviewer of *Il messaggero*, who questioned the viability of *Fanciulla*, were unable to appreciate Puccini's new artistic expression. Following the reviews, Puccini felt the need to explain his modern approach to the critics:

> I hold that the "Girl" is an opera completely different from the others preceding it, in spite of the fact that many insisted on finding in it reminiscences of "Bohème" and "Tosca." It is my strongest opera, and the most full of color, the most picturesque, particularly in orchestration. As a melodramatic composition [*struttura*] it seems to me my most modern opera, and the most advanced from the harmonic point of view. Besides, being conscious of all this while I was writing it, I endeavored to keep whole and entire that Italian melodic definiteness [*finalità*] which no Italian composer should forget, and I think that I have succeeded.[77]

In late August, *La fanciulla* was performed in Brescia's Teatro Grande with both Zangarini and Civinini in attendance. Puccini was well received by the townspeople and personally greeted by the mayor. One report noted that as the composer arrived at the theater for rehearsals, "he received an ovation

---

75. *I giudizi della stampa* (The Judgment of the Press), from the program for the production of *La fanciulla del West* at the Teatro Grande di Brescia, 1911; see appendix B, no. 12. All the reviews quoted here from the Roman premiere were printed in the Brescia program. Similar comments appear in Gara, *Carteggi pucciniani*, 390–92.

76. *I giudizi della stampa;* see appendix B, no. 13.

77. "Rome Satisfied with Its *Fanciulla*," *Musical America* 14, no. 8 (1 July 1911): 18.

from conductor [Giorgio] Polacco and all the musicians."[78] The cast included Melis (Minnie), Martinelli (Johnson), and Domenico Viglione-Borghese (Rance). Shortly thereafter, in September, it was performed at the Teatro del Giglio in the city of Puccini's birth, Lucca. The Lucca program included a section of sentimental poetry written by an unidentified author and dedicated to the town's favorite son:

> Melody, who once here in melancholy lulled
> your infant whimperings with her maternal voice,
> your genius gave back to us happy,
> having taken the loveliest path from country to country.
>
> We sound your music to the heavens
> and we shout your name alongside hers;
> so that to all the world is revealed
> our sweet homeland, as sweet as your song.[79]

After a warm reception in Lucca, Puccini traveled to Britain for an English-language performance in Liverpool on 6 October, where he wrote to Seligman that *Fanciulla* was produced "with reduced dimensions,"[80] the reduced orchestra version created for smaller theaters and budgets; the composer, of course, preferred the full version, although Tito Ricordi supported the versatility of the contracted one. After a successful production in Turin on 11 November, the next performance was at the San Carlos Theatre in Naples on 5 December, from which Puccini wrote Seligman complaining that although it had gone well, the conductor, Leopoldo Mugnone, was not suitable for the opera, "which needs life, whereas he is flabby and drags out the *tempi* to indecent lengths. But the performances are always crowded and that is the important thing."[81]

The new year found Puccini in Budapest for the Hungarian premiere on 29 February 1912. On 2 April *Fanciulla* premiered in Monte Carlo; the Monte Carlo Opera Company also performed the French premiere in Paris on 16 May during their guest season. Tullio Serafin conducted the Paris Opéra production, in Italian, with Melis, who played Minnie in Boston, Caruso (Johnson), and Titta Ruffo (Rance). The *New York Times* reported that the opera was ex-

---

78. "Italians Pay Homage to Puccini," *Musical America* 14, no. 18 (9 September 1911).

79. *La fanciulla del West*, program from Teatro del Giglio di Lucca, September 1911; see appendix B, no. 14.

80. Seligman, *Puccini among Friends*, 210.

81. Ibid., 212.

tremely well received: "Among those present were Prince Albert of Monaco and many Americans. The Monte Carlo Opera Company interpreted the opera. Caruso . . . was in excellent voice."[82] The next major hurdle for the composer and his opera was the first performance at La Scala in Milan, the site of *Madama Butterfly*'s disastrous premiere. On 17 February 1904 *Madama Butterfly* was greeted with boos and shouts of protest by hecklers in La Scala's audience. Puccini suspected that his enemies had sabotaged his Japanese tragic opera and never forgave or forgot the incident. In fact, the composer never permitted *Madama Butterfly* to be performed again at La Scala during his lifetime.[83] Reluctant to let his latest opera face the potentially hostile Milanese audience, Puccini withheld *Fanciulla* from La Scala until 29 December 1912, after it had already been performed in many European capitals (as well as Buenos Aires, in July 1911). "Finally," wrote a Milan critic, "an opera by Puccini will return to La Scala with *La fanciulla del West*."[84] It was performed there thirteen times with Martinelli (Johnson), Ernestina Poli-Randaccio (Minnie), and Carlo Galeffi (Rance), and Serafin conducting. The work received a mixed reception.

Fanciulla did not premiere in Germany until 28 March 1913 at Berlin's Deutsches Opernhaus, where, according to the *New York Times*, it was "greeted with respectful attention" by the public. Critics were less enthusiastic: "the audience which filled the house was lukewarm. The types represented in the opera are as incomprehensible to a German as men from Mars would be. The pieces strike them as crude melodrama. The critics, moreover, find little to praise in the music. They say that Puccini is steadily going down hill and has reached his lowest level in this opera."[85] Another report said that months before the performance, talk in Berlin's opera circles suggested that *Fanciulla* was "much inferior both musically and dramatically to other Puccini works, notably 'La Boheme" and 'Madama Butterfly,'"[86] and following the performance the music critic of the *Tageblatt*, Leopold Schmidt, commented that "we had expected nothing good from Puccini's new opera."[87] Perhaps anticipating the German reaction, Puccini complained bitterly about the opera's cast and conductor. In a letter to Elvira ten days before the premiere, Puccini described the rehearsals as "so-so. I suffer because I do not see things progressing, as they

82. "Paris Likes Puccini Work," *New York Times*, 17 May 1912.

83. For a detailed account of *Madama Butterfly*'s premiere at La Scala, see Girardi, *His International Art*, 195–99, and Budden, *Puccini*, 240–43.

84. "Ultime notizie," *Corriere della sera* (Milan), 13 July 1911.

85. "*The Girl* Puzzles Berlin; Germans Don't Comprehend Its Types, or Like Puccini's Music," *New York Times*, 29 March 1911.

86. "Slap at Berlin Critics," *New York Times*, 1 January 1911.

87. "Critiques of *The Girl of the Golden West* Show German Feeling," *New York Times*, 6 April 1913.

should. Today we are changing the baritone; the one we are going to take has a small and ugly voice, but at least he is more of an artist. The prima donna is a nincompoop. The conductor is a mischief-maker. They don't understand a word either of Italian or of French. It is a tremendous effort for me."[88] Curiously, he wrote Elvira eleven days later that the performance was a "magnificent event." However, one can, indeed, come to the same conclusion as Budden that "the company was evidently second-rate and the prospects of success doubtful."[89] Most accounts show that the German press and public at the time did not understand or appreciate the dramatic boldness, the western esthetic, or the new direction of the opera. The work was produced in some twenty German theaters before a successful premiere on 24 October in Vienna with Jeritza as Minnie and Alfred Picaver as Johnson. In a letter from the Met archives, Puccini described her performance, which was at the beginning of her career, as "dignified"; she later became a celebrated interpreter of this role and a favorite of Puccini's.

"Misunderstood Masterpiece"

Although *La fanciulla del West* made the rounds of the world's leading opera houses, it failed to find a place in the standard repertoire alongside Puccini's other popular operas. Early Puccini biographers proffered many different reasons for this lack of immediate acceptance. Some, like Vincent Seligman, speculated that the interruption caused by the Doria Manfredi tragedy negatively affected the composer's inspiration and confidence. He also felt the hiatus in Puccini's composing had an impact on the work: "I often wonder to what extent 'Minnie and her friends' suffered from their temporary abandonment. It seems reasonable to suppose that the 'lack of genuine inspiration,' of which the critics were later to complain, was due, at least in part, to the breaking of the original thread."[90] Others blame the Wild West setting, with its complex action, or the expense of mounting such an elaborate production, with its large sets and costly staging, and the need for four tenors. Yet another reason offered is the work's so-called happy ending. But the opera's early critics were unable to appreciate or accept the works unquestionable originality; and, as Budden says about Puccini and his remarkable opera, "Now at last time has caught up with him and accorded *La fanciulla del West* the place in the

88. Marek, *Puccini*, 272–73.
89. Budden, *Puccini*, 341.
90. Seligman, *Puccini among Friends*, 184, 199.

Puccini canon it deserves."[91] In the past fifty years, *La fanciulla* has been viewed with renewed interest by opera lovers and opera houses throughout the world, and has been performed and recorded numerous times (see pl. 30).[92] Musicologists have come to see the work as "an opera that has been too generally underestimated,"[93] indeed, "one of the most fascinating of Puccini's operas."[94] Girardi concurs, adding that *Fanciulla* should be counted among those "masterpieces that have been misunderstood for too long."[95] In reality, it is Puccini's unmistakable style, as Gary Tomlinson says, that "stands comparison with any other operatic idiom from the 40 years after Wagner's death. And to my hearing, the best single act Puccini ever wrote is the first of 'La fanciulla del West.'"[96]

Such commentaries suggest that *La fanciulla* has come back to life after being virtually buried by the avalanche of publicity and narrowly focused interpretations of the opera's early critics. It would seem that Belasco's 1910 wish that *"The Girl of the Golden West* will live in music"[97] may be realized through the efforts of conductors and directors who recognize *Fanciulla* not only as a major turning point in Puccini's career but also as the composer's "stylistic leap"[98] into the new musical language of the twentieth century.

91. Budden, *Puccini*, 304.

92. See appendix E for a discography and videography of *La fanciulla del West.* Fittingly, *Fanciulla* was the first opera performed in the newly built Metropolitan Opera House: in April 1966 it was used for an acoustic test of the new theater. Appearing on that occasion were Beverly Bower (Minnie), Gaetano Bardini (Johnson), and Cesare Bardelli (Rance). On 16 September 1966 Samuel Barber's *Anthony and Cleopatra* officially opened the new house.

93. Ashbrook, *Operas of Puccini*, 146, 150.

94. Osborne, *Complete Operas of Puccini*, 190.

95. Girardi, *His International Art*, 326.

96. "Puccini Turns Respectable," *New York Times Book Review*, 15 December 2002, 14.

97. "Operatic Performance Described by the *Sunday American* by David Belasco," *New York Sunday American*, 11 December 1910.

98. Girardi, *His International Art*, 316.

PART III

Critical Perspectives

CHAPTER SIX

Operatizing America

From the moment New York's critical establishment turned its gaze on *La fan-ciulla del West* in 1910, interpretive discourse on the opera has focused primarily on two issues: its "Americanness" and its purported message of redemption.[1] Together they have yielded a body of criticism that is remarkable for its failure to query the historical contingency of its central concept (what, after all, was "Americanness" in 1910?) and its uncritical acceptance of the composer's claims concerning the characters' redemption. This chapter explores the first of these topics by considering the opera's so-called American qualities and the reception they received in 1910. The discussion situates *Fanciulla* within the historical frames of operatic exoticism and musical nationalism and benefits greatly from the perspectives offered in recent writings on opera's constructions of nation, race, ethnicity, gender, and class.[2]

Both operatic exoticism and nationalism were outgrowths of Europe's colo-

---

1. "Operatizing" was the word used by Blanche Bates to describe the process by which Puccini and his librettists transformed Belasco's stage play *Girl of the Golden West* into the opera *La fanciulla del West.*

2. Particularly pertinent to the present discussion is Richard Dellamora and Daniel Fischlin, eds., *The Work of Opera: Genre, Nationhood, and Sexual Difference* (New York: Columbia University Press, 1997), especially its introduction and essays by Susan McClary, Ralph Locke, and Ruth Solie: see McClary, "Structures of Identity and Difference in Bizet's *Carmen,*" 115–29; Locke, "Constructing the Oriental 'Other': Saint-Saëns's *Samson et Delila,*" 161–84; and Solie, "Fictions of the Opera Box," 185–209. See also Jonathan Bellman, ed., *The Exotic in Western Music* (Boston: Northeastern University Press, 1998), and Herbert Lindenberger, "Opera/Orientalism/Otherness," in *Opera in History from Monteverdi to Cage* (Stanford, Calif.: Stanford University Press, 1998), 160–90. Additional sources by Naomi André, Steven Baur, Bruce A. McConachie, Michael Pisani, Nancy Rao, and Judy Tsou are cited in the bibliography.

nization of much of the globe and the concomitant drive to establish sovereign nation-states in Europe. Conquest of the Americas, Asia, and Africa yielded rich subject matter for European audiences whose curiosity about the customs, belief systems, clothing, and sexual habits of the "new" worlds was insatiable.[3] At the same time, the continually evolving political concept of the nation-state, which required clearly drawn distinctions between national populations, was supported by Herderian notions of "the folk": the idea that there existed essential national identities that could be defined according not only to language, racial type, and ethnicity, but to music as well.[4] Johann Gottfried Herder's *Volkslieder* (1778–79) and David Herd's collections of Scottish texts were seminal in the development of the view that "every nation, at least every ancient and unmixed nation, hath its peculiar style of musical expression, its peculiar mode of melody, modulated by the joint influence of climate and government, character and situation, as well as by the formation of the organs."[5]

Although Meyerbeer's *L'africaine* (1865), Verdi's *Aida* (1871), Leo Delibes's *Lakmé* (1883), and Puccini's *Butterfly* (1904) are perhaps the most famous examples of operatic exoticism (with scenes set in Africa, Egypt, India, and Japan, respectively), they were preceded by dozens of other works such as Jean-Philippe Rameau's opera-ballet *Les indes galantes* (1735), C. W. Gluck's *Le cinesi* (1754), C. H. Graun's *Montezuma* (1755), W. A. Mozart's *Die Entführung aus dem Serail* (1782), Gaspare Spontini's *Fernand Cortez* (1809), Gioachino Rossini's *L'italiana in Algeri* (1813), and Carl Maria von Weber's *Oberon* (1826). Numerous additional examples are to be found in the repertoires of *Singspiel, opéra comique, masque,* and operetta.[6] Opera looked not only to distant continents for its exotic subjects; Europe's own working classes and ethnic minorities also provided sources of fascination for patrician audiences and were featured in such works as Bizet's *Carmen* (1875), Pietro Mascagni's *Cavalleria rusticana* (1890), Wolf-Ferrari's *I gioielli della Madonna* (1911), and Puccini's *Il tabarro* (1918).

3. Edward Said, *Culture and Imperialism* (New York: Knopf, 1991); Said, *Orientalism* (New York: Pantheon, 1978).

4. Johann Gottfried Herder's late-eighteenth-century collections of *Volkslieder* (1778–79) were seminal in this development. See Thomas Churchill's translation of Herder's *Outlines of a Philosophy of the History of Man* (London: J. Johnston, 1800), and Wolf Koepke, *Johann Gottfried Herder: Innovator through the Ages* (Bonn: Bouvier, 1982). See also the discussion of Herderian Nationalism in Helen Carr, *Inventing the American Primitive: Politics, Gender and the Representation of Native American Literary Traditions, 1789–1936* (New York: New York University Press, 1996), 106–13.

5. David Herd, *Ancient and Modern Scottish Ballads, etc., 1776* (Edinburgh: Scottish Academic Press, 1973), ix; quoted in Carr, *Inventing the American Primitive,* 108.

6. Peter W. Schatt, *Exotik in der Musik des Jahrhunderts: Historisch-systematische Untersuchungen zur Metamorphose einer ästhetischen Fiktion* (Munich: Emil Katzbichler, 1986).

Fanciulla's place within this long lineage was met with chagrin by most early American critics, who resisted seeing their countrymen portrayed as "them" in the us/them formulation that lies at the heart of operatic exoticism. Indeed, New York's critical establishment and operagoing public identified itself largely through its cultural kinship with Europe; the idea that the United States might be considered culturally distant and on a level with Turks, gypsies, geishas, Nubians, and other such types was anathema. The United States was itself a colonial power by 1910 and considered itself Europe's equal on the world stage.[7] It is hardly surprising that *Fanciulla*'s early reviews reflect annoyance that Americans had been made the object of the voyeuristic imperial gaze on the opera stage.

The exotic is expressed in opera on the most obvious levels through choice of subject matter, costume, set design, and makeup. Musically, a number of devices delineate the alien culture: unusual orchestral effects; harmonic, melodic, and rhythmic crudities; and, most strikingly, the use of indigenous musics (or, at least, musics that seem to be indigenous). The last lends a crucial air of authenticity even though the appropriated musics are played by European orchestral instruments and their harmonic and melodic structures are altered to fit the western European tonal idiom. In the tradition of the work's predecessors, *Fanciulla*'s sets, costumes, and makeup serve to conjure up the strange and remote American West while Europeanized versions of the distant locale's music construct the presence of the exotic Other. Puccini deployed musical material from Native American and African American sources throughout the opera: Jake Wallace's aria is based on a Zuni melody;[8] the motif associated with Johnson and the West is an adaptation of the African American cakewalk; and the music associated with Billy and Wowkle is saturated with "Indian" musical signifiers.

While Puccini's portrayal of America as exotic seemed perfectly normal to European audiences and worthy of scant critical attention, it resonated quite differently in New York, not only for the reasons mentioned above but because many prominent American artists, writers, and composers were at the time deeply preoccupied with finding ways to express American national identity through their respective art forms. Debate over what was and what

---

7. In addition to extending its continental dominion to the Pacific, the United States had by 1910 established territorial claims in Panama, Puerto Rico, the Philippines, and Wake Island and maintained political control in Cuba.

8. Allan Atlas, "Belasco and Puccini: 'Old Dog Tray' and the Zuni Indians," *Musical Quarterly* 75, no. 3 (Fall 1991): 362–98.

was not "American" raged in the halls of academe, music conservatories, and schools of art and found its way into the pages of newspapers and magazines.[9]

Fanciulla's reception was colored by this larger debate, which, for many decades preceding the premiere, found some artists arguing for the use of Native American and African American cultures as touchstones for Americanness and others arguing against it. Supporters contended that Native Americans were the indigenous "folk" and fit logically, it seemed, the Herderian model. Others found it unacceptably contradictory to revere as an American cultural icon a population whose relationship with the U.S. government was so tortured.[10] The same argument was used to counter the Czech composer Antonín Dvořák's advocacy of the use of African American spirituals as a point of departure for the construction of American musical national identity.[11] While European immigrants were regarded as another potential source of material, they were, after all Europeans, and the whole point of the American nationalist project was to accentuate distinctions between the United States and Europe: using the folk songs of European immigrants would, clearly, do the opposite. The search for a distinctly American voice continued to preoccupy U.S. writers, composers, choreographers, and visual artists long after 1910;[12] the storm over *Fanciulla's* Americanness, or lack thereof, provides a useful historical marker in terms of the debate's musical dimension.

Puccini, the Press, and Americanness

As mentioned in the introduction to chapter 5, the unprecedented level of advance publicity for *Fanciulla* in the weeks preceding its premiere raised expectations of an operatic Americanness that Puccini never intended to create. The

9. Robert Clark, *History, Ideology, and Myth in American Fiction, 1823–52* (London: Macmillan, 1984); Mick Gidley, *The Vanishing Race: Selections from Edward S. Curtis's* The North American Indian (Oxford: David and Charles, 1976); Sam B. Girgus, ed., *The American Self: Myth, Ideology, and Popular Culture* (Albuquerque: University of New Mexico Press, 1981); Gail Levin, "American Art," in *"Primitivism" in Twentieth-Century Art: Affinity of the Tribal and the Modern,* ed. William Rubin (New York: Museum of Modern Art, 1984).

10. Arthur Farwell defended the former position and wrote numerous articles advocating it in journals such as the *New Music Review, North American Review,* and *Musical World.* Some of these are reprinted in Gilbert Chase, ed., *The American Composer Speaks: A Historical Anthology, 1770–1965* (Baton Rouge: Louisiana State University Press, 1966). See additional sources by Adrienne Fried Block, Francis Brancaleone, Richard Crawford, and Harry Perison cited in bibliography.

11. Betty Chmaj, "Fry versus Dwight: American Music's Debate over Nationality," *American Music* 3, no. 1 (1985): 63–84; Alan Howard Levy, "The Search for Identity in American Music, 1890–1920," *American Music* 2, no. 2 (1984): 70–81.

12. The feat is thought to have been achieved in music, finally and definitively, by Aaron Copland. See Aaron Copland and Vivian Perlis, *Copland: 1900 through 1942* (New York: St. Martin's Press/Marek, 1984); Howard Pollack, *Aaron Copland: The Life and Work of an Uncommon Man* (New York: Henry Holt, 1999).

promised American quality of the opera was no doubt found to be an effective selling point and was relentlessly repeated in the press despite Puccini's
protests. Puccini's opinion on the matter was printed at least once among the
dozens of newspaper and magazine articles that were written during late November and early December. The *Musical Leader* was virtually alone in recording Puccini's objections and seemed to share both his rhetorical style and his
emphatic denial:

> How could Puccini write an American opera? How could he realize the
> American type? What did he know of the western mining camps? . . .
> In the first place, Puccini did not write an American opera and no one
> scouted the idea that he did more than he, when he saw the first bill-
> boards in front of the Metropolitan announcing "The Girl of the Golden
> West" as an American opera.
>   "American opera!" he cried aghast. "This is no American opera; it
> is pure Italian opera," and the billboards were changed.[13]

Puccini seemed shocked that few were able to place his work within the context of operatic exotica, a tradition whose lack of verisimilitude mattered little
to audiences and critics. One critic, Algernon St. John-Brenon, did, however,
note *Fanciulla*'s place in a long line of such operas, remarking that "a similar
strain is put on our imagination in two-thirds of the operas that we accept
without question. The Spaniards of 'Carmen' sing French, the Egyptians in
'Aida' sing the language of Victor Emmanuel, the gods of [the] 'Ring'—and
this is the strangest of all—lisp the mellifluous accents of Goethe and the del-
icatessen."[14] With little interest in the genre's historical lineage or current per-
tinence, and over Puccini's publicly stated objections, the press's pre-premiere
fixation on the opera's American aspects continued unabated after the first
performance.

In the days following the premiere there was near-consensus among New
York newspaper writers that Puccini, Zangarini, and Civinini had failed, with
their words and music, to capture a quality of Americanness. Reviews were
rife with opinion on what was and was not considered to be truly American,
and, as might be expected of hastily written newspaper reviews, they dwelled
upon superficial detail and easily grasped affect. Americanness was said to
be missing not only in the music, but also in certain elements of staging and

13. "Premiere of Puccini's New Opera, *The Girl of the Golden West*," *Musical Leader*, [15] December 1910.

14. Algernon St. John-Brenon, "*Girl of the Golden West* in Opening Storms Metropolitan Throngs," *New York Telegraph*, 11 December 1910.

costume and in the gestures and physical bearing of the European principals. Even Blanche Bates felt compelled to express her fear that "unless an American girl should be cast for the role [of Minnie] . . . a European with no national sympathy for that section of America, simply could not grasp the subtleties of the part." [15]

Of *Fanciulla's* American music, the *Sun's* reviewer wrote, "The opera is lacking in what the painters call 'quality.' . . . There is no page in his score that paints the primeval West nor the elemental man who hewed and blasted his way into it." The *World's* critic felt that Puccini's music was "too elaborate and too modern in harmonic structure to suggest the primitive elemental types whose thought and action it is intended to illustrate." [16] Sylvester Rawling, critic for the *Evening World,* found Puccini's allusions to popular music unconvincing: "There is nothing American about the score of 'La Fanciulla del West,' except a suggestion of ragtime, and the suave, mellifluous Italian phrases fall strangely upon the ear from the mouths of the rough and uncouth miners in a camp of forty-niners in California." [17] More than one reviewer listed approvingly the songs Belasco had used during the scene changes and intermissions of his stage play and lamented Puccini's decision to omit them; Belasco had included American favorites such as "Camptown Races," "Bonnie Eloise," "O, Susannah," "Carry Me Back to Old Virginny," "Old Dan Tucker," "Wait for the Wagon," "Old Dog Tray," and "Clementine." [18] Another critique appeared under the headline "Puccini Hears That Dixie Tune." The reporter recounts a dinnertime conversation between Puccini and Henry Savage (an impresario who owned a portion of the opera's performance rights) in the presence of Tito Ricordi:

> "There is one part of your score, my good Puccini," said Mr. Savage in choice Italian, "which needs rewriting with a strong infusion of American ragtime as the lied [*sic*] motif." . . . Signor Ricordi dropped his eyeglass into the spaghetti a la Cova, with which he was fortifying his musical constitution. "When you introduce a blackface minstrel act into 'The Girl,'" said Mr. Savage, "you have the gentleman of color twang his banjo to a weird Indian melody instead of a thrum of ragtime. That

15. "Blanche Bates, 'So Overcome from Weeping . . . That She Almost Collapsed,'" *American,* 11 December 1910.

16. Both *Sun* and *World* reviews quoted in "Puccini's Operas as Heard by Critics," *New York Herald,* 12 December 1910.

17. "*Girl of the Golden West* Given a Rousing Reception," *Evening World,* 12 December 1910.

18. See "Incidental Music for *Girl of the Golden West* by William Furst" (1905), in the New York Public Library for the Performing Arts, Belasco Collection.

is not right, and it is not American. You ought to have him pick the banjo to the tune of 'Suwanee Ribber' or 'Dixie,' you know, to be strictly true to life." [19]

Evidently the types of improvements suggested by Savage had been put to Puccini before. In an article appearing a month prior to Puccini's dinner with Savage, Viola Justin quoted the composer as saying, "I think I have succeeded in getting plenty of atmosphere in 'Girl of the Golden West' without employing the coon song to obtain it." [20]

Another element of minstrelsy was the focus of additional complaints about the opera's lack of "authentic" Americanness: the makeup of Jake Wallace, described in the cast of characters as a "traveling camp-minstrel." One observed, "Segurola, the camp minstrel, blacked his face but kept his hands white," [21] while another commented, "Only Andrea de Segurola as the minstrel seemed a bit out of the picture, for he wore a black mask instead of the traditional burnt cork, though the rest of his appointments were perfectly good." [22] For Fanciulla's second performance, "Andrea de Segurola this time did not have his face blackened." [23]

While the music and atmosphere of Fanciulla were criticized for their shortage of minstrel elements, the opera's cast was found wanting for being excessively European. Numerous reviewers echoed the Musical Leader's sentiments: "After the cast was announced there came a new flood of questions and of criticism: How could Mme. Destinn represent that type of woman, she so essentially German? How could Caruso look the part of Johnson, the horse thief?" [24] The unvarnished essentialism of remarks of this type is underscored in accounts of Belasco's efforts to coach the European stars in American stage gestures. The Sunday Telegraph reported:

So Mr. Belasco had been called in to devote this week to making this polyglot crew act as much as possible like Americans of the '49 period. Mr. Belasco has Signor Viviani at his elbow as an interpreter and he

19. Telegraph, 13 December 1910.

20. "Every Woman a Song and Nothing More, to Puccini," Evening Mail, 19 November 1910. The term "coon song" was understood to mean songs in the style of blackface minstrelsy.

21. "An International Premiere, America Proud of Girl of the Golden West," Sun, 12 December 1910.

22. Evening Post, 11 December 1910.

23. "Girl of the Golden West Gains with Repetition," [Evening Post], [21] December 1910. Given the time and energy that Belasco and Puccini devoted to details of costume and gesture (as discussed in chapter 5), their apparent indecision over Jake Wallace's appearance is most surprising. See chapter 8 for further discussion.

24. See note 13.

moves among the singers showing one a gesture, another the way to walk across the stage in Western fashion and then a third singer asks his advice as to the most correct Western fashion of drawing a gun.[25]

As mentioned in chapter 5, even a kiss was thought to have a distinctly American mode of execution for which the European principals required instruction.

The portrayal of the work's two Native American characters, Billy Jackrabbit and Wowkle, elicited from reviewers little more than cursory comment: "Marie Mattfeld sang the music of Wowkle effectively. Georges Bourgeois made a good Indian."[26] Given the reviewers' doubts that Europeans could effectively portray Minnie and Johnson, it would seem to follow that their misgivings would have extended to the Native American characters as well, yet, there were no complaints of inauthenticity concerning their stage depiction. The only problem concerning the portrayal of Billy and Wowkle was reported as a "mistake" in the libretto; it called for Billy to place the noose around Johnson's neck in act 3. The New York Times correspondent reported that Belasco caught this "mistake" early in rehearsals: "'You mustn't let the Indian tie Johnson,' cried Mr. Belasco suddenly. 'All these men hate Johnson and want to see him hanged, but there is such a thing as caste in the West, and if the Indian bound him they would all let him go.'"[27]

Incorrect gestures, makeup, and local musical color dominated reviewers' critiques of the opera's Americanness, while its prominent use of racial, ethnic, gender, and class themes elicited no response. Somewhat surprisingly, writers closer to the present day also locate Fanciulla's American qualities solely in superficial aspects and do not acknowledge the opera's structurally important musical and dramatic uses of American social divisions and hierarchies, at least not beyond summary statements that seem intended to dispose of the topic as quickly as possible.[28] These uses are particularly apparent in three story lines that run parallel to the principal narrative of the love between Minnie and Johnson. In these subplots, characters are placed in dramatic and musical opposition in ways that mirror the unique clash of classes, races, ethnicities, and cultures in the western United States circa 1849–1910. The first

25. "Belasco at Rehearsals: Drilling Singers for The Girl of the Golden West in American Ways," Sun, 3 December 1910.

26. See note 23.

27. "Teaching the West to Singers of It," New York Times, 5 December 1910.

28. Comments such as "if the viewer can get over two Indians . . . singing in bad Italian . . . there is much to enjoy" typify the manner in which such topics were handled by critics of Fanciulla. See John Louis DiGaetani, "Comedy and Redemption in La fanciulla del West," Opera Quarterly 2, no. 2 (Summer 1984): 91. About Belasco's treatment of this topic, Budden concludes, "Political correctness was never a consideration for Belasco"; Puccini, 293.

involves the story's female characters, Minnie, Wowkle, and Nina; the second concerns the triad of male characters, Johnson, Rance, and Billy; and the third pits the ostensibly classless and homogeneous group of miners against the threatening Mexican and Chinese Others.

Minnie, Nina, and Wowkle

Fanciulla's very first lines introduce the Minnie-Nina polarity: the miners, designated as "Voices in the Distance," exclaim, "To the Polka [Minnie's saloon]! / To the Palmeto [Nina's bordello]!" thus juxtaposing the two options open to the revelers. Nina is portrayed as the sexually feral, scheming, and untrustworthy Hispanic vixen. Minnie describes her as "a phony Spaniard, a native of Cachuca, a siren who uses lots of makeup to make her eyes seem languid. You ask the boys!"[29] Though we never actually see Nina, comments about her ethnicity and character identify her as a New World cousin of Bizet's Carmen.[30] Nina's only similarity to Minnie is that she runs a business that caters to men. Mere mention of Nina's name elicits strong disapproval from Minnie and later, increasingly jealous reactions as she suspects and then learns that Johnson has had a sexual liaison with her. She asks Johnson in act 2: "This evening at the Polka, you didn't come to see me. . . . What brought you here then? Perhaps it's true that you got lost on your way to Micheltorena's?"[31] A few moments later she asks again, apropos of nothing, "Did you ever know Nina Micheltorena?"[32]

Minnie, in contrast to Nina, is portrayed positively and appears chaste and pure; much is made of the fact that she has never danced and has never been kissed. Chastity is an important element of Minnie's identity and is highlighted in contrast to Nina's licentiousness, a trait emblematic of her south-of-the-border ethnicity. Minnie's chastity seems to be the source of her power over the miners and the sheriff. She defines and defends her moral position throughout the opera, as in acts 1 and 2 when she fends off the sheriff's advances.[33]

The Minnie-Nina contrast echoes that of Snow White and the Queen in the Brothers Grimm's familiar fairy tale, while Johnson's kiss, signaling Minnie's sexual awakening, serves a function similar to the Prince's kiss that restores

29. Civinini and Zangarini, Italian libretto, 27.

30. For a study of the interplay of music, text, ethnicity, and sexuality in *Carmen*, see Susan McClary, *Georges Bizet*, Carmen (Cambridge and New York: Cambridge University Press, 1992).

31. Civinini and Zangarini, Italian libretto, 50.

32. Ibid., 57.

33. Ibid., 29–30, 65.

life to Snow White. However, unlike the fairy tale, in which Snow White's awakening is presented as having positive effects for everyone except the Queen, Minnie's sexual awakening is portrayed as immensely disruptive. It disturbs all her prior social relationships and destroys the mother-son bond between Minnie and the miners. Everything changes after the kiss of act 2:

> Johnson *(holding his arms out to Minnie):*
>   A kiss, at least a kiss, just one!
> Minnie *(throws herself in his arms):*
>   Here it is! It's yours!
> *(The door opens and slams violently several times; a furious wind and blasts of snow blow into the room, disturbing everything. Minnie and Johnson embrace and kiss each other with great emotion, forgetting everyone and everything.)* [34]

Minnie's desire and the resulting kiss set in motion a sequence of events that leads to the oedipal crisis of act 3, in which the miners nearly kill the man who has taken their mother figure from them. Puccini underscores the disruption caused by Minnie's newfound sexuality with an orchestral maelstrom that combines the opera's two most significant themes, those introduced in mm. 1–12 of the prelude. The love theme's smooth and lilting quarter and eighth notes (see ex. 2.1, mm. 7–12) are transformed by the kiss into a compulsively repetitive rhythm whose tension builds to a *fortissimo* climax. Tension is suddenly released in a wash of steady sixteenth notes, with a tempo marking of *largo sostenuto molto*. The harmonic instability of the descending whole-tone motif (the so-called motif of redemption) resolves simultaneously to a full C-sharp minor triad, played *espressivo e dolcissimo* (see ex. 2.10).

Though the kiss is imbued with extraordinary musical and dramatic power, Minnie's sexual desire is not controlled by Johnson. Her agency is clear in the series of actions leading up to and following the kiss: she welcomes Johnson to her cabin and prepares to greet him there dressed in what she believes to be a sexually attractive way. Though Minnie remains chaste, the scene contains obvious sexual references that make consummation seem imminent: Minnie invites, though does not facilitate, her deflowering by removing the roses she has anchored in her cleavage, and the pre-kiss banter even includes a coy reference to a euphemism for orgasm.[35]

Minnie's determined agency in her sexual awakening is confirmed by her dramatic rescue of Johnson in the opera's final act: the kind, stable Minnie of

---

34. Ibid., 53.
35. Ibid., 52. Minnie asks Johnson, "Quante volte siete morto?" (How many times have you died?).

act 1 is, by act 3, moved to threaten her friends with grievous violence in defense of Johnson, the object of her desire. While most interpretations of *Fanciulla* focus on Johnson's redemption via Minnie's love, the sexual component of their interactions is in itself a driving force of the opera's action and generates some of its most memorable musical moments. In addition to the compelling orchestral music of the kiss, act 1's duet, beginning with "Mister Johnson, siete rimasto indietro," and Johnson's "Quello che tacete" must be counted among these.

In contrast to the complex musical representation of Minnie and Johnson's passion, Billy and Wowkle's musical interaction at the beginning of act 2 seems perfunctory and disengaged. Although Wowkle's ripe sexuality is signaled by the presence of her baby, no passion of the kind displayed by Minnie and Johnson is evident in her dialogue with Billy. Wowkle and Billy seem untroubled that their sexual relationship lacks the seals of approval conferred by church and state—an attitude that Minnie finds unacceptable. In act 1, in a scene that was cut from the opera in 1911 but restored by Leonard Slatkin in the 1990s, Minnie hammers home the point:

Minnie:
    And Wowkle? Have you married her?
Billy *(slyly)*:
    Too late to marry now. . . We have baby. . .
(This excuse elicits another round of laughter. Minnie beckons him. He approaches her reluctantly. The Girl takes the stolen cigars from his pocket.)
Minnie:
    This beggar seduced her one day. . .
    Scoundrel! And they have a six month-old baby!
    Woe to you if don't marry her to-morrow!
    Now, get out!
(Grabs him by the ear, and to general laughter, puts him out.) [36]

Billy was surrounded by miners as Minnie reprimanded him, as shown in a diagram of stage movements in the opera's production book (see fig. 6.1).[37]

36. Ibid., 26. In Ricordi's English translation of 1910, Elkin translates *pezzente* as "thieving redskin" instead of the more precise "beggar," even though the Italian word has no racial connotations. In this instance and many others, Elkin's English version of the libretto restores the racial epithets of Belasco's original. See also Elkin's translation of the words *ladri* (thieves) and *bandito* (bandit) as "Mexican greasers" and "greaser." Civinini and Zangarini, libretto, English version, 22–23.

37. *La fille du West, Opera en trois actes (du drame de David Belasco), livret de Guelfo Civinini et Carlo Zangarini, musique de Giacomo Puccini, mise en scène de Jules Speck, régisseur de la scène du Metropolitan Opera New York* (Paris: Ricordi, [c. 1912]), 22.

comme pour les interroger. Sur la 5ième mesure, page 73, Billy ent
ouvre doucement la porte du fond, se glisse en scène va au
comptoir, et avale avidement ce qui reste au fond de deux ou
trois verres, dont il lèche les bords. Erin, en l'apercevant, le d
que à Minnie en riant.
"Guarda, Minnie". – Minnie se retourne, Billy la regarde, se tour
vers elle, et riant d'un rire sournois, se frappe et se frotte l'
tomac en disant: "Buono"... tous rient. Nick, qui à ce moment
rentrait de la salle de bal, vient à lui et lui allonge un coup de
pied en disant: "Va via di qua etc. – Billy descend vers Minnie a
une humilité hypocrite.

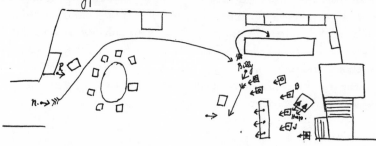

Billy, comptant sur ses doigts dit: ...una due...tre...etc. tous éclatent d
rire. – E vendible l'hai sposato?... Billy répond d'un air sournois". Spo
abbiamo bimbo..." Un nouvel éclat de rire accueille cette réponse...
ne s'avance vers lui, elle lui sort de la poche un cigare qu'il
volé, puis, sur le point d'orgue de la 2ième mesure page 77, le pr
par l'oreille et le met à la porte au milieu de la risée général
Insulté elle revient au comptoir. Les mineurs remettent leurs tab
rets en place. Erin et Harry vont replacer le banc sous l'escalie
droite. En revenant, Erin et Harry approchent la table carrée
peu plus en scène (ils doivent la placer de façon à ce que la -
mière de la lampe éclaire la figure de Minnie pendant son du
avec Johnson...) Joe reporte sa chaise à la table de Pharaon, à la
ce qu'il occupait pendant la partie. Rance reste toujours à gauche
il s'est levé et est allé près de la cheminée. Ashby l'a quitté et es
allé dans la salle de bal. Il revient en scène sur les 1res mesures, p.
78. Deux mineurs jouent à saute-mouton (un saut)
Animer la fin de la scène jusqu'à l'arrivée de "la Posta".

Figure 6.1. Diagram from the production booklet for *Fanciulla*, prepared by Ricordi shortly after
the opera's premiere, showing Minnie's and Billy's stage actions during their act 1 dialogue—a scene
that was later cut. *La fille du West: opéra en trois actes (du drame de David Belasco): Livret de Guelfo Civinini
et Carlo Zangarini, musique de Giacomo Puccini, mise en scène de Jules Speck, régisseur de la scène du Metropolitan
Opera* (Paris: Ricordi, [c. 1912]). (Courtesy of Sidney Cox Library, Cornell University)

The fact that Billy and Wowkle's sexuality is unregulated by law or religion distances them from the rest of the opera's characters. Musically, Billy and Wowkle's racial and cultural difference is reinforced by the use of "Indian" musical markers (see the discussion in chapter 2). While Nina has no musical markers to set her apart from the other female characters, her "difference" is, nevertheless, necessary to the story. Without Nina and Wowkle the sexual aspect of Minnie's character would lack dramatic definition, and the compulsive quality of the music accompanying her sexual awakening would lack context.

Johnson, Rance, and Billy

Class differences, while certainly apparent in the opera, are more sharply delineated in the play. Johnson's relatively sophisticated and educated manner of speaking is contrasted throughout the play with that of Minnie and the Polka's denizens. In the play's act 2 dialogue, Belasco distinguishes Minnie from Johnson not only through differences in their grammar, spelling, and syntax, but also through Minnie's ignorance of the poet Dante.[38]

Billy and Wowkle are separated linguistically from Johnson and also from the colloquial vernacular of the miners through Belasco's use of "Indian" English—punctuated by grunts, "ugh"s, incorrect pronoun usage, and omitted definite and indefinite articles. A third type of language is presented with the appearance of the Mexican "greaser" Castro and is characterized by Belasco's use of stereotypical Spanish misspellings and mispronunciations. Belasco's three clearly stratified tiers of language are replaced in Puccini's opera by two tiers: linguistically, Johnson and Castro join Minnie, Rance, Ashby, and the miners, while Billy and Wowkle's manner of speech, like their music, is noticeably different.

Johnson and Rance are more alike in the libretto than they are in the play, but there are few other similarities. Johnson represents the city sophisticate, claiming northern California's principal cities, Sacramento and San Francisco, as his homes. Mention of those cities, especially when uttered by Rance, is negative in tone and alludes to the hostility between urban and rural interests that polarized California (and American) politics around 1910. In act 1, Johnson's unusual request for whisky and water identifies him as a San Franciscan.

38. In the play Minnie alludes to "Dant [sic]" without seeming to know who the poet was. Johnson corrects her tactfully. The opera omits this dialogue, perhaps in deference to Italian audiences, who might have been offended by the irreverent reference to Dante. See David Belasco, The Girl of the Golden West, a Play in Four Acts (New York: S. French, 1915; reprints, 1933, 1942), 72.

Nick clarifies: "At the 'Polka' we drink our whisky straight!"[39] In act 2, Rance goads him by calling him "the lord of Sacramento."[40]

In addition to personifying an urban-rural split, Johnson and Rance represent two male sexual and class stereotypes: Johnson is the suave, cosmopolitan, sexually knowing ladies' man, Rance the inarticulate, desperate, and repulsive brute. The element of violence separates the two men. While Johnson is an outlaw, it is established that he is a "gentleman robber" and does not usually resort to violence.[41] Rance's pistol or fists are ever present: in most of his scenes he uses or threatens to use force, as in act 1, when he interrogates Johnson, and again in act 2, when he uses force against Minnie.[42]

The music of Rance's "Minnie, dalla mia casa" conveys his roiling emotions through its restless, disjunct melodic movement and thematic discontinuity (see ex. 2.5). Though Johnson's passionate, conjunct, and harmonically coherent "Ch'ella mi creda" contrasts sharply with Rance's music, its simple, hollow accompaniment acts as a subtext, suggesting a lack of substance or depth beneath the smooth melodic surface (see ex. 2.18). Johnson is at his best musically when he is singing with Minnie, as in the duet at the end of act 1, signifying the ennobling effects of her presence on his character. Musically, this is most explicit when he sings Minnie's theme during the duet (ex. 6.1).

Example 6.1. Johnson: "No, Minnie, non piangete" (act 1, 4 mm. after 117)

39. Civinini and Zangarini, Italian libretto, 29.

40. Ibid., 67.

41. Johnson bears a strong resemblance to the legendary "social bandit" Joaquín Murieta, the subject of numerous dime novels published in the United States during the second half of the nineteenth century. See María Herrera-Sobek, *Northward Bound: The Mexican Immigrant Experience in Ballad and Song* (Bloomington: Indiana University Press, 1993), 11–33.

42. Civinini and Zangarini, libretto, 34, 65.

Example 6.1. *(continued)*

Sie - te u - na cre - a - tu - ra d'a - ni - ma buo - na e

pu - ra . . . e a - ve - te un vi - so d'an - ge - lo! ___

con grande espressione

dim.

diminuendo

Rance and Johnson also occupy opposite positions in relation to the rule of law in American society. Sheriff Rance, representing the law and the state, is portrayed as unethical and corrupt, while Johnson, the man outside the law, is portrayed sympathetically as the rugged individual, forced to operate outside the legal economic system in order to support his mother and siblings after the death of his father. His act 2 solo, "Non mi difenderò" (see ex. 2.13), establishes that his crimes—against property, not individuals—are forgivable. Such crimes, perpetrated against large, wealthy companies such as Wells Fargo, are typically lauded in American western myth and are seen as justified acts of retaliation by the individual against an exploitative, privileged elite.[43] Hence Johnson, though he is a criminal, and a Mexican criminal at that, takes his place among a certain type of American outlaw-hero made famous in the

43. See Eric Hobsbawm's description of the "noble robber," quoted in Herrera-Sobek, *Northward Bound*, 16.

era of dime novels and silent movie westerns. Indeed, the theme most closely identified with the spirit of the American West, the syncopated music of the prelude (see ex. 2.1, mm. 30–34), is the theme most often associated with Johnson.[44]

While Johnson and Rance are positioned differently in relation to the law, Billy is seen in the opera as completely outside the law and society, having neither a positive nor a negative relationship to it. By contrast, Belasco's Native Americans occupy a less marginal position, as evidenced by their rarely mentioned scene in the play's act 3 (not included in the opera), in which Billy and Wowkle sing a politically charged rendition of "My Country 'Tis of Thee." They sing the song perfectly, not in the stereotypically fractured English that characterizes their dialogue elsewhere in the play. Billy and Wowkle's sarcasm is even noted by the miners who listen to it:

> (*The boys all try to make each other sing. While they are chafing each other, Wowkle and Billy Jackrabbit rise and sing.*)
> Billy Jackrabbit and Wowkle:
> "My country 'tis of thee,
> Sweet land of liberty,
> Of thee I sing!"
> Sonora:
> Well, if that ain't sarkism!
> Billy Jackrabbit and Wowkle:
> "Land where our fathers died" . . .
> Sonora (*quickly during the pause between the two lines*):
> You bet they died hard!
> Billy Jackrabbit and Wowkle:
> "Land of the Pilgrim's pride,
> From every mountain-side
> Let freedom ring!"
> (*When the song is ended, the Indians sit down again.*)[45]

Through this short but potent scene Belasco credits the Native American characters with an awareness of their disenfranchised social, political, and economic position. In the opera, Puccini and his librettists substitute nothing comparable, leaving Billy and Wowkle with no opportunity to demonstrate such awareness.

---

44. It accompanies both his entrance and the first scene.
45. Belasco, *The Girl*, 117.

1. A portrait of Giacomo Puccini taken while he was working on *La fanciulla del West*, his seventh opera. The photograph was signed by the composer at Torre del Lago, December 1907. (Metropolitan Opera Archives, New York)

2. A previously unpublished photo of *Fanciulla*'s librettist, Carlo Zangarini, c. 1910–11. (Courtesy Geminino Zangarini family, Bologna)

3. The Miners. One of several cast photographs from the premier production at the Metropolitan Opera, New York, 1910. (Metropolitan Opera Archives, New York)

4. Emmy Destinn as Minnie in the premier production, 1910.
(Metropolitan Opera Archives, New York)

5. An autographed sketch of Minnie's theme and a publicity photo of Puccini as they appeared in the *New York Times* on 11 December 1910. (Metropolitan Opera Archives, New York)

6. Enrico Caruso as Dick Johnson/Ramerrez in the premier production, 1910.
(Metropolitan Opera Archives, New York)

7. Pasquale Amato as Sheriff Jack Rance in the premier production, 1910.
(Metropolitan Opera Archives, New York)

8. Front cover of the sheet music for three numbers from *La fanciulla del West*, distributed by the Ricordi Company. They include the minstrel Jake Wallace's nostalgic song, Minnie's aria from act 1, and Johnson's aria "Ch'ella mi creda" from act 3. (Rosalind Gray Davis collection. © Archivio Storico Ricordi. All rights reserved. Reproduced by permission)

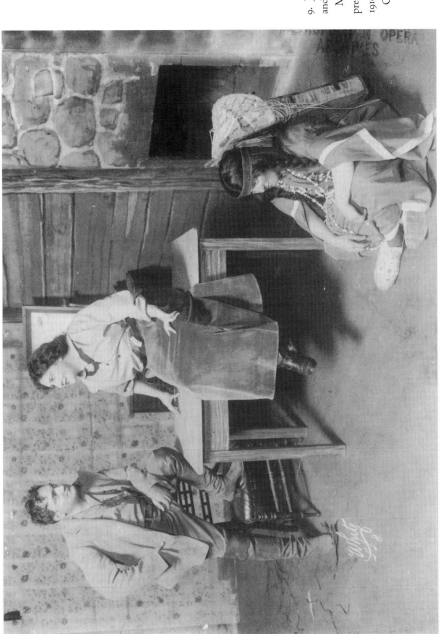

9. Johnson, Minnie, and Wowkle (Marie Mattfeld) in the premier production, 1910. (Metropolitan Opera Archives, New York)

10. Minnie aiding the wounded Johnson, act 2. From the premier production, 1910. (Metropolitan Opera Archives, New York)

11. The Card Game, act 2, as produced at the premier production in 1910.
(Metropolitan Opera Archives, New York)

12. The Forest Scene, act 3; Set for the premier production, 1910. (Metropolitan Opera Archives, New York)

13. The Hanging Scene, act 3, as produced at the opera's premiere, 1910. (Metropolitan Opera Archives, New York)

14. One of the few published photographs of Sybil Seligman, a longtime friend and confidante of Puccini. (Metropolitan Opera Archives, New York)

15. Photographic portrait of Elvira Puccini, née Bonturi, wife of Puccini and mother of Antonio, the composer's only child. (From Leopoldo Marchetti, *Puccini nelle immagini* [Milan: Garzanti, 1949])

16. A facsimile of Puccini's letter to Carlo Zangarini dated 28 September 1907 conveying the composer's early characterization of Minnie. (Marvin Gray Collection)

HOTEL BRISTOL
WIEN

Caro Zeta
T'ho scritto
a Bologna —
perchè Tito mi disse
del suonatore di
Flauto che tu
dovevi finire!
e mi crucciai al
pensiero di doverti
troncare il lavoro.
Ora ti so a Torre
e mi fa tanto piacere

Spero che questa mia
ti raggiunga —
Butt. andrà giovedì
la prova generale andò
benissimo — commozione
immensa in tutti —
Grande poesia nella
musica e in scena —
però dunque bene.
Ora a noi —
Mi raccomando la
nostra Girl — sempre
più la penso sempre
più me ne innamoro.
Penso seriamente
al 3° atto — quello
io non lo vedo ancora
bene

17. A facsimile of the letter Puccini wrote to Zangarini expressing his frustration at the lack of a special "gimmick" in Fanciulla's third act. He uses the *coro a bouche fermée* of *Madama Butterfly's* second act as an example of the proper approach. Puccini wrote on both sides of the letter, and his handwriting is visible on the front and back of the paper. (Marvin Gray Collection)

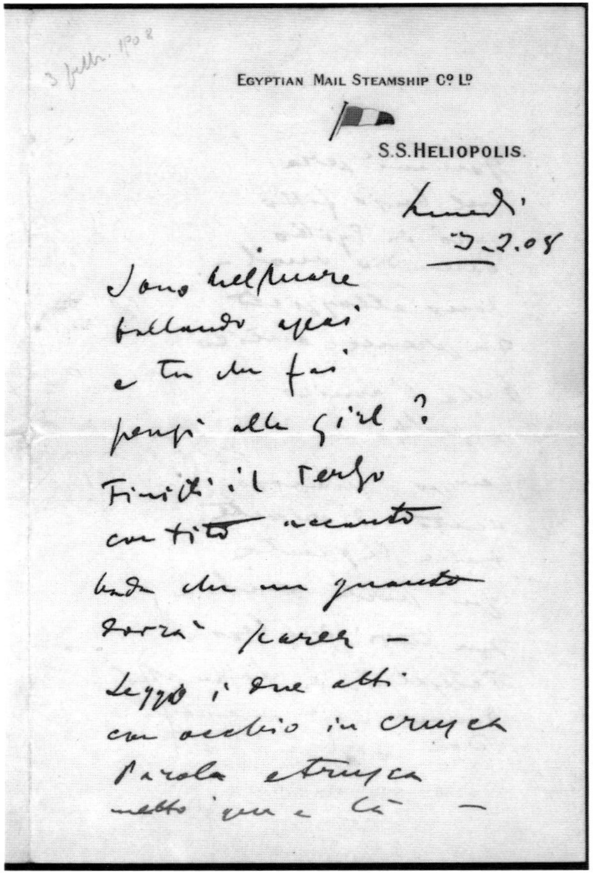
3 febbr. 1908

EGYPTIAN MAIL STEAMSHIP Cº Lᴰ

S.S. HELIOPOLIS.

Lunedì
3-2-08

Sono nel mare
ballando assai
e tu che fai
pensi alle girl?
Finito il terzo
con tutto accento
bada che un quanto
sarà parere —
Leggo i due atti
con occhio in crusca
parola etrusca
metto qua e là —

18. Puccini wrote this poem, containing many witty allusions, aboard the SS *Heliopolis* while traveling to Egypt for a vacation. The letter is an example of how the composer often wrote in rhyme. (Marvin Gray Collection)

LIBRETTISTI:

GUELFO CIVININI

19. Puccini's second librettist for *Fanciulla*, Guelfo Civinini, reproduced from the 1911
performance program of *La fanciulla del West* at the Teatro del Giglio, Lucca.
(Courtesy Geminino Zangarini family, Bologna)

20. Puccini with his wife, Elvira, and son, Tonio, at Torre del Lago in 1908. (From *Carteggi pucciniani*, Eugenio Gara, ed. [Milan: Ricordi, 1958]. © Archivio Storico Ricordi. All rights reserved. Reproduced by permission)

21. Doria Manfredi. The photograph comes from Doria's obituary, which was printed in the Milan newspaper *Corriere della sera* in January 1909.

22. A facsimile of the letter in which Puccini urges Zangarini to make an important addition to the libretto of *Fanciulla*'s third act. (Marvin Gray Collection)

23. On 13 July 1910 Puccini wrote two letters to Zangarini while he was finalizing *La fanciulla*. This facsimile of the first letter makes several important references to a crucial section at the end of the third act. (Marvin Gray Collection)

24. The four men responsible for the premiere of *La fanciulla del West*: Giulio Gatti-Casazza, David Belasco, Arturo Toscanini, and Puccini. Photographed at the time of the premiere, 1910. (Metropolitan Opera Archives, New York)

25. Puccini and Tito Ricordi on their way to New York in 1910. (From *Carteggi pucciniani*, Eugenio Gara, ed. [Milan: Ricordi, 1958]. © Archivio Storico Ricordi. All rights reserved. Reproduced by permission)

26. Newspaper caricature of Puccini arriving in New York City with
his latest opera. The *New York Telegraph* featured the title of the American
play rather than the Italian name of the work.
(Metropolitan Opera Archives, New York)

GIULIO GATTI-CASAZZA   GIACOMO PUCCINI   DAVID BELASCO   ARTURO TOSCANINI

First Performance
on any stage of
Giacomo Puccini's
Opera
The Girl of the Golden West
(La Fanciulla Del West)
Founded on the Drama written by
David Belasco

Metropolitan Opera Company
Giulio Gatti-Casazza, General Manager

Metropolitan Opera House
NEW YORK
DECEMBER 10ᵀᴴ 1910

John Brown
BUSINESS COMPTROLLER

27. Reproduction of a handbill distributed by the Metropolitan Opera to publicize
the premiere of *La fanciulla del West*. (Metropolitan Opera Archives, New York)

Scenes and Stars in "The Girl from the Golden West"

SCENE FROM THE GIRL OF THE GOLDEN WEST.

"THE GIRL" PROVES PUCCINI TRIUMPH

Opera Based on Belasco Play Electrifies Great Audience at the Metropolitan.

CARUSO AS A WESTERNER

Composer, Playwright, Society and Star Cast Join in Making Premier Notable Occasion.

THE GIRL OF THE GOLDEN WEST

"La Fanciulla del West"

Giacomo Puccini.

The Cast.

Minnie	Emmy Destinn
Johnson	Enrico Caruso
Jack Rance	Pasquale Amato
Nick	Albert Reiss
Ashby	Adamo Didur
Sonora	Dinh Gilly
Sid	Angelo Bada
Trin	Giulio Rossi
Bello	Vincenzo Reschiglian
Harry	Pietro Audisio
Joe	Glenn Hall
Happy	Antonio Pini-Corsi
Larkens	Menotti Frascona
Billy	Georges Bourgeois
Wowkle	Marie Mattfeld
Jake Wallace	Andrea de Segurola
Jose Castro	Edoardo Missiano
Rider of the Pony Express	Lamberto Belert

Conductor .. **Arturo Toscanini.**

By Telegraph from a Staff Correspondent.
New York, Dec. 10.—Dedicated to Queen Alexandra of England, thus keeping an old promise made in London when "Madame Butterfly" was given during the "Summer of 1906, Giacomo Puccini's 'Girl of the Golden West' (La Fanciulla del West) had one of the most extraordinary first-time-on-any-stage productions at the Metropolitan Opera House this evening. Everything conspired to make ...

... this set. The fact that Minnie wins in this game of lives, as well as a game of cards, gives Puccini a chance to do some striking tempestuous musical description.

The Farewell.

The third act takes one again out into the open, into the California forests, where her lover, who has been captured by the posse, is about to be lynched, but who is saved by Minnie riding to his rescue on horseback at breakneck pace. She converts the crowd, at first hostile, into her own partisans, convinces them that if they will let her and her lover go, that she will redeem the man, and with him she will start life anew in some more favorable clime.

And so "he ...

28. One of the many dramatic headlines and articles heralding the premiere of *La fanciulla*. (Metropolitan Opera Archives, New York)

29. Rehearsal photo of *Fanciulla* as revived at the Metropolitan Opera in New York on 2 November 1929. Pictured are, back row, left to right: Lawrence Tibbett (Rance), Ernst Lert (stage director), Giulio Setti (chorus master), and Frederick Jagel (Johnson); front row, left to right: Giulio Gatti-Casazza, Maria Jeritza (Minnie), and David Belasco. Jagel was scheduled to sing Johnson later in the season; Giovanni Martinelli sang the role at the premiere. (Metropolitan Opera Archives, New York)

30. Catherine Malfitano and Placido Domingo at the bar in act 1; from a rehearsal of the Los Angeles Opera's production of *Fanciulla*, September 2002. (Robert Millard/LA Opera)

31. Jeannette MacDonald and Nelson Eddy as they appeared in Sigmund Romberg's 1938 musical film version of The Girl of the Golden West. (*The Girl of the Golden West* ©1930 Turner Entertainment Co. A Warner Bros. Entertainment Company. All Rights Reserved)

32. Cover of *L'ultimo dei Moicani,* composed by Paul Allen to a libretto adapted by
Carlo Zangarini from *The Last of the Mohicans* by James Fenimore Cooper (1826),
c. 1916. (Courtesy Geminino Zangarini Family, Bologna)

The Miners: Nation and Other

Through scenes featuring the miners' interactions with Billy and Castro, a sense of American nationhood develops as defined by the tension of a self/Other split: the miners represent the stable, culturally homogeneous core of Cloudy Mountain's society, while figures representing the Other remain, dramatically and musically, on the periphery. Billy is set apart as Other through his music, gestures, stage actions, and interactions with the boys in the Polka and Minnie. In act 1 his entrance is described thus: "Billy enters with furtive steps; he approaches the bar and gulps down the dregs of two or three glasses, licking the brims."[46] A second group, the Mexicans, also represents a threatening Other against whom the miners must protect themselves. Ashby says of Johnson that "he commands a band of Mexican thieves: a tough, clever bunch that's ready for anything. Stay on your guard."[47] A Chinese Other is also present but appears only in the miners' epithets, as in the first act, when Sonora ridicules Rance as "Chinese face" or "yellow mug" for believing that Minnie will eventually succumb to him.[48]

In contrast to the menacing Others represented by Billy, Castro, and the unseen Chinese, the miners are portrayed through their actions and music as sympathetic characters who long for the simple pleasures of home and mother.[49] The impression is formed early in the first act with the ensemble number led by Jake Wallace (see ex. 2.2). The miners are also presented as the guardians of civic values, enforcers of justice, and upholders of morality: they punish a cheater (an Australian) and study the Bible in the first act; form a posse to catch the Mexican bandits in the second; and invoke the will of a seemingly Christian deity as justification for freeing Johnson in the third.[50]

On the fringe of the miner's group is Jake Wallace. In blackface, he embodies the most complex representation of the Other in the opera. He is white and, by impersonating a black singer, evokes the unique American tradition of blackface minstrely.[51] Yet, he does not actually sing a "coon song," as Puccini

46. Civinini and Zangarini, libretto, 25.

47. Ibid., 20.

48. Ibid., 21. The libretto's Italian expressions for these terms are *faccia di cinese* and *muso giallo*, respectively. In Ricordi's 1910 English version, Elkin translates these as "yellow-faced old Chinaman" and "old yellow face."

49. Ibid., 15–16.

50. Ibid., 87–88.

51. It was reported that "when Puccini expressed an interest in hearing some Negro spirituals and minstrel songs [during his 1907 visit to New York], one of his hosts arranged for a troupe of black singers to entertain at an evening in his honor." Marie Ponzo, "Homage to the West, Italian Style," *Identity Magazine*, January 1977, 64.

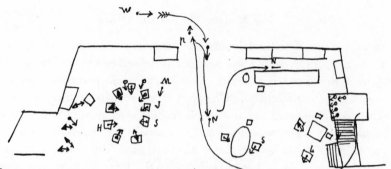

Wallace, en paraissant sur la mesure 2/4 de la page 21, attaque "La mia mamma" et se fait étonné du silence qui l'accueille; tous les mineurs se tournent vers lui et de la main lui font signe de continuer. Wallace descend d'un pas ou deux et continue. Les artistes et choristes, assis à la table de Phardon restent assis tout le temps. Seul Harry se lève pour dire sur place "O mia casa" etc page 30. Tout l'ensemble qui suit (page 23) doit être chanté avec beaucoup de sentiment.

Figure 6.2. Diagram from the production booklet for *Fanciulla* showing Jake Wallace's stage
position during his act 1 aria "Che faranno i vecchi miei." *La fille du West: opéra en trois actes
(du drame de David Belasco); livret de Guelfo Civinini et Carlo Zangarini, musique de Giacomo Puccini, mise en scène
de Jules Speck, régisseur de la scène du Metropolitan Opera* (Paris: Ricordi, [c. 1912]).
(Courtesy of Sidney Cox Library, Cornell University)

put it, or music that would have been typical of minstrelsy around 1849, as
interpreted in 1910. Rather, as Allan Atlas has shown convincingly, Wallace's
"Che faranno i vecchi miei" (see ex. 2.2) is Puccini's version of a Zuni melody.[52] Henry Savage's ability to identify the tune as "a weird Indian melody"
suggests that it may even have been familiar to members of the 1910 audience.
The structural importance of "Che faranno i vecchi miei" as one of the opera's three principal musical themes, in addition to the dramaturgical weight
of the scene in which it first appears, indicates that Wallace's role is pivotal
despite his seeming irrelevance to the plot.

Wallace can be interpreted as embodying both Other and self, black and
white. And while the Zuni-inspired song he sings bridges the gulf between
these opposed forces, its ephemeral nature signifies the alienated opposites'
doom: the song's unifying effect lasts just for the few minutes of its duration
and cannot be sustained. Significantly, Wallace enters the social space of the

52. Puccini's source was probably Carlos Troyer's Wa-Wan Press arrangement of a Zuni "Festive
Dance." See Atlas, "Belasco and Puccini," 362–98.

Polka only while he is singing. When he stops and the fragile, temporary union of alienated opposites comes to an end, he leaves the Polka, returning the unreconciled opposites he embodies back to the fringe of social consciousness. Wallace's position on the fringe of the Polka is represented graphically in the diagrams of the Metropolitan's stage director, Jules Speck (see fig. 6.2).[53] Interestingly, it was the character of Wallace that most engaged Puccini's imagination when he first saw Belasco's stage play in 1907.[54]

Expectations and Promises

It is clear from the foregoing discussion that *Fanciulla*'s early reception was marked by false expectations and unrealistic promises. The public expected Puccini to craft an operatic paean to the American character and spirit for consumption on the world's opera stages. Instead, he delivered a work that placed all of *Fanciulla*'s characters in the subordinate position of exotic objects. Advance publicity promised "an American opera" and implied that *Fanciulla*'s music would give much-needed direction to the long and tortuous search for a national musical identity. Instead, Puccini's music, save for its ragtime and Native American–derived themes, was well within the parameters of contemporaneous European opera.[55] However, as the analysis of the three structurally important subplots demonstrates, Puccini and his librettists operatized America in ways that were neither expected by nor promised to American audiences; they exploited and accentuated the unique divisions and hierarchies of American society extant in 1848 (as interpreted in 1910) in order to develop the opera's story and to delineate character. Indeed, *Fanciulla* is distinguished by the tight musicodramatic coherence and depth of these three American story lines.

53. See note 37.

54. Osborne, *Complete Operas of Puccini*, 176.

55. This is certainly the impression given by the reviews that appeared in Ricordi's monthly *Ars et Labor*, July 1911. The newspaper critics Giovanni Pozza, Gustavo Macchi, Pietro Suzzi, Nicola D'Atri, Enrico Beni, and Lionello Spada commented positively on recent performances in London and Rome and did not mention issues of "authenticity" or Americanness in their reviews; *Ars et Labor*, July 1911, 557.

CHAPTER SEVEN

Redemption and Other Critical Orthodoxies

"The Girl of the Golden West—a drama of love, and moral redemption"
From the preliminary note to *La fanciulla del West*

Unlike the debate over *Fanciulla's* Americanness, which was sparked by the Metropolitan Opera's publicity campaign and fueled by the artistic community's preoccupation with American identity, the idea that redemption is at the heart of the opera comes from Puccini himself. Backed by the powerful notion of "the composer's intentions," the belief that redemption is the opera's dramatic and musical goal carries the weight of ultimate authority despite the fact that for Minnie no redemption actually takes place. The discussion below examines Puccini and Zangarini's own words regarding the invention of the redemption plot and concludes that while they carefully crafted Johnson's redemption, the composer and librettists left Minnie's fate at best unresolved.

Plotting Redemption

Early in his work on *Fanciulla* Puccini identified the need to replace Belasco's final act with "*something* that makes people say from sheer amazement: bravo, by God!" [1] The composer perceived as anticlimactic the play's talky act 3 and very brief, bittersweet act 4 (a quiet, panoramic view of the lovers at daybreak in a prairie landscape, one week after their departure from Cloudy). In his

---

1. MGC 12.

act 4 Belasco carefully calibrated the stage lights' intensity to increase steadily throughout in order to simulate the brilliance of sunrise,[2] and though stunning on its own terms, this did not strike Puccini as a satisfactory ending. By August 1907 he had envisioned the thrilling manhunt-rescue-exit sequence as a substitute for Belasco's acts 3 and 4.[3] Only later, after putting his brain "through the wringer," did he craft the redemption plot as a necessary dramatic adjunct to the new ending.[4] That he concocted a redemptive theme worthy of both Bayreuth and Hollywood is hardly surprising given Puccini's taste for westerns and the then-prevalent appetite—both his own and the audience's—for Wagner-style cryptoreligious entertainments. This theme evolved over a period of months in 1907–8, and in fact its details were not finally in place until five months before the 1910 premiere. When completed, the redemption plot provided new structural pillars for the opera and dramaturgical motivation of sufficient gravity to support the weight of the new climax.

Although by mid-July 1907 Puccini had imagined "a big scene in which she [Minnie] pleads for his [Johnson's] freedom,"[5] he was still not sure what to do with the schoolroom scene preceding it.[6] He vacillated and had good reasons both to keep it and to cut it. In favor of keeping the *class di asen* (literally, "classroom of asses")[7] was the fact that its short though pointed discussion of the Prodigal Son story contained the rationale for the miners' forgiveness of Johnson. In favor of cutting it was Puccini's perception that it interrupted the flow of action leading up to the new manhunt-rescue. Belasco's passage reads:

> *Girl:* . . . of late a man in trouble has been on my mind . . . an' I fell to
>   thinkin' of the Prodigal Son—he done better at last, didn't he?
> *Sonora:* I never heard that he was a cardsharp. . .
> *Girl:* But suppose there was a moment in Sid's life when he felt called

2. See the author's detailed directions for lighting effects in David Belasco, *The Girl of the Golden West: A Play in Four Acts*, (New York: S. French, 1915; reprints, 1933, 1942, 151–57). The novel lighting effects of Butterfly's vigil were also a product of Belasco's fertile theatrical imagination.

3. MGC 6 and 7.

4. MGC 12: "We really need to put our brains through the *wringer* and search and search and search."

5. Puccini to Sybil Seligman, 14 July 1907.

6. The "schoolroom" refers to the dance-hall area of the Polka, which had been converted into an "Academy." Here Minnie gave lessons to the miners in the rudiments of reading, writing, and counting. Though most of Belasco's act 3 takes place in this location, the "schoolroom scene" refers specifically to the dialogue between Minnie and the boys as they begin a reading lesson on the first day of school.

7. This was Puccini's tongue-in-cheek term for Belasco's schoolroom scene. See Puccini to Giulio Ricordi, 15 July 1907; Adami, *Letters*, 183.

upon to find an extra Ace. Can't we forgive him? . . . Some of us are
lucky enough to be born good—others have to be elected . . . It jest
came over me that we mustn't be hard on sinners.[8]

The composer's letter to Zangarini of 28 September 1907 indicates that Puccini had started to imagine alterations to the schoolroom scene in order to
make it work with his new conception of Minnie's heroic rescue of Johnson.
Contrary to Belasco's scenario, in which Minnie exits after the dialogue quoted
above and reappears moments later to argue for Johnson's release, Puccini envisioned a single, spectacular entrance for Minnie timed precisely to coincide
with the moment of Johnson's greatest peril. He described the problem thus:
"it seems to me that it is not worth the effort to have her enter and exit for
the *cardsharp-ace*[9] story only to return at the *critical* moment . . . couldn't the
cardsharp-ace story be done at the *high point*, that is, when she has arrived to defend *him?*"[10]

Not convinced that Belasco's "cardsharp-ace story" sufficed as dramatic
motivation for Minnie to risk everything to save Johnson and for the blood-
thirsty miners to remove the noose from Johnson's neck, Puccini wrote in October 1907: "It's lacking a 'gimmick' [*trovata*] and it needs it. What will it be?
Who knows?"[11] Zangarini's memoir of *Fanciulla*'s creation establishes that the
long-sought *trovata* was devised shortly thereafter—sometime during the late
fall or early winter of 1907. The librettist explains that it was during one of
their walks in Torre del Lago that the composer, in a flash of inspiration, conceived the idea for the act 1 Bible scene (in which the word "redemption" is
first heard via Minnie's recitation of Psalm 51): "a graceful, intimate little scene
in the first act, in which Minnie, the girl, reads a Bible verse to the rough but
good-hearted miners dawned upon him during a discussion with me. . . . And
all of a sudden . . . this simple *trovata* gave a new motivation to the beloved
protagonist."[12]

8. The context makes clear that this is Minnie's veiled plea for *Johnson's* forgiveness, even though she is
ostensibly defending Sid against continued punishment for the cheating incident of act 1. Belasco, *The Girl*,
115–19.

9. Puccini refers to this dialogue with the shorthand "cardsharp-ace story" (*la storia baro-asso*) because of
its key words, referring to the cardsharp (*baro*) Sid and the hidden ace (*asso*) with which he cheated; MGC 9.

10. Here Puccini underlines "him" to clarify that Minnie is now defending Johnson explicitly and no
longer obliquely through the story of Sid.

11. MGC 12. The word *trovata* in this context means "theatrical gimmick."

12. "Una graziosa, intima scenetta del primo atto, là dove Minnie, la fanciulla, legge ai rudi e buoni
cercatori d'oro un versetto della Bibbia, gli balenò improvvisa, in una discussione con me. . . . E d'un tratto
le anime e il lago e il cielo si rischiararono a quella semplice *trovata*, che donava però la grazia di una inten-

The idea to link the new notion of redemption to the schoolroom scene in act 3 and to invest the material with structural weight appears to have occurred to Puccini in early 1908, but it fell to Zangarini to integrate the *trovata* into act 1, which was already written, and the new act 3, which had not yet even been outlined. In April 1908 Puccini wrote to him, "I'm expecting the prose outline of the third [act]. . . . Keep an eye on the idea of redemption, which must linger above the whole work." [13] Zangarini appears to have had considerable trouble executing Puccini's directives to plant the redemption material into the libretto in such a way that it would "linger above the whole work." At this point Civinini was engaged to assist in the deployment of the important, new structural element. In May 1908 Puccini wrote to Civinini, "I am awaiting the revised proofs of act 1. . . . In the duet, I should mention redemption only once. Write and give me news of act 3." [14] Two years later, in mid-July 1910 Puccini was still refining the *trovata*'s treatment in act 3: "After the word *redemption* on page 14b, Minnie remains ecstatic. . . . Since after Minnie's word 'redemption' there is a long orchestral postlude, during it I would have Sonora play his last cards." [15] "Redemption," underlined each time it appears in this letter, underscores its importance as the theatrical gimmick through which Puccini and his librettists crafted the necessary musicodramatic support for *Fanciulla*'s new climax.

Puccini did not, of course, publicly disclose the tortuous origins of the redemption plot. Rather, through an interview given to Arnaldo Fraccaroli of Milan's *Corriere della sera*, the composer instigated the idea that redemption was, and always had been, the opera's central feature. Puccini granted the interview just as he was finishing the opera, and Fraccaroli was the first reporter to quote the composer at length about the new work. It is here that redemption enters the interpretive discourse on *La Fanciulla*, and it is here that we first learn that Puccini identifies the overture's opening gesture as "the motive of redemption." Fraccaroli quotes Puccini:

> The opera opens with a few emphatic phrases; rather than violent, robust. Among them one hears some of the most [significant] motives of the opera, for instance, the motive of the redemption—do you

---

zione nuova all'amata figura della protagonista." Zangarini, "Vigilia pucciniana," *Il resto del Carlino*, 20 Sept 1910.

13. MGC 20.

14. Adami, *Letters*, 187–88. This probably refers to Minnie's act 1 dialogue with Joe, which precedes the opera's first mention of redemption in the new Bible scene.

15. MGC 28.

remember?—the redemption of Johnson, the bold and passionate adventurer who is saved by the love and self-denial of Minnie.[16]

The Metropolitan's publicity office acquired Fraccaroli's article, translated it into English, and distributed it to the New York press corps. Puccini's words, as told to Fraccaroli and translated by the Metropolitan's publicity office, then appeared in countless New York newspaper articles; they repeated the translated quotation almost verbatim and, as is typical of newspaper writing, without attribution. It reads as if Puccini had personally contacted the *New York American:*

> Mr. Puccini has furnished the following synopsis of the action of his latest work: "The opera begins with a few phrases, emphatic rather than violent, robust. Among them one hears some of the most striking motives of the opera; for instance, the motive of the redemption. Do you remember? The redemption of Johnson, the bold and passionate adventurer who is saved by the love and self-denial of Minnie." [17]

Amplified by daily repetition in various newspapers and with memories of *Parsifal's* redemption still fresh in the minds of journalists and their readers,[18] this quotation fell on fertile ground: the idea quickly took root that redemption was the central focus of Puccini's opera. Though Puccini specifies that it this redemption was "the redemption of Johnson," critics—perhaps focusing on the blanket nature of the redemption promised in the opera's preliminary note—extended the concept to embrace Minnie and even the miners.

Redemption's place in *Fanciulla's* reception history can be approached from at least three different perspectives: Puccini's (why did he foster the idea that *Fanciulla* was, principally, about redemption?), the audience's (why did they devour the notion of redemption so hungrily?), and scholars' and critics' (why have the composer's stated intentions held sway for decades despite *Fanciulla's*

---

16. Arnaldo Fraccaroli, "Puccini Talks about His New Opera: *The Girl of the Golden West.*" Undated translation of "Puccini e *La fanciulla del West,*" *Corriere della sera,* 15 October 1910. The typist omitted the word "significant" from the sentence, though the syntax makes clear that it was an accident rather than a deliberate shading of the remark. Fraccaroli's original text reads: "L'opera si apre con poche battute violenti: anzi, più che violente, robuste. Vi sono fugacemente accennati alcuni dei motivi più significanti dell'opera: un divampare di energia e uno spunto del motivo della redenzione. Ricordate? La redenzione di Johnson, l'avventuriero ardito e passionale che è salvato dall'amore e dalla abnegazione di Minnie."

17. "Puccini Describes *The Girl of the Golden West,*" *New York American,* 3 December 1910. Other newspapers, including the *Telegraph* and the *New York Sunday Times,* repeated the same phrases nearly verbatim in their early December editions.

18. *Parsifal* had its U.S. premiere at the Met in 1903. It too was greeted with a storm of newspaper coverage and was probably the largest media event generated by an opera prior to 1910.

prominent presentation of themes other than, or in addition to, redemption?) As discussed in chapter 3, Puccini was determined to break free from the *musica zuccherata* [sugary music] of his earlier operas and to position himself as a composer of "serious" works.[19] He had arrived at a point in his career when he was beginning to consider how historians would judge his music; his emphasis on *Fanciulla's* novel musicodramatic elements and its redemption theme was part of a larger objective to project artistic gravitas and to attempt to mold his historical reputation. While Puccini certainly met his goal of departing from the music of his past, he seemed impelled to wrap his new music, new dramatic conception, and new heroine in the old and very safe audience-pleasing language of Wagnerian redemption.

Audience reception of redemption in the United States at the time of *Fanciulla's* premiere must be placed within the context of Wagnerism, while the Wagner craze itself must be understood within the then-current discourse on music as a means of "moral uplift" in the socially unstable times following the United States' western expansion.[20] As Joseph Horowitz observes in his account of *Parsifal's* numerous incarnations in New York and Boston, Wagnerism in the United States met an urgent need for religious certainty among "Christians adrift in a spiritual void," and *Parsifal's* "narcotic music was both escapist and cathartic."[21] Although this need was felt to be especially urgent at the turn of the twentieth century owing to the anxieties produced by the "barbarity of [the United States'] westward progress [and] the guilts stirred by its libidinous territorial drive," the desire for, and belief in, redemption long predated Wagner.[22] According to the religious leader Lyman Abbott, writing at the turn of the century, "Americans had lived, from the beginning, in the hope of universal redemption. It was the energizing principle, the motive power, that drove the strange, crude, unwieldy vehicle that became the United States on its dangerously accelerating course."[23] Seen within this con-

19. Gara, *Carteggi pucciniani*, no. 362, p. 266.

20. Steven Baur, "Music, Morals, and Social Management: Mendelssohn in Post–Civil War America," *American Music* 19 (2001): 64–130. See also the work of one of Wagner's principal proponents, Hugh Reginald Haweis, *Music and Morals* (New York: Harper and Brothers, 1874), whose monograph went through twenty-four printings between 1872 and 1934.

21. There were concert performances of *Parsifal* in 1886, 1890, and 1891, and, finally, a long-awaited fully staged version in 1903. See Joseph Horowitz, *Wagner Nights: An American History* (Berkeley and Los Angeles: University of California Press, 1994), 189–90, 259.

22. Ferenc Szasz, "The American Quest for Religious Certainty, 1880–1915," in Girgus, *The American Self*, 88–104; Carr, *Inventing the American Primitive*, 144; Joseph Horowitz, "Sermons in Sacred Tones: Sacralization as a Theme in American Classical Music," *American Music* 16, no 3 (1998): 311–40. See also Ralph Locke, "Music Lovers, Patrons, and the 'Sacralization' of Culture in America," *Nineteenth-Century Music* 17, no. 2 (1993): 149–73.

23. Horowitz, *Wagner Nights*, 190.

text, it is not surprising that *Fanciulla*'s redemption plot, played out against an "authentic" western American backdrop, would have been embraced so readily by U.S. audiences: it reinforced long-established and widely held beliefs in redemption and satisfied tastes for stories of "redemptive history."[24] A similar observation could be made about numerous frontier plays[25] and Hollywood westerns in which a romance between a U.S. settler and a Mexican or Native American served as the dramatic device through which U.S. presence in the West was explained in terms of mutual desire, and violent acts were redeemed by love.[26]

Scholars' and critics' acceptance of Puccini's emphasis on redemption is due, in large part, to a tradition of privileging "the composer's intentions" in matters of meaning over performers' interpretations or audience perceptions. This has been especially true if the composer's intentions are recorded in his or her own words. Even if, as in *Fanciulla*'s case, the opera itself suggests other plot lines of equal or, possibly, greater importance, there is reluctance to entertain views that contradict the composer's view of his or her own work. Though Puccini would have us focus our attention on Johnson's redemption, Minnie's transformation through her sexual awakening and the resulting consequences for her and the miner's community is an equally compelling story line deserving of rigorous examination and critical attention.

Is Minnie Redeemed Too?

The idea of blanket redemption was further propagated as a key to understanding the opera in the decades following the redemption-saturated flurry of newspaper articles accompanying *Fanciulla*'s New York premiere. In 1966 the conductor Fausto Cleva wrote, "This is more than the story of an individual.

24. Carr, *Inventing the American Primitive*, 52, 143, traces the origins of redemptive history as a theme in American literary traditions; see n. 22.

25. See Roger Hall, *Performing the American Frontier, 1870–1906* (Cambridge and New York: Cambridge University Press, 2001), 206–11. Hall considers both Belasco's *Girl* and Puccini's *Fanciulla* in terms of the conventions established by the 1,200 frontier plays written between 1849 and 1917.

26. One very explicit example of this is the film *Rebellion*, directed by Lynn Shores (Hollywood: Crescent Pictures, 1937). The film starred Tom Keene and Rita Hayworth (billed as Rita Cansino) and was produced by E. B. Derr, with story and screenplay by John T. Neville. For discussions of redemptive narratives of the American West in literature and on film, see Gretchen M. Bataille, ed., *Native American Representations: First Encounters, Distorted Images, and Literary Appropriations* (Lincoln: University of Nebraska Press, 2001); James A. Clifton, ed., *The Invented Indian: Cultural Fictions and Government Policies* (New Brunswick, N.J.: Transaction, 1990); Michael Hilger, *From Savage to Nobleman: Images of Native Americans in Film* (Lanham, Md.: Scarecrow Press, 1995); Jacquelyn Kilpatrick, *Celluloid Indians: Native Americans and Film* (Lincoln: University of Nebraska Press, 1999); Peter C. Rollins and John E. O'Connor, eds., *Hollywood's Indian: The Portrayal of the Native American in Film* (Lexington: University Press of Kentucky, 1998).

Its theme of redemption applies not just to Johnson but to everybody."[27] Girardi maintains that "the entire musical structure of *La Fanciulla del West* is built with a view to the happy ending,"[28] while Allan Atlas recounts Minnie's move "toward her musical goal—the redemption *tinta.*"[29] Some authors, including Ashbrook, Carner, John DiGaetani, and Catherine Clément, posit a cause-and-effect relationship between Johnson's redemption and the opera's so-called happy ending for all. Ashbrook writes, "Its happy ending is . . . implicit in the values stressed by the story."[30] Carner observes that "all ends happily in the victory of virtue over vice, of true and pure love over lust,"[31] while DiGaetani concurs that "[Minnie] had redeemed him and his change happily illustrates the opera's central affirmation."[32] Clément celebrates the ending of the opera: "finally we have the flawless exception, and happiness dearly won. They go, the bandit and the girl, off into the rising sun, and the sky resounds with the cheers that go with them."[33] But there are no cheers: according to the opera's stage directions, the miners are "sobbing," "dejected," and "crying."[34]

Though the opera's preliminary note and Psalm 51 promise redemption for all, only Johnson's redemption, facilitated by Minnie's heroic rescue, is ever demonstrated. Everyone else, even Minnie herself, suffers as a result. As Puccini wrote, "The idea of redemption . . . linger[s] above the whole work"; however, for all but Johnson, it is only the *idea* of redemption and its use as a cleverly engineered theatrical device that are manifest in the opera.[35] In this Puccini again appears to follow Wagner: Minnie's pure love and unfailing loyalty place her in the tradition of Elisabeth (*Tannhäuser*), Senta (*Der fliegende Holländer*), and Elsa (*Lohengrin*), all characters whose sacrifice is tied to the hero's redemption.

A requisite component of Johnson's redemption is, according to Puccini, Minnie's self-denial, a point explored by only a few critics. Because of it, Al-

27. Fausto Cleva, "Poem of the West," *Opera News*, 8 January 1966, 24. Cleva conducted the Metropolitan Opera of New York's 1961 revival of *Fanciulla*.

28. Girardi, *His International Art*, 285.

29. Atlas, "*Lontano—tornare—redenzione,*" 375.

30. Ashbrook, *Operas of Puccini*, 144.

31. Carner, *Critical Biography*, 454.

32. DiGaetani, "Comedy and Redemption," 93.

33. Catherine Clément, *Opera, or, The Undoing of Women*, trans. Betsy Wing, foreword by Susan McClary (Minneapolis: University of Minnesota Press, 1985), 94–95.

34. Civinini and Zangarini, libretto, 86–89.

35. Recent Puccini biographies proclaim the opera's "clear moral message about redemption" (Mary Jane Phillips-Matz, *Puccini: A Biography* [Boston: Northeastern University Press, 2002], 206) and assert that "the drama is articulated with perfect clarity and [is] rendered wholly believable by the music" (Budden, *Puccini*, 304).

bert Innaurato perceives something other than a happy ending: "There is a terrible sadness here. . . . I think in his heart he [Puccini] knew that there is something silly in this B-picture happy ending that really leaves nothing resolved."[36] Byron Nelson takes the thought a step farther and sees elements of tragedy in *Fanciulla's* ending: "the opera is a tragedy for the community . . . and an ambivalent moment for the lovers as well . . . [who are] like Adam and Eve expelled from the Garden."[37] The lack of resolution noted by Innaurato and in Nelson's Eden analogy acknowledges the unhappiness and material instability that will surely result from Minnie's heroic actions.[38] Johnson is indeed saved, but the cost is so high in terms of Minnie's self-denial and loss of community that the ending, at least for Minnie and the miners, can be read as a tragic one. After all, Johnson is still a "wanted" man, and his reprieve is only temporary; Minnie and her lover are both doomed to a life evading the law, forced to reestablish themselves in a threatening and uncertain American wilderness.

Other Critical Orthodoxies

Repeated in some form or another in most *Fanciulla* critiques are received appraisals of the opera, which may be summarized as follows: *Fanciulla* "fails" because of its weak libretto; the premise of the opera is irredeemably ridiculous; Minnie's beatification and Rance's demonization robbed Belasco's play of its strengths; the opera lacks a sufficient quantity and quality of melodies; and Puccini's assimilation of his contemporaries' innovations was a transparent attempt to mask his creative drought and quiet the concerns of his academic detractors.[39] Each of these will be examined in light of newly available documents or alternate interpretations of the opera and its sources.

The "Weak" Libretto

Fanciulla's libretto is among the most frequently cited reasons for the opera's failure to equal the successes of *La Bohème, Tosca,* and *Madama Butterfly.* Its weaknesses have been attributed to the pedestrian approaches of the librettists, the

36. Albert Innaurato, "Heartbreak Saloon: How Puccini Poured Out His Personal Anguish in *Fanciulla*," *Opera News,* 11 April 1992, 10.

37. Byron Nelson, "The Isolated Heroine and the Loss of Community in Puccini's Belasco Operas," *Yearbook of Interdisciplinary Studies in the Fine Arts* 2 (1990): 404.

38. Belasco viewed them as "outcasts from Paradise." Marker, *David Belasco,* 160.

39. Girardi calls it his "crisis" period. Girardi, *His International Art,* 259.

delay caused by the events surrounding Doria Manfredi's suicide, the libretto's unclear focus, or the story's lack of conviction.[40] Harold Schonberg's 1977 article asserts glibly, "A generation ago *La fanciulla del West* was not discussed in intellectual music circles. The libretto was considered too embarrassing, and that was enough to kill it."[41] Indeed, "cowboys singing in Italian" is, according to many critics, beyond the operatic pale—a position that seems difficult to support in light of the standard repertoire's countless non-Italian, non-European characters who sing in Italian, equally preposterously, without comment.[42]

The idea of the failed libretto originates with the oft-recounted "dismissal" of Zangarini in 1908 and the hiring of Civinini shortly thereafter to replace him. Given the difficulties of the novel subject matter and its language, the obstacles experienced by Puccini, Zangarini, and Civinini in turning Belasco's play into a libretto were, no doubt, more complex than mere disagreements over working habits and conflicting theatrical sensibilities. The task entrusted to Zangarini and Civinini was not only to translate and versify Belasco's play, but also to capture and render in Italian the qualities of slangy American English and English as spoken by those for whom it is a foreign language. As discussed in the previous chapter, different American dialects are used both in the play and the opera to delineate a hierarchy among the characters and are necessary to the story lines. In trying to preserve the distinctions between the characters Zangarini's and Civinini's word choices clashed with Puccini's on numerous occasions.[43] Civinini even went to the trouble of distancing himself publicly from the libretto and disavowing responsibility for its unconventional language and meter.[44] Further difficulties arose from the need to write

---

40. "Something rather different and inferior to the stage play emerged from the hands of the new librettists Guelfo Civinini and Carlo Zangarini, who reduced the script to a much more conventional, sentimental, and artificial work"; Roxana Stuart, "Uncle Giacomo's Cabin: David Belasco's Direction of *La fanciulla del West*," in *Opera and the Golden West: The Past, Present, and Future of Opera in the U.S.A.* (Rutherford, N.J.: Fairleigh Dickinson University Press, 1994), 143. "The standard line concerning *Fanciulla* is that the main effect of this tragedy [Manfredi's suicide] was the painfully slow progress made, and perhaps that the composer's concentration and inspiration had lapsed in this work"; Innaurato, "Heartbreak Saloon," 10. "Dramatic and moral confusion carries through into the libretto . . . that beautiful melodies and a ravishing score could not pass over"; John Paul Russo, "Puccini, the Immigrants, and the Golden West," *Opera Quarterly* 7, no. 3 (Fall 1990): 19; "What cannot be accepted is the play's intolerably false sentiment, that is, its underlying idea of moral redemption"; Carner, *Critical Biography*, 455.

41. Harold Schonberg, "Don't Sneer at Puccini's Horse Opera," *New York Times*, 16 October 1977.

42. Algernon St. John-Brenon, "*Girl of the Golden West* in Opening Storms Metropolitan Throngs," *New York Telegraph*, 11 December 1910.

43. "To my ear the language is not what is needed . . . you must still sweat over it"; Puccini to Zangarini, 10 March 1908 (MGC 18).

44. "Il libretto della *Fanciulla del West*, una lettera di Guelfo Civinini," *Corriere della sera*, 4 December 1910.

wholly new pivotal scenes in acts 1 and 3 for which the librettists had no models in the play to use as guides. The linguistic and dramaturgical tasks were monumental; hence, the delays in delivering act 3 to the composer and the disputes over linguistic minutiae that several MGC letters bring to light.[45]

Although *Fanciulla's* subject matter, language, and added scenes posed unusual and daunting problems for the librettists, it is simplistic to blame the "weak" libretto for the opera's curious status among Puccini's works. Indeed, given the interrelationship of an opera's numerous component parts, no work's success or failure hinges solely on its text.[46] While *Fanciulla's* libretto certainly provided more than the usual number of opportunities in an opera for sarcastic lampoons, critics and audiences were more seriously bothered by its premise and its focus on a robust, honest, self-determined, and financially independent woman.

Premise Is Ridiculous

From its debut as a stage play in 1905 through subsequent performances in New York and other American cities, *The Girl of the Golden West* was widely considered to be Belasco's best play and was lauded for its realism and courageous female lead character. Yet in 1910, when transferred to the opera stage, the premise was considered preposterous. That *Fanciulla's* premise was considered suitable for a stage melodrama but ridiculous for an Italian opera has less to do with the relative propriety of opera's sources than with the very specific, if unspoken, expectations of the conservative opera establishment, who were accustomed to seeing and hearing women portrayed in conventional roles and relationships as defined by turn-of-the-century patriarchy.[47] Characters resembling the "New Woman," who had begun to emerge in novels and dramas of the period, were, it would seem from the tone of *Fanciulla's* reviews, most unwelcome in opera.[48] The New Woman, icon of the women's suffrage movement and other causes such as feminist legal reform, family planning, and labor unionism, threatened to destabilize the social, political, and economic or-

45. MGC 12, 18, 20, 24, 25, 27, 28.

46. Carolyn Abbate and Roger Parker, eds., "Introduction: On Analyzing Opera," in *Analyzing Opera: Verdi and Wagner* (Berkeley and Los Angeles: University of California Press, 1989), 1–24.

47. On social class and nineteenth- and turn-of-the-century opera audiences, see Bruce A. Mc-Conachie, "New York Operagoing, 1825–50: Creating an Elite Social Ritual," *American Music* 6 (1988): 181–92; Solie, "Fictions of the Opera Box," 185–208; Karen Ahlquist, *Democracy at the Opera: Music, Theater, and Culture in New York City, 1815–1860* (Urbana: University of Illinois Press, 1997).

48. For a discussion of the appearance of the New Woman in frontier dramas, western novels, and film, see Shelley Armitage, "Rawhide Heroines: The Evolution of the Cowgirl and the Myth of America," in Girgus, *The American Self,* 179.

der by which opera's privileged patrons maintained their wealth and social status.[49] Clément contends that "opera lovers do not like this antiheroine" and
that Minnie troubles audiences because she does not conform to the expected
standard of female operatic victimhood established through such characters as
Violetta, Mimi, Carmen, and Butterfly, among others: "[This opera] shows a
woman out to win her love, a woman who wins painlessly, without defeat,
without coming undone." [50] While one may disagree with Clément that Minnie "wins painlessly," she does, at least temporarily, win love, and she emerges
from the opera alive and without a terminal illness, unlike the "undone" heroines Clément describes. Minnie's survival, her centrality, and her portrayal as
equal or superior to the male characters all seem to be at the heart of early criticisms of the opera's "ridiculous" premise. Writers of subsequent decades
reiterate this sentiment and focus on the improbability of the opera's plot
twists—particularly the card scene in act 2 and the "impossibility" of Minnie herself.[51]

Minnie is frequently described in comic terms, and writers seem compelled
to reduce her to a single sentence filled with compound descriptors, the silliness
of which, it is implied, reflects the silliness of Minnie's character. Martin Bern-
heimer wrote in 1991, "It is easy to make a campy caricature of the gun-toting,
Bible-quoting, booze-slinging, card-cheating, essentially unkissed saloonkeeper who would do anything for love." [52] Allan Atlas describes Minnie in
similar terms as "the gun-slinging, Bible-quoting, never-before-kissed owner
of the Polka Saloon." [53] Daniel Gerould likens Minnie to typical stage heroines of the 1870s who can "outrun, out-ride, out-shoot, out-lasso, and out-yell
any man in town." [54] And Carner, while managing to refrain from sardonic,
hyphenated prose, still stuffs Minnie into a single sentence: "This rare compound of hoyden, glorified barmaid and pure angel handles the revolver as
easily as she pours whisky, keeps a whole gang of miners under her thumb yet
takes offense at the slightest impropriety, thinks nothing of cheating yet as-

49. For studies of the New Woman from a variety of perspectives, see Adele Heller and Lois Rudnik,
eds., *1915, the Cultural Moment: The New Politics, the New Woman, the New Psychology, the New Art, and the New Theatre
in America* (New Brunswick, N.J.: Rutgers University Press, 1991), 69–117; Keith Newlin, ed., *American Plays
of the New Woman* (Chicago: Ivan R. Dee, 2000); Lyn Pykett, *The "Improper" Feminine: The Women's Sensation Novel
and the New Woman Writing* (London and New York: Routledge, 1992), 137–43; Ellen Wiley Todd, *The "New
Woman" Revised: Painting and Gender Politics on Fourteenth Street* (Berkeley and Los Angeles: University of California Press, 1993).

50. Clément, *Undoing*, 94–95.

51. Schonberg; see n. 41.

52. "Carol Neblett: A New Girl of the Golden West," *Los Angeles Times*, 24 June 1991.

53. Atlas, "*Lontano — Tornare — Redenzione*," 360.

54. Daniel Gerould, *American Melodrama* (New York: Performing Arts Journal Publications, 1983), 26.

pires to higher things and talks of moral redemption through the agency of pure love."[55] He concludes that Minnie is "a wholly stagey creation, histrionically effective but psychologically impossible."[56]

The tongue-in-cheek descriptions of Minnie (especially her handling of a gun) call to mind the countless caricatures of the New Woman that appeared in newspapers and journals of the first decades of the twentieth century. In 1910 women had not yet won the right to vote, and the New Woman was shown in clumsy relationship to symbols of authority and power such as the ballot box, the paycheck, and military and academic regalia, while the "traditional" woman was portrayed comfortably and happily handling symbols of traditional female roles such as brooms, diapers, laundry, and cooking utensils.[57] Both Minnie and the New Woman pushed the boundaries of conventions governing women's activities, their place in society, and their sexuality, and both received a chilly reception in the press.[58] Despite her cartoonish characterizations Minnie remains, according to Cleva, "the strongest heroine in any Puccini opera. She has a will, knows what she wants from the very beginning."[59] For these reasons Clément may have been right to suggest that *Fanciulla's* premise was ahead of its time and that its unusual heroine was "made for tomorrow."[60]

Saint Minnie and Rance the Villain

The opera's treatment of Minnie and Rance is thought to depart significantly from Belasco's, and Puccini's alterations are usually described as diminishing rather than improving those characters. But did Puccini, Zangarini, and Civinini change Minnie and Rance that much? Reviewers of the 1910 premiere, many of whom had firsthand knowledge of Belasco's play, did not seem to think so. The opera seemed very close to Belasco's original, according to one observer: "Signor Puccini's librettist has followed the text of Mr. Belasco's melodrama so closely (until the last act) that his libretto might be called a

55. Carner, *Critical Biography*, 455.

56. Ibid., 454.

57. Alice Sheppard, *Cartooning for Suffrage* (Albuquerque: University of New Mexico Press, 1994); Lisa Tickner, *The Spectacle of Women: Imagery of the Suffrage Campaign, 1907–14* (Chicago: University of Chicago Press, 1988).

58. Patricia Marks, *Bicycles, Bangs, and Bloomers: The New Woman in the Popular Press* (Lexington: University Press of Kentucky, 1990).

59. Cleva, "Poem of the West," 25.

60. Clément, *Undoing*, 94–95.

translation of the original book." [61] That the creators of *Fanciulla* radically altered Belasco's conception of the main characters is an idea that appears to have originated in a piece written by Blanche Bates, Belasco's original Minnie.

After attending the opera's dress rehearsal, Bates, "so overcome from weeping . . . that she almost collapsed," managed to compose a letter to the editor of the *American*. In Sunday's edition, 11 December 1910, she shared her reactions to Puccini's characterization of Minnie with the *American*'s readers. In a carefully worded statement she hints at her ambivalence about the new, operatic Minnie: "From the beginning of the opera, Puccini's moulding of the characters was apparent to me. . . . Puccini so wrote that La Fanciulla is of the base or slope of the mountain rather than of the peak. She is more the peasant, the material, with scarcely a suggestion of the mental, which so pervades the character in the drama." [62]

By contrast, reviewers reporting to their readers in detail the plot of the Metropolitan's new opera scarcely mentioned Puccini's "moulding of the characters" or the added Bible scene in act 1, or the deleted schoolroom scene of Belasco's act 3. The changes that seemed to engage the reviewers most concerned act 3's newly minted manhunt and rescue scenes and the novelty of the staging (with live horses). Critics in subsequent decades, however, have made much of the Bible scene, contending that it gives Minnie a nunlike or saintly aura that she did not have in Belasco's play. Nelson contends that the Bible scene "depicts Minnie's love and grace as the source of her power. . . . Minnie has personally transformed the rough mining community into a kind of monastic community governed by love." [63] Finding a uniquely sectarian quality in *Fanciulla*, Nelson continues: "in the hands of its Italian Catholic adapters [the opera becomes] a mythic celebration of incarnate grace." [64] Daniel Gerould presents a secular angle: "The Italianization of *The Girl of the Golden West* resulted in the reimposition of traditional hierarchies, transforming Belasco's modern heroine into a more conventional figure who is all passion and palpitation. . . . Puccini turned the clock back." [65]

Puccini is credited with adding a religious dimension to Minnie's character and inserting it into the opera via the Bible scene; however, in light of new

61. "Sensational Production at the Opera: *The Girl of the Golden West* and Its Music," *New York Tribune*, 12 December 1910.

62. "Blanche Bates, 'So Overcome from Weeping . . . That She Almost Collapsed,'" *American*, 11 December 1910.

63. Nelson, "The Isolated Heroine," 402.

64. Ibid., 403.

65. Gerould, *American Melodrama*, 25, 27.

epistolary evidence it would seem that this dimension was a by-product of the redemption *trovata* rather than a deliberately crafted, new aspect of Minnie's character. In other words, if Puccini's alterations made Minnie seem saintly, it was by default rather than by design; in delivering Psalm 51 Minnie becomes redemption's agent, but not its incarnation. An additional point, that Puccini's musical treatment sharpens both her sexuality and her all-too-human capacity to allow her judgment to be clouded by sexual desire, may be made to counter the idea that Puccini beatified his heroine.

Puccini is also said to have removed layers of complexity from the character of Sheriff Rance by making him into a Scarpia-type villain with no apparent positive traits. Carner writes, "Puccini remains faithful to his old principle of whitewashing the lovers and blackening the villain. . . . The Rance of the opera . . . is more savage and sinister than he is in Belasco; so as not to fall too far behind Scarpia, he too makes an attempt at rape on the open stage, to which he is never tempted in the play." [66] Carner's view of the evil Rance is certainly supported by the visual record of the 1910 performance. Photographs show Amato (in the role of Rance) displaying the demeanor and wearing the costume of the typical silent movie villain: dark, downward-drooping moustache, menacing eyes, cigar, dark clothing, and a tall stovepipe hat. However, this image, present in Belasco's original, was a stock character of the melodrama stage and not a Puccini invention. Indeed, Rance's attempted "rape on the open stage" seems more a product of Carner's imagination than Puccini's. If anything, *Fanciulla* portrays Rance as an abject, pathetic figure whose desire for Minnie can only express itself in repugnant ways. His act 1 aria, "Minnie, dalla mia casa," is hardly the savage utterance of a Scarpia.

Lacks Melodies, Memorable Arias

Another common criticism of *Fanciulla* is that it does not offer an audience the memorable arias one expects of a Puccini opera. A reviewer for the *New York Evening Post* wrote shortly after the premiere, "What the public has always wanted . . . above all things, is melody. . . . There is surprisingly little of this in *The Girl of the Golden West*." [67] Decades later, Stanley Jackson complained of "a score that was neither truly American nor Italian in flavour and, above all, lacked memorable arias," [68] while Carner asserts that "Puccini fails to produce

66. Carner, *Critical Biography*, 456.
67. "Puccini's New Opera," *New York Evening Post*, 12 December 1910.
68. Stanley Jackson, *Monsieur Butterfly: The Story of Puccini* (New York: Stein and Day; London: Allen, 1974), 191.

memorable music owing to his inability to identify himself entirely with this heroine."[69] He goes on to say that "the lyrical glow which marks the love scenes of his previous operas is all but absent."[70] Russo jumps on board: "the vocal writing is as technically proficient as it is unmemorable, which Carner himself admits."[71] Charles Osborne, however, differs: "Those who consider that *La Fanciulla* is lacking in Puccinian tunes or think that it is a poor opera *because* it lacks such tunes are those who also fail to recognize that Verdi's *Falstaff* is not a less great work than his *Rigoletto* but a different kind of great work."[72] This reference to Verdi's innovative *Falstaff*, which had premiered only seventeen years before *Fanciulla*, reminds us that Puccini had struck out consciously in a new direction and designed the arias purposefully so that they were not separable numbers. Rather, they became reflective moments that emerged from and dissolved back into the musical continuum without disruptive breaks for full cadences, applause, and cheers for the soloists. Budden compares Puccini's vocal writing in *Fanciulla* to "the early Baroque 'recitar cantando,' with a consequent diminution of the lyrical element" and suggests that this, along with a new harmonic complexity, "outstripped the popular tastes of his day."[73] While Puccini made his intention to establish a new direction clear, both to his publisher and to his audience, critics nevertheless lambasted him, observing in his efforts a clumsy attempt at a Wagner-inspired *unendliche Melodie.*

Critics also have observed in *Fanciulla* a failure to deploy leitmotivic material with Wagnerian consistency. Carner writes, "With characteristic inconsistency he associated it [the "swaying, yearning theme" of mm. 1–12] with several other dramatic motives: the love between hero and heroine, moral redemption, and homesickness."[74] The "swaying yearning theme" contains, in fact, a separable motif (mm. 1–2, ending on the first beat of m. 3) that is deployed independently throughout the opera. Though this is the motif that the composer labeled "the motif of redemption,"[75] Puccini uses it in a variety of dramatic contexts. The scenes do, however, appear to be linked. Music echoing the motif of the opera's first few measures appears fleetingly at Nick's act I line, "Certo: ho capito / che siete il preferito" (Certainly, I know that she

---

69. Carner, *Critical Biography,* 462.

70. Ibid., 465.

71. Russo, "Puccini, Immigrants, and the Golden West," 19.

72. Osborne, *Complete Operas of Puccini,* 190.

73. Budden, *Puccini,* 304–5.

74. Carner, *Critical Biography,* 462–63.

75. Fraccaroli, see notes 16 and 17.

prefers you) and again, very briefly, during Larken's breakdown, "mandatemi via!" (Send me away!); in full during the Bible scene as Minnie sings, "Ciò vuol dire, ragazzi, che non v'è / al mondo peccatore / cui non s'apra una via di redenzione" (And that means, boys, that there's no sinner in the world that can't find a path to redemption); clearly though briefly in Minnie's act 2, pre-kiss conversation with Johnson, at the line "Allor sono occupata. È aperta l'Accademia" (I'm busy then. The academy is open); and prominently as Minnie and Johnson kiss, at "Eccolo! È tuo!" (Here it is! It's yours!).[76]

This important motif may be interpreted as signaling the presence of chance—the close, yet unseen presence of imminent chaos.[77] The descending whole-tone scale, saturated with irresolution, strangeness, and unpredictability, conveys a vague, unsettling sense that things could become unhinged at any second. To consider the opera's opening motif as chance rather than as redemption (or something swaying or yearning) makes sense of its appearance in seemingly unrelated situations and credits Puccini with thoughtful deployment of musical markers to bring coherence to this fast-moving work.

In addition to the recurring motifs and themes of the prelude, *Fanciulla* contains many other memorable melodies in the form of orchestral passages, ensembles, or arias. Among the arias, certainly the most compelling in terms of a traditional number is Johnson's act 3 "Ch'ella mi creda." Rance's "Minnie, dalla mia casa" also functions as a traditional revelatory aria, while "Che faranno i vecchi miei," sung by Jake Wallace and the miners in act 1, is possibly the opera's best-known tune.

Minnie's theme, arguably the most developed and complex of any of the melodies associated with the main characters, is not presented in the prelude, nor does she ever sing her own melody; it is presented by the orchestra when Minnie makes her entrance and makes subsequent appearances thereafter, most notably in the climactic rescue scene. Significantly, only Johnson actually sings the sumptuous melody of Minnie's theme—at the very end of act 1, when he tells her, "Voi non vi conoscete. / Siete una creatura / d'anima buona e pura ... / e avete un viso d'angiolo!" (You don't know yourself. You're a creature of good and pure nature. And you have the face of an angel!).[78] Johnson's stunning rendition of Minnie's melody confirms Minnie's influence over him but also suggests that only through him can she come to

---

76. See these passages in the piano-vocal score: in act 1, 5 mm. before rehearsal no. 19, 1 m. after rehearsal no. 25, and 10 mm. before rehearsal no. 52; and in act 2, 8 mm. before rehearsal no. 22 and 2 mm. after rehearsal no. 27.

77. This point is discussed in chapter 2.

78. See ex. 6.1.

know her true self. The fact that the miners hum her melody at the same moment (from offstage) reinforces the idea that elements of Minnie's character must be reflected back to her through others before she can understand them or harness their power herself.

When Minnie's theme reappears in the final act, it is given full orchestral treatment and literally vanquishes all other melodies that vie with it for sonic dominance. Rance's emphatic repetition of the word "Impiccatelo!" (Hang him!)[79] is no match for Minnie's orchestral melody, now presented with a palpable physical force that was nowhere in evidence at its first appearances in act 1. Minnie's music, though presented in varied orchestral guises, tempos, and harmonizations throughout the opera, does not develop from a generative motif but is presented fully formed at its first appearance, possibly signifying Minnie's depth of character. Throughout the opera the theme gains dimension and sheer force, mirroring Minnie's own growth via the opera's wrenching plot twists. Minnie's richly harmonized and orchestrated music stands in stark contrast to the simplicity of Johnson's "Ch'ella mi creda," underlining the vastly different worlds they inhabit.

While all of this music is certainly memorable, the fact that the arias were deliberately scaled down in length and dramatic intensity may have disappointed those with an interest in performing excerpts from the opera. Had Puccini treated his grand melodies traditionally, Minnie's theme music would not have been given only to the orchestra and to Johnson; rather, Minnie herself would have sung it in a show-stopping aria that would have enjoyed endless performances on the professional recital stage in addition to hundreds of thousands of renditions in music conservatories and domestic parlor settings. Even though Puccini resisted his old formulas, the thousand copies of the piano-vocal score that Ricordi shipped to the United States following *Fanciulla*'s premiere sold out rapidly, a fact likely to have remained unchanged even if Ricordi had allowed recordings to be made.

Caruso was most eager to meet this demand for recorded excerpts from the opera and expressed a desire to make a record of "Ch'ella mi creda." However, Ricordi withheld permission and thus lost the opportunity to capitalize on the wave of publicity that blanketed New York at the time of the premiere and to fix the opera's music in the imaginations of large numbers of opera lovers. Had Ricordi permitted Caruso to proceed, it is likely that the record would have sold thousands of copies. Critics would perhaps be less likely to dismiss the music as unmemorable or the opera as lacking in melodies if the work had

---

79. See act 3, rehearsal no. 30 and measures following.

had the chance to circulate normally among musically literate listeners via recital performances and recordings.

Puccini and His Critics

Though Puccini attempted to address complaints that he had succumbed to formulaic methods of composition and had begun to repeat himself, he could not quell the contempt of the influential Ildebrando Pizzetti and Fausto Torrefranca, whose harsh invective hinted at deep divisions within the musical world that were beginning to appear around 1910.[80] The division between academic and commercially viable music was growing, as was the split between composers who sought to please audiences by appealing to their conservative tastes and those who considered such efforts to be loathsome pandering to the bourgeoisie.[81] Well aware of the controversy, Zangarini defended Puccini against "the intellectuals who call *commercial* everything in the theater that succeeds and does not bore" (È invalso l'uso tra gli intelletuali di chiamare *commerciale* tutto ciò che in teatro ha successo e non annoia).[82] The more powerful Torrefranca wrote soon thereafter, "Puccini embodies most perfectly all the decadence of modern music and represents all its cynical commercialism, all its pitiful impotence and its triumphant international vogue."[83]

---

80. Pizzetti reprinted his 1910 *La voce* article, "Giacomo Puccini," in his book *Musicisti contemporanei* (Milan: Fratelli Treves, 1914), 49–106. 1910 was also the year Torrefranca wrote *Giacomo Puccini e l'opera internazionale* (Turin: Fratelli Bocca Editori, 1912). Pizzetti softened his earlier criticisms and admitted as much in his 7 December 1958 commemoration; Pizzetti, *Commemorazione di Giacomo Puccini nel primo centenario della nascita* (Milan: Edizione della Scala, 1958). See also Pizzetti, "Omaggio a Puccini," in Sartori, *Puccini*, 123–27.

81. It is likely, given his materialistic predilections (a well-publicized pleasure in bourgeois luxury items such as speedboats, multiple villas, and expensive cameras, clothing, and cars) that Puccini felt no conflict between his bourgeois audience's aims and tastes and his own. Puccini's international celebrity, gained through his avowed role as a composer both *for* the bourgeoisie and *of* the bourgeoisie, may have caused what Greenwald termed "the taint of success." Helen Greenwald, "Recent Puccini Research," *Acta musicologica* 65, no. 1 (January–June 1993): 23. Though Pizzetti and Torrefranca's early denunciations managed to negatively influence Puccini's status among scholars, others rose to the composer's defense before Carner's pathbreaking studies in the 1940s. Among them were Adolf Weissmann (1923), Mario Rinaldi (1932), Thomas Burke (1935), and Renato Mariani (1936). Later defenders against the bourgeois taint include Giannandrea Gavazzeni (1950), Adriano Lualdi (1957–58), and Alfredo Bonaccorsi (1962).

82. The passage in which this appears seems particularly pointed. Attributing their displeasure to "a melacholic taste for nostalgia" (*un malinconico sapore di nostalgia*), he continued, "Now the music of Puccini, who, after Verdi, is the standard-bearer of lyric opera in Italy and abroad, is branded as *commercial*" (*Ora anche alla musica di Puccini, che, dopo Verdi, è il maggiore trionfatore delle scene liriche d'Italia e dell'estero, hanno appioppato il marchio di* commerciale). Zangarini, "Vigilia pucciniana," *Il resto del Carlino*, 20 Sept 1910.

83. He also denounced Puccini's "obfuscation and indifference to the Italian language, more specifically, to Italian prosody and its fundamental role as a structural determinant of nineteenth-century opera. Thus Puccini's works epitomized for Torrefranca the dissolution of verse forms in opera." Greenwald, "Recent Puccini Research," 24.

While Torrefranca singled out for criticism Puccini's betrayal of the Italian lyric tradition in favor of a gratuitous, international modernism, *Fanciulla*'s reviewers sought to explain the composer's new sounds and structures in less vituperative terms as borrowings from Wagner, Debussy, and Strauss. Reginald de Koven wrote on 11 December 1910, "There can be little doubt that the opera . . . which is presented to us as a lyric drama . . . is a direct derivative from Wagner's single art."[84] Numerous other reviewers observed that Puccini had borrowed harmonic and atmospheric effects from Debussy's *Pelléas et Mélisande* and ideas for orchestration from Strauss's *Salome*, operas that had appeared in the years directly preceding *Fanciulla* and that Puccini had seen and admired.[85]

The tradition of explaining Puccini's music for *Fanciulla* in terms of his contemporaries continues to the present, with the added implication that his borrowings were pale imitations of the work of his betters. Byron Nelson states that "Puccini's musical idiom . . . fell short of the modernist advances represented in 1910 by such near-contemporary works as Strauss's *Salome*, Stravinsky's *Le Sacre*, and Bartok's *Bluebeard's Castle*," while Joseph Kerman writes, "Puccini throughout his career borrowed and bowdlerized up-to-date techniques for his own conservative ends. Puccini cannot be said to have made any positive operatic innovation beyond the stage represented by the works of Massenet and Verdi's *Falstaff*."[86] Donald Jay Grout too suggests that Puccini's synthesis of others' innovations ultimately fell short: "his music sounds better than it is."[87] Kerman, Nelson, and Grout's perspective would appear to originate in the still-dominant paradigm that conceives western European music history in terms of a single continuum marked by ever greater degrees of melodic, harmonic, rhythmic, and aesthetic complexity; accordingly, historical importance and critical acclaim are conferred upon those whose innovations are judged to advance music along this continuum and withheld from those

84. "Opera or Lyric Drama? *La fanciulla del West* Marks Dividing Line," *New York World*, 11 December 1910. Girardi notes four key similarities between *Fanciulla* and operas by Wagner: he links *Fanciulla*'s theme of redemption with that of Wagner's *Parsifal*, interprets Minnie within the context of the Valkyries, compares Minnie and Johnson's kiss with that of Siegmund and Sieglinde in *Die Walküre*, and likens *Fanciulla*'s chromaticism to that of *Tristan und Isolde*; Girardi, *His International Art*,.

85. *Pelléas et Mélisande* was also deemed a failure but is now considered one of Debussy's masterpieces. See Lydia Goehr, "Radical Modernism and the Failure of Style: Philosophical Reflections on Maeterlinck-Debussy's *Pelléas et Mélisande*," *Representations* 74 (Spring 2001): 19–46.

86. Nelson, "The Isolated Heroine," 398. See also Luigi Torchi's review of *Tosca*, in which the author suggests that Puccini's opera was not Wagnerian enough. "*Tosca*: melodramma in tre atti di Giacomo Puccini," *Rivista musicale italiana* 7 (1900): 78–114. Joseph Kerman, *Opera as Drama* (Berkeley and Los Angeles: University of California Press, 1988), 208.

87. Donald J. Grout, *A Short History of Opera*, 2d ed. (New York: Columbia University Press, 1965), 444–45.

perceived to merely imitate the innovators. Hence, Puccini at the time of *Fan-ciulla* is usually categorized as a stylistic fence sitter who grafted borrowed modernist sounds onto an essentially outdated nineteenth-century idiom.

Rather than perpetuating the tired orthodoxies that consider Puccini a mu-sical scavenger, a Wagner manqué, or a "pushy salesman,"[88] or that charac-terize his audiences as naive, recent critical writings have sought to place Puc-cini within the political discourses of early-twentieth-century nationalism and protofascism and the aesthetic realms of modernism and early film. Tambling's ideas that *Fanciulla's* hurried pace, brief scenes, violence, nihilism, sadism, and collapse of community may represent elements of a nascent "culture of fas-cism" suggest new directions in Puccini research:[89]

> One aspect of modernity may be the recognition of a loss of centre. . . .
> *La fanciulla del West* may be thought of as a decentered text, presenting
> a society based on primitive lynch law; the violence there looks forward
> to Turandot, which shows an absolutist, primitive, non-bourgeois soci-
> ety. . . . There is no society for Minnie and Johnson to relate to. . . .
> I conclude that Puccini seems not to believe in anything holding bour-
> geois society together. . . . There is no unity. . . . The absence indicates
> that the myth of the nation-state could not hold, and nor could accom-
> panying bourgeois values.[90]

He goes on to propose "psychoanalytic issues which are modern—Johnson/ Ramerrez as a split self, Rance as a psychotic whose nihilism recalls Iago's Credo, but whose sadism is new and post-Freudian."[91]

Jürgen Leukel explores Puccini's modernism through an examination of film technique as applied to musical composition and suggests that Puccini employed musical equivalents of the filmic cut, interpolation, and disssolve in

---

88. "In recent operatic history he is the most aggressive purveyor of longing for a song-before-commodification. But a part of us knows better, however swayed we might be, than to trust pushy sales-men." Gary Tomlinson, *Metaphysical Song: An Essay on Opera* (Princeton, N.J.: Princeton University Press, 1999), 149.

89. "To come to some assessment of Puccini and his politics is important, but it could be better done now by working outside the value-judgements implicit in Joseph Kerman's famous, if negative, reading, which presuppose the possibility of a single coherent way of taking the text, one that does justice to all its features. It might be better to stress the contradictions that mark Puccini's work." Jeremy Tambling, *Opera and the Culture of Fascism* (New York: Clarendon Press, 1996), 125. John DiGaetani and Anthony Arblaster consider Puccini's treatment of crowds ("easily swayed and clearly need[ing] leadership and direction") as another element of protofascism in his works. See Anthony Arblaster, *Viva la Libertà! Politics in Opera* (Lon-don and New York: Verso, 1992), 253.

90. Tambling, *Opera and Fascism*, 128–29.

91. Ibid., 128.

order to create musicodramatic complexity comparable to the visual complexity of film.[92] Girardi also explores Puccini's general interest in cinema and proposes that in *Fanciulla* he "made one of the most vital early contributions to the idea of such generic blendings [of opera and film]."[93]

Other approaches to Puccini's music have included investigations into his long-range tonal planning, musicodramatic pacing, and deployment of thematically and affectively related motifs.[94] In addition, social-historical contextual studies and analyses of his operas' reception are broadening the focus of critical discourse on Puccini and initiating a new chapter in Puccini historiography.[95] It would appear from the diversity of these approaches that a plurality of positions regarding Puccini has emerged to dislodge and supplant in the twenty-first century the orthodoxies that were so influential at the time of *Fanciulla's* premiere and that shaped critical opinion for much of the twentieth.

92. Jürgen Leukel, "Puccinis kinematographische Technik," *Neue Zeitschrift für Musik* 143, no. 6–7 (1982): 24–26.

93. Girardi, *His International Art*, 327.

94. See Helen Greenwald, "Puccini, *Il tabarro*, and the Dilemma of Operatic Transposition," *Journal of the American Musicological Society* 51, no. 3 (1998): 521–58; Allan Atlas and Roger Parker, "A Key for *Chi?* Tonal Areas in Puccini," *Nineteenth-Century Music* 15, no. 3 (1992): 229–34; Allan Atlas, "Multivalence, Ambiguity and Non-Ambiguity: Puccini and the Polemicists," *Journal of the Royal Music Association* 118, no. 1 (1993): 73–93. See Allan Atlas, "Pacing and Proportion in the Act I Love Duet of Puccini's *La Bohème*," *Acta musicologica*, forthcoming; Atlas, "*Lontano—tornare—redenzione*," 359–98.

95. Susan Vandiver Nicassio, *Tosca's Rome: The Play and the Opera in Historical Perspective* (Chicago: University of Chicago Press, 1999), is among these.

CHAPTER EIGHT

Staging *La fanciulla del West* in 2010

Inevitably, the year 2010 will see a spate of new productions commemorating *Fanciulla*'s centenary. How might these early-twenty-first-century interpretations differ from their twentieth-century counterparts? What new considerations might directors, producers, singers, and set and costume designers take into account? How might they reconceptualize the work so as to mitigate the opera's inherent difficulties? Has the passage of time made this opera easier or more difficult to produce? As many of the opera's challenges stem from notions concerning its western American setting, it seems necessary to start the process of production with a clear concept of its western qualities.[1]

Do *Fanciulla*'s western qualities constitute mere local color, or are they integral to the story, as in a western film or novel? It may be useful for the director to formulate a response to the question to what degree is *Fanciulla* an opera working within the conventions of the western, and to what degree is it a western operating within the conventions of opera? Belasco's story as reconfigured by Puccini offers unique challenges to directors in that few operas seek to combine genres so distinctly different as the opera and the western. Both genres' conventions are rigidly defined and, in many fundamental ways, radically opposed to one another. Might a director first identify areas of overlap and opposition, and then attempt to accentuate the positive qualities of both?

---

1. Girardi explores the influence of Hollywood westerns c. 1903–11 on *La fanciulla* in "Il finale de *La fanciulla del West* e alcuni problemi di codice," in *Opera e libretto* II, ed. Gianfranco Folena, Maria Teresa Muraro, and Giovanni Morelli, 417–37 (Firenze: Olschki, 1993).

Or are the conventions of opera and the western so firmly established that they are hopelessly at cross-purposes? In that case, should one set of conventions predominate over the whole work? In other words, do the conventions of one inexorably trump the other? Or have directors loosened conventions (and, in turn, broadened audience expectations) to the point that a hybrid opera-western is conceivable?

Puccini highlights a principal feature of the western genre in his stage directions: the omnipresent and overpowering influence of the landscape. About the role of the landscape in westerns, Jane Tompkins observes:

> The interaction between hero and landscape lies at the genre's center. . . . In the end, the land is everything to the hero; it is both the destination and the way. . . . The rhythms of the landscape's appearance and disappearance in the hero's consciousness, the way it impinges on his mind, body, and emotions, are fundamental to the experience Western narratives provide.[2]

Given Puccini's documented interest in the setting of the opera (particularly that of its final scene, a clearing in a redwood forest)[3] and the poignant music, which emphasizes the rupture caused by Minnie and Johnson's imminent exile from it, it seems desirable to amplify rather than downplay the western's thematic elements of landscape.[4] The rustic nature of the opera's two other settings, the Polka saloon and Minnie's cabin, are also in keeping with locale conventions of the western and challenge an opera set designer either to evoke the dark, dreary atmosphere of a rough-hewn mining village or to create an obviously romanticized set. The former would be in keeping with Belasco's desire for realism, while the latter would make no pretense of realism and would accentuate *Fanciulla*'s idealized, imagined West as seen through the eyes of a turn-of-the-twentieth century Italian composer.

---

2. Jane Tompkins, *West of Everything: The Inner Life of Westerns* (New York: Oxford University Press, 1992), 81, 78.

3. Puccini's enthusiasm for the forest settings is evident in his 27 August 1907 letter to Zangarini (MGC 6). The stage directions specify that act 3 take place on "the extreme edge of the great Californian forest, where it gradually slopes downward on a ridge of the Sierras. An open space surrounded by enormous, straight and bare pine trees which form a gigantic colonnade round it. . . . A trail is seen winding between the trees [and] here and there the snowy peaks of the highest mountains are visible. . . . In the indistinct light of the early dawn, the lofty mass of reddish trunks is wrapt in a thick mist"; Civinini and Zangarini, libretto, English version, 91.

4. In the Metropolitan's 1992 production (conducted by Leonard Slatkin and sung by Barbara Daniels, Placido Domingo, and Sherill Milnes), the director, Giancarlo Del Monaco, chose to set the final scene in the town's main street rather than in a forest clearing. The darkness of his conception is entirely contrary to Puccini's and Belasco's vision of a steadily increasing dawn light.

The landscape also figures prominently in the characterization of Minnie, whose bond with nature is similar to that of typical heroes in western films and novels. If this work were conceived as a film, Minnie's heroic relationship to the landscape could be conveyed in ways that are unimaginable in a conventional theater. The medium of film may yet prove to be the ideal means by which the affective features of the western landscape—so important to *Fanciulla's* atmosphere and characterizations—are evoked.[5] The following passage, by Tompkins, aptly characterizes Minnie's relationship to nature, except, of course, for the pronouns: "Perhaps more than anything, nature gives the hero a sense of himself. For he is competent in this setting. He knows his horse will lead him to water, knows how to build a fire and where to camp. He can take care of himself."[6] The problematic pronouns point to two crucial aspects of *Fanciulla* in which operatic conventions override those of the western and undermine key aspects of its emphasis on masculinity. First, opera's unavoidable reliance on text makes the western's "strong, silent type" an impossibility. A prime trait of the male western hero is his economy of speech or the suppression of vocality; by extreme contrast, opera's hypervocality denies male characters a principal marker of western masculinity. *Fanciulla's* leading men and all-male chorus are, then, feminized by their volubility, when viewed through the lens of the western. Second, and also contrary to standard notions of masculinity in western narratives, a female character is central to the story. Minnie not only displaces the male as hero, but also uses his most iconic props—a gun and a horse—with the same sense and show of entitlement to power as male heroes. Clearly, in the case of the play of gender in *Fanciulla*, opera's conventions trump those of the western.

Finally, the director in 2010 might also weigh the background and expectations of the audience when imagining his or her new production. Unlike audiences of 1910, the modern listener will not have been exposed to western-themed dime novels, nor, like audiences around 1960, will they have been weaned on Hollywood's version of the history of the American West. Audiences in 2010 will, at the very least, be aware of pluralistic historical perspectives and will have come of age during the first waves of public discourse on American multiculturalism. Indeed, the director will, most likely, be a member of this generation—a fact that may affect the handling of the opera's Native American and Mexican characters and its unseen Chinese population.

---

5. Marcia Citron's important book *Opera on Screen* (New Haven: Yale University Press, 2000) provides a history of filmed operas in addition to close readings of selected works such as Syberberg's *Parsifal*, Zeffirelli's *Otello*, Rosi's *Carmen*, and Ponelle's *Don Giovanni*.

6. Tompkins, *West of Everything*, 81.

Will the director leave the libretto's epithets intact? Will he or she cut or change words that have been traditionally translated as "half breed," "red-skin," "greaser," "yellow face," or "chink" (as in Ricordi's 1910 translation by R. H. Elkin) in anticipation of negative audience reaction? If such words are flashed above the stage in now-ubiquitous supertitles, will a director insist on program notes to explain his or her decision to include the epithets thus translated and attempt to place them in the social-historical context of 1910, when such words were common in western plays and novels?

How will directors conceptualize the characters and coach the singers playing Castro, Billy, and Wowkle, and even Johnson? Will the Native Americans' gestures convey subservience and passivity, or will they show something of the resistance to authority that is in Belasco's original play?[7] Will future directors follow Slatkin's lead and restore the scene in act 1 in which Minnie demeans Billy? Will Castro and Johnson's Mexican Otherness be accentuated or minimized? Will Jake Wallace appear in blackface, as he did in the premiere performance?

As demonstrated in chapter 6, Jake Wallace is, by virtue of the musical and structural importance of "Che faranno i vecchi miei," a pivotal character in *Fanciulla*. New productions may want to revisit the issue of his appearance— a problem that remained unresolved at the premiere. Puccini and Belasco's apparent indecision about his makeup (and indeed, his identity) may be attributed to the changing nature of blackface minstrelsy in the second half of the nineteenth century.[8] Whereas in 1850 a blackface minstrel could be presumed to be a white performer wearing burnt-cork makeup, in 1900 it was increasingly common for black performers (who often wore blackface makeup also) to take these roles in traveling minstrel shows. So neither the word "minstrel" nor the unclear stage directions of Belasco's play and Puccini's opera tell us conclusively who Jake Wallace really is.[9] Directors in 2010 will have to make up their own minds.[10]

---

7. Chapter 6 compares Belasco's treatment of Wowkle and Billy with Puccini's.

8. Finson, *The Voices That Are Gone*, 229–39. See also Dale Cockrell, *Demons of Disorder: Early Blackface Minstrels and Their World* (Cambridge and New York: Cambridge University Press, 1997); Lott, *Love and Theft*; and Mahar, *Behind the Burnt Cork Mask*.

9. In addition to the newspaper reports quoted in chapter 6 regarding Wallace's makeup, there is this description in Belasco's play: "He is carrying a banjo, his face half blackened." Belasco, *The Girl*, 8. In the novelization of *The Girl of the Golden West*, Wallace is described similarly as "a Minstrel who [was] robed in a long linen duster, his face half-blacked, and banjo in hand" and again as "a typical camp minstrel from the top of his dusty stove-pipe hat to the sole of his flapping negro shoes"; David Belasco, *The Girl of the Golden West*, (New York: Grosset and Dunlap, 1911), 43–44.

10. Complicating matters further for Puccini and Belasco was the matter of the color line on the opera stage. If they had wanted Wallace to be an African American, a white singer (wearing dark makeup) still

Before the director in 2010 ponders any of these issues, he or she will have to decide whether or not to attempt an "authentic" performance that seeks to reconstruct and execute Puccini's directions as he and his collaborators understood them. Will they look to the 1910 premiere as the authoritative version and try to recreate those characterizations, sets, and costumes? Or will they reconceive Minnie's character as a tragic heroine in light of her self-abnegation and Puccini's statements concerning the redemption "gimmick"? Some, judging the composer's intentions to be unknowable and finding the conventions of opera and westerns to be too confining, may eschew the very notion of an authoritative or historically informed version. They may forgo the western setting and sensibility altogether in favor of the expressive freedom claimed by such late-twentieth-century directors as Peter Sellars.[11]

Such directors seeking to imprint their own vision on the production might also look to the several screen adaptations of *Girl of the Golden West* for inspiration. These include Cecil B. DeMille's silent film of 1915; First National's 1923 version, "regarded as one of the most outstanding silent films ever made"; and a 1930 remake with sound, also by First National.[12] The 1938 musical film (with music by Sigmund Romberg, starring Nelson Eddy and Jeanette MacDonald) may be particularly provocative in terms of genre blending (see pl. 31).[13] Director, composer, and screenwiters blurred the boundaries separating the Hollywood western and operetta through shameless addition of scenes, dialogue, characters, and extravagant production numbers.[14] The production's guiding principles appear to have been the musical film templates that had become standard by 1938 and the desire to exploit Eddy and Mac-Donald's talents in ways that the frequently paired duo's audience had grown to expect. Certainly, such contingencies always have and always will play a role in shaping new productions and will influence the director's choices in 2010

---

would have had to play the role, given de facto prohibitions against nonwhite performers onstage. The contralto Marian Anderson was, in 1955, the first African American to perform at the Metropolitan (in the role of Ulrica in Verdi's *Un ballo in maschera*).

11. Sellars's radical reworkings of Mozart's *Don Giovanni*, *Le nozze di Figaro*, and *Così fan tutte* (1991) continue to spark controversy. See Citron, *Opera on Screen*, chapter 6, for a discussion of Sellars's productions.

12. DeMille's Paramount production starred Theodore Roberts as Rance, Mabel Van Buren as Minnie, and House Peters as Johnson. First National's 1923 version featured J. Warren Kerrigan as Johnson, Sylvia Breamer as Minnie, and Russell Simpson as Rance. Ann Harding, James Rennie, and Harry Bannister starred in the 1930 sound version. See Hall, *Performing the American Frontier*, 211.

13. *The Girl of the Golden West*, directed by Robert Z. Leonard (Metro-Goldwyn-Mayer, 1938). The film featured music by Sigmund Romberg and a screenplay by Isabel Dawn and Boyce DeGaw. Walter Pidgeon and Buddy Ebsen appeared in secondary roles.

14. Even the characterizations are substantially different.

even if he or she embraces notions of authenticity or strives for historical correctness.

The 2010 productions will also count among their contingent factors advances in theater technology, a century's worth of perspective on the history of the American West, and dueling philosophies of opera production; these will facilitate practically any vision a director may have and indeed inspire entirely new conceptions and interpretations. On the other hand, scholarly analyses of primary sources such as autograph sketches, production booklets, unpublished letters, and libretto drafts, in addition to comparisons of early printed editions of the opera's music, may encourage attempts to recreate "authentically" *Fanciulla*'s 1910–12 productions in the United States and Europe (see chap. 1, n. 13). Either approach would illuminate this work, whose logistical and interpretive difficulties have made it the least performed of Puccini's mature works and prevented it from developing a performance tradition comparable to those of *Manon, Tosca, Bohème,* and *Butterfly.* The year 2010 may prove to be a milestone in this regard, with productions of *La fanciulla del West* that match the originality of music, stage, and set direction enjoyed by Puccini's other mature operas.

Giacomo Puccini's Letters to Zangarini, Table and Italian Texts

Date in Puccini's hand	Postmarked as Sent	Postmarked as Arrived	Origin	Destination
MGC 1 15 May 1907	Milan / Ferrovia[1] 16 May 1907 8 P.M.		Via Verdi 4, Milan	Piazza Duomo 43–45 City (Milan)
MGC 2 22 July 1907	Torre del Lago / Lucca 22 July 1907		Torre del Lago, Toscana	Piazza Duomo 43–45, Milan
MGC 3 25 July 1907	Torre del Lago / Lucca 25 July 1907	Milan / Center 26 July 1907 10 A.M.	Torre del Lago, Toscana	Piazza Duomo 43–45, Milan
MGC 4 None	Torre del Lago / Lucca [1] August 1907[2]		Torre del Lago, Toscana	Piazza Duomo 43–45, Milan

1. "Ferrovia" refers to a city or town post office located in the local railroad station. Literally translated, *ferrovia* means "railroad."

2. Until quite recently, Italians often did not write "1" for the first day of the month but simply the month and year.

Date in Puccini's hand	Postmarked as Sent	Postmarked as Arrived	Origin	Destination
MGC 5 None	Boscolungo 14 August 1907	Milan / Ferrovia 14 August 1907 6 P.M.	Boscolungo, Abetone (Serra bassa)	Milan (Piazza Duomo crossed out)
MGC 6 None	Boscolungo 27 August 1907	Milan / Center 27 August 1907 4 P.M.	Boscolungo, Abetone	Piazza Duomo 43–45, Milan
MGC 7 29 August 1907	Boscolungo 29 August 1907	Milan / Center 30 August 6 P.M.	Boscolungo	Piazza Duomo 43–45, Milan
MGC 8 None	Torre del Lago / Lucca 12 September 1907	Bologna / Center 13 September 1907 8 P.M.	Torre del Lago	Via Farini no. 4, Bologna (43–45 Piazza Duomo, "Milan" crossed out)
MGC 9 None	Torre del Lago / Lucca 28 September 1907	Bologna / Center 29 September 1907 3 A.M.	Torre del Lago	Bologna
MGC 10 None	Torre del Lago / Lucca 13 October 1907		Torre del Lago	Hotel Florence, Malfatti, Viareggio
MGC 11 23 October 1907	Milan / Ferrovia 24 October 1907 4 P.M.	Torre del Lago / Lucca 25 October 1907	Via Verdi 4, Milan	Torre del Lago "(Pisa)"
MGC 12 No date Probably October / November 1907 [3]	No envelope	None	Hotel Bristol, Vienna	No address

3. See chap. 3, n. 69.

Date in Puccini's hand	Postmarked as Sent	Postmarked as Arrived	Origin	Destination
MGC 13 17 November 1907	As first sent: Torre del Lago / Lucca 18 November 1907	Bologna / Center 18 November 1907 8 P.M.	Torre del Lago	Sent to Via Farini, Bologna, and re-sent on 19 November 1907 to Piazza Duomo 43–45, Milan
	As re-sent: Bologna / Ferrovia 19 November 1907 12 noon	As arrived: Milan / Ferrovia 19 November 1907 2 P.M.		
MGC 14 None	Torre del Lago / Lucca 19 November 1907		Torre del Lago	Piazza Duomo 43–45, Milan
MGC 15 22 November 1907	Torre del Lago / Lucca 23 November 1907	Bologna, Center 23 November 8 P.M.	Torre del Lago	Via Farini, Bologna
MGC 16 5 December 1907	Torre del Lago / Lucca 6 December 1907		Torre del Lago	Piazza Duomo 43–45, Milan
MGC 17 3 February 1908	No postmarks; no envelope		Aboard the SS *Heliopolis,* Egyptian Mail Steamship Co.	No address
MGC 18 10 March 1908	Torre del Lago / Lucca 10 March 1908	Milan / Center 12 March 1908 10 A.M.	Torre del Lago	Piazza Duomo 43–45 Milan ("Via Farini, Bologna" crossed out)
MGC 19 None	Torre del Lago / Lucca 4 April 1908	Milan / [/] 5-APR [illegible]	Torre del Lago	Piazza Duomo 43, Milan

Date in Puccini's hand	Postmarked as Sent	Postmarked as Arrived	Origin	Destination
MGC 20 None	Torre del Lago / Lucca 15 April 1908	Milan / Center 16 April 1908 5 A.M.	Torre del Lago	Piazza Duomo 43, Milan
MGC 21 None	Bagni di Lucca 7 August 1909 8 P.M.		Grand Hotel des Thermes, Bagni di Lucca	Piazza Duomo 43, Milan
MGC 22 2 (January) 1910[4]	Milan / departure 3 January 1910 2 P.M.	Bologna / Center 4 January 1910 8 A.M.	Via Verdi 4, Milan	Via Farini, Bologna
MGC 23 24 January 1910	Milan / departure 24 January 1910 6 P.M.		Via Verdi 4, Milan	45 Piazza Duomo, City (Milan)
MGC 24 30 (January) 1910	[No postmarks; no stamps]		Via Verdi 4, Milan	45—P. Duomo, City (Milan)
MGC 25 None	Milan / departure 28 May 1910 6 P.M.	Bologna / Center 29 May 1910 3 A.M.	Via Verdi 4, Milan	Via Farini, Bologna
MGC 26 2 July 1910	Torre del Lago / Lucca 2 July 1910		Torre del Lago	43 Piazza Duomo, Milan
MGC 27 13 July 1910	Torre del Lago / Lucca 14 July 1910		Torre del Lago	43 Piazza Duomo, Milan
MGC 28 13 July 1910 [second letter]	Torre del Lago / Lucca 14 July 1910		Torre del Lago	43 Piazza Duomo, Milan
MGC 29 31 July 1910	Torre del Lago / Lucca 31 July 1910	Milan / Arrived 1 August 1910 10 A.M.	Torre del Lago	Piazza Duomo 43, Milan

4. Parentheses indicate illegible dates on the letters.

In the following transcriptions Puccini's abbreviations, underlinings, other marks, and occasional misspellings have been preserved. Small capitals are used to denote printed letterheads.

MGC 1

VIA VERDI, 4, MILANO
Carissimo Zangarini
La parola aspettata venne – Quando posso vederla?
Saluti
GPuccini
15. 5. 07
[On verso:] Sig Carlo Zangarini / Piazza Duomo 43–45 / Città
[Postmarked as sent:]
Milano / Ferrovia
16/5/07—8 S[era]

MGC 2

TORRE DEL LAGO, TOSCANA.
22 luglio 907
Caro Zangarini
Il Sig Giulio credo che le manderà il copione tradotto malamente – io le manderò l'originale appena l'avrò ricevuto. Il 3° e 4° valgono . . . pochetto ma mi pare ci sia panno per trarne bene – io ho delle idee e dovremo vederci – in Agosto andrò all'abetone – da Bologna a lassù non c'è molto cammino e se vuole potremo abboccarci[.] Io avrò l'auto per mandarlo a prendere a Pracchia – Intanto legga e guardi se può riuscire ad ingrandire il contorno specie dei minatori (triplicandoli) e farne il coro – e cercare una scena all'aperto – l'ultima (cioè il 3° atto) ma siamo in inverno! qui è lo scoglio.
        basta; legga e ponderi e trovi e troverà certo.
        Saluti aff
        Suo GPuccini
[On verso:] Carlo Zangarini / Piazza Duomo 43–45 / Milano
[Postmarked as sent:]
Torre del Lago / Lucca
22/7/07

MGC 3

TORRE DEL LAGO, TOSCANA.

Caro Zangarini

oggi le spedisco l'originale e le fotografie – queste ultime aiutano e fanno più evidente il dramma – mi accusi, la prego, ricanti di tutta questa roba – e mi dica al più presto, perché ho ansia, la sua impressione.

Aff saluti

GPuccini

25–7–07

[On verso:] Carlo Zangarini / Piazza Duomo 43–45 / Milano

[Postmarked as sent:]

Torre del Lago / Lucca

25/7/07

[As arrived:]

Milano / Centro

26/7/07—10 M[attina]

MGC 4

TORRE DEL LAGO, TOSCANA.

Domenica

Carissimo Zangarini

Ho letto 2 atti perché non ne sono arrivati altri – Ora li mando al Sig G[iulio]. Cerchi di vederlo. Il I° atto è un po' confuso ma c'è roba. – il 2° è bellissimo – però io ho idee di altre movenze di ingrandimenti. . . . ma di questo, dopo la lettura finita. –

Io credo d'aver in mano ciò che mi occorre. –

Saluti cordialissimi

da GPuccini

[On verso:] Carlo Zangarini / Piazza Duomo 43– / Milano

[Postmarked as sent:]

Torre del Lago / Lucca

[1]/8/07

MGC 5
BOSCOLUNGO ABETONE,
(SERRA BASSA.)
Caro Zangarini
Se trovasi corti passi da Tito Ricordi e si faccia dare il copione
originale inglese e le fotografie della bella fanciulla dell'ovest –
(io la chiamerei così).
Poi le dico che sono qui[.] ho un [sic] automobile – Pracchia è
la sosta del treno –
Con Tito combini di venire o solo – Ho bisogno di definire
questa cosa che mi ha preso – Ho delle idee – Belasco o no si deve
fare –
affettuosi
saluti
da GPuccini
[On verso:] a Carlo Zangarini / ~~Piazza del Duomo 43–45~~ /
Milano
[Postmarked as sent:]
Boscolungo
14/8/07
[As arrived:]
Milano / Ferrovia
14/8/07—6 S[era]

MGC 6
Abetone Lunedì
~~TORRE DEL LAGO, TOSCANA.~~
Caro Zangarini
Sempre più la malattia californiana mi prende. Ho fatto diverse
fotografie della più bella parte della foresta dove sono i più alti
e grandi alberi e tutto per la scena del 3° atto – Sono fermo che
dovrà essere all'aria aperta in una grande spianata d'una foresta con
alberi colossali e con 10 o più cavalli e 60 uomini. Sarà un terzo atto
magnifico! – Forza –
Saluti—G Puccini
[On verso:] a Carlo Zangarini / Piazza Duomo 43–45 / Milano
[Postmarked as sent:]
Boscolungo
27/8/07

[As arrived:]
Milano / Centro
27/8/07—4 S[era]

MGC 7
 29.VIII.07
 Boscolungo
 ~~TORRE DEL LAGO, TOSCANA~~
 Caro Zangarini
    Sapevo che Cawbois [*sic*] non erano i nostri uomini – ma mi
 piaceva chiamarli così per simpatia. – Pensiamo al 3° atto – io lo vedo
 grandioso – nella foresta grandiosa – Lei mi accenna alla caccia al-
 l'uomo – mi viene un'idea – Perché non fare della spianata o della
 veranda che appena si affaccia alla scena, il quartiere generale (tanto
 per dire) dove convergono di tempo in tempo al principio (mentre
 c'è il dialogo tra lo sceriffo e Nick e può esserci anche il 2° sceriffo
 il quale aspetta l'esito della caccia) gruppi di uomini a cavallo e a
 piedi portando notizie . . . contradittorie circa le tracce del brigante
 e finalmente arriva un gruppo a cavallo che trascinerà un uomo
 legato – è lui – di qui avanti fare come dice il dramma colle nostre,
 anzi sue modificazioni.
    È un'idea che ho buttato giù – discutibile – cancellabile –
 cestinabile – è per dire che non scrivo vangelo – Lei sia il vaglio –
    Saluti aff. GPuccini
 [On verso:] a Carlo Zangarini / Piazza Duomo 43–45 / Milano
 [Postmarked as sent:]
 Boscolungo
 29/8/07
 [As arrived:]
 Milano / Centro
 30/8/07—6 S[era]

MGC 8

| Scrivetemi sempre a   TORRE DEL LAGO, | TOSCANA. |

Giovedì
Caro Zangarini
    vado per 5 o 6 giorni ad una villetta in collina a Chiatri – poi
ritorno a Torre del Lago – incubate e pesate bene – raccomando
semplificare tanto specie il I° atto – e pensate alla grandezza del

3° – per il 2° non c'è niente da fare di nuovo – sempre in attesa –
Spero vederci qui a Torre presto –

    Aff saluti

    GPuccini

[On verso:] Carlo Zangarini / ~~43–45 Piazza Duomo / Milano~~
Via Farini No 24 – Bologna [in a different hand]
[Postmarked as sent:]
Torre del Lago / Lucca
12/9/07
[As arrived:]
Bologna / Centro
13/9/07—8 S[era]

MGC 9

Bisognerà vederci presto –
TORRE DEL LAGO, TOSCANA.
Sabato
Caro Z –

    Ho avuto i 2 atti – il I° va quasi bene – mi pare la <u>fine</u> fredda –
Il 3° non mi capacita la I^a entrata di Minnie – mi sembra che per la
storia <u>baro-asso</u> non valga la pena di farla entrare e uscire per poi
ritornare al momento <u>Topico</u> – allora era meglio (se non ci fosse
pletora di duetti) farla venire per duettare col tenore – non le pare?

    E la storia <u>baro asso</u> non può farsi nel <u>pieno</u> cioè quando sarà
arrivata per difendere <u>lui</u>?

    Aff saluti

    GPuccini

[On the verso of this letter is the following note in a different
hand:]
Caro Charlie,
Ho aperta la lettera perché ho capito che era di Puccini e credevo
fosse forse necessario telegrafare. Ma visto che non occorre te la
respingo. Il tempo è ancora incerto e forse rimarremo giù anche
oggi. Addio copriti bene con questa umidità.

    Saluti da tutti.

    Katie

[Address:] Carlo Zangarini / Farini 24 / Bologna
[Postmarked as sent:]
Torre del Lago / Lucca
28/9/07

[As arrived:]
Bologna / Centro
29/9/07—3 M[attina]

MGC 10

Torre del Lago, Toscana.
non ti secco né ti noio
ma ti sprono, se no muoio.
Colla Girl mi togli quiete!
Se ci penso! ma son liete
di speranza l'ore attese —
(Siamo quasi a fin di mese)
Pensa caro che son tutti
cogli occhiacci torvi e brutti
aspettando l'opra nostra —
ma sia presto sulla giostra
giri, ruoti, falci, uccida
chi ha gli orecchi di re Mida
Forza chiedi al Tosco mare
per poter ben lavorare
Raccomandati a Malfatti
che ti dia lepri non gatti
Ti saluta o Zangarini
il tuo Giacomo Puccini
[On verso:] A Carlo Zangarini
Hotel Florence
— Malfatti — <u>Viareggio</u>
[Postmarked as sent:]
Torre del Lago / Lucca
13/10/07

MGC 11

VIA VERDI, 4, MILANO.
23. X. 07
Caro Z.
    alle 11.^{20} stasera parto — Oggi ho parlato tanto e simpatica-
mente di te col Sig Giulio, Tito[,] Toscanini, Gatti Casazza,
Simoni. Niente Tosca alla Scala[:] Il Sig Giulio irremovibile! non
puoi credere quanto me ne dolga! Sarebbe stata una così bella
ripresa e veniva così bene! Pazienza — Spremi il tuo forte cervello

per la Girl! Pregoti dire al mio cacciatore, ad amanzio[5] che gli ho
spedito degli uccellini per la voliera – Saluti affettuosi da
    GPuccini
[On verso:] a <u>Carlo Zangarini</u> / <u>Torre del Lago</u> (Pisa)
[Postmarked as sent:]
Milano / Ferrovia
24/10/07—4 S[era]
[As arrived:]
Torre del Lago / Lucca
25/10/07

MGC 12

HOTEL BRISTOL WIEN

Martedì

Caro Zeta

    T'ho scritto a Bologna – perche [*sic*] Tito mi disse del Suona-
tore di Flauto che tu dovevi finire! e mi crucciai al pensiero che
dovevi troncare il lavoro. Ora ti so a Torre e mi fa tanto piacere[.]
Spero che questa mia ti raggiunga – Butt[erfly] andrà giovedì[.] La
prova generale andò benissimo – Commozione immensa in tutti –
Grande poesia nella mise en scene – Pare dunque bene. Ora a noi –
Mi raccomando la nostra Girl – Sempre più la penso sempre più
me ne innamoro. Pensa seriamente al 3° atto – quello io non lo vedo
ancora bene[.] Materia c'è da farne una bella cosa – ma ci manca
ancora qualcosa di speciale[,] di imprevisto[,] di non ancor udito. . .
La trovata ci manca e ci vuole – quale sarà? chi lo sa? Bisogna davvero
mettere il nostro cervello sotto <u>Strizzo</u> e trovare trovare – trovare. . .

> Qui fa un effetto grande il finale 2° perché è espresso con una
> poesia speciale

    Ho inquadrato questa cosa – perche [*sic*] è la trovata di Butter-
fly – in altro campo in altro ordine di idee ci vuole il finale 2°
di Butterfly anche nella Girl – non coro a bouche fermées, non
quello – tu capisci – ma un <u>quid</u> che faccia dire dallo stupore–:
bravi per dio – Pensa dunque e forza caro Zangarini
    Salutissimi affmi
    GPuccini
[No postmark or envelope]

5. probably *Amanzio*, the name of the *cacciatore* [hunter].

MGC 13

TORRE DEL LAGO, TOSCANA.

17. II. 07

Ho comprato un cane che si chiama Nick! Grazie delle [*sic*]
Frutta che potevi spedire a Torre già che c'eri – E Minnie? Mi
raccomando come chi con tutte le insistenze ed ansie può farlo

Pensa al gran Terzo –

Ciao

aff

Puccini

[On verso:] Carlo Zangarini / ~~Via Farini~~
[in a different hand] Piazza Duomo 43–45 / Milano
Love Darling Send your news
[in another hand] Ricordati i libri della biblioteca.
Saluti
Frida.
[Postmarked as first sent:]
Torre del Lago / Lucca
18/11/07
[As arrived:]
Bologna / Centro
18/11/07—8 S[era]
[As re-sent:]
Bologna / Ferrovia
19/11/07—12 M[attina]
[As arrived:]
Milano / Ferrovia
19.XI. 07 2 S[era]

MGC 14 [Postcard]

Grazie squisite frutta!
ma non grazie per gita milanese!!
Vorrei relegarti a Giannutri!

aff tuo

GPuccini

[On verso:] Carlo Zangarini / Piazza Duomo 43–45 / Milano
[Postmarked as sent:]
Torre del Lago / Lucca
19/11/07

MGC 15

ore 10 sera   22 nov 907

Caro Zanga, mentre il vento mugghia e nel lago rimbombano le
notturne schioppettate, io preludio a minnie – e tu sarai al lavoro –
come sia contento della piega sana che prenderà il libretto non sto
a dirtelo – ma, mio caro, bisogna sbrigarsi – il tempo passa e pensa
che abbiamo promesso l'opera per l'anno venturo! Spremi, mangani
il tuo cervello e sia vicino il giorno che mi annunzierai compiuto il
West –

ciao tuo GPuccini

[On verso:] A Carlo Zangarini / Via Farini / Bologna

[Postmarked as sent:]

Torre del Lago / Lucca

23/11/07

[As arrived:]

Bologna / Centro

23/11/07—8 S[era]

MGC 16

TORRE DEL LAGO, TOSCANA.

5. 12. 07

Caro Z.

Sta bene – Lunedì ti attendo e con che ansietà! ma non man-
carmi – Spero che verrai finalmente con tutto – sono in forma,
pronto – ho il cervello che vuole Minnie e li compagni sui [*sic*]

aff tuo GP –

[On verso:] Carlo Zangarini / Piazza Duomo 43–45 / Milano

[Postmarked as sent:]

Torre del Lago / Lucca

6/12/07

MGC 17

Egyptian Mail Steamship C°. L^D.

SS Heliopolis

Lunedì

3–2.–08

Sono nel mare   Finisti il terzo
ballando assai   con Tito accanto
e tu che fai   bada che un guanto
pensi alla Girl?   dovrà parer –

Leggo i due atti
con occhio in Crusca
parola etrusca
metto qua e là —
Domani sera
nel buio fitto
sarò in Egitto
come Dio vuol —
Sono alloggiato
da prence antico
balla l'amico
la polka vil!
Tempo piovoso
vento d'oriente
tutta la gente
qui parla mal —
Son tutti inglesi
tedeschi e franchi
donne coi fianchi
donne bambù[.]
[No postmark or envelope.]

L'Elvira è morta
stesa sul letto
io circospetto
studio il lavor —
fumo egiziane
bevo miniera
ma questa sera
bevo cognac —
o bolognese
conferenziere
tutte le sere
ti leggerò —
Tanti saluti
dall'alto mare
se vuoi suonare
copriti ben —
Ciao
    tuo
      GPuccini

MGC 18

TORRE DEL LAGO, (TOSCANA.)

10. 3. 08

Caro Zanga

    Invece di darmi notizie del 3° atto mi spoetizzi con animo lieto sulla solita tiritera teatrale cremonese! — Pensa, caro amico, al nostro lavoro! Ho sottocchio il primo e secondo — più li leggo e più trovo che hanno bisogno di <u>riguardi</u> — non tanto per l'<u>andazzo</u> scenico, perché quello va — salvo qualche lunghezza — ma il <u>linguaggio</u> per me non è quello che vuolci — la forma anch'essa ha bisogno di ritorni — dunque non lasciarti andare alla tranquillità — hai ancor camicie da sudare!

    Ciao   scrivi — parto per Roma il 14 — andrò al Grand Hotel.

    aff. tuo GPuccini

[On verso:] a Carlo Zangarini / ~~Via Farini~~ / ~~Bologna~~

[in a different hand] Piazza Duomo 43−45 / Milano

[Postmarked as sent:]

Torre del Lago / Lucca
10/3/08
[As arrived:]
Milano / Centro
12/3 / 08 —10 M[attina]

MGC 19
Torre del Lago, Toscana.
Caro Zangarini
 Lunedì sarò a Milano[.] ho urgente bisogno di parlarti e mi
trattengo solo per questo –
 Dunque fammi trovare un tuo biglietto in portineria mia nel
quale mi dici l'ora in cui mi appunti e il dove se da me o io da te –
come credi meglio – È urgente che io ti veda. – Ciao
  tuo aff
  GPuccini
[On verso:] Espresso Espresso [in red ink]
A Carlo Zangarini / Piazza Duomo 43 / Milano
[Postmarked as sent:]
Torre del Lago / Lucca
4/4/08
[As arrived:]
Milano / [/]
5 —APR [illegible]

MGC 20
Torre del Lago, Toscana.
Caro Zangarini
 Ricevuto tua lettera – Per ora non avevi niente di nuovo – di
nuovo attendo il tracciato in prosa del 3° – E ora che son passate
tante bufere tu devi farlo a dimostrare come senti il teatro con vi-
sione pratica e ben equilibrata non tralasciando di tener d'occhio
il pensiero redenzionista che deve aleggiare su tutto il lavoro –
dimostratici dunque nella pienezza tua –
 Ciao tuo sempre
 GPuccini
[On verso:] A Carlo Zangarini / Piazza Duomo 43 / Milano
[Postmarked as sent:]
Torre del Lago / Lucca
15/4/08

[As arrived:]
Milano / Centro
16/4/08 — 5 M[attina]

MGC 21

Caro Z

Potresti venire qui qualche giorno per lavorare al libretto per certe correzioni causate da esigenze musicali? È questione di poco lavoro ma mi saresti molto utile anzi necessario — Ben inteso che avrai la rifusione spese. attendo risposta pronta per decidere anche per le mie cure.

Aff saluti
GPuccini
7 ag. 909
Bagni di Lucca
[On envelope:] Carlo Zangarini / Piazza Duomo 43 / Milano
[Postmarked as sent:]
Bagni di Lucca
7/8/09 — 20

MGC 22

VIA VERDI, 4, MILANO.
2. 10.
Caro Zanga
Grazie dei tuoi auguri[6]
che giungono assai puri
anche se dopo sturi
e il tappo va nei muri [.]
Io passo giorni scuri
a scrivere siluri
a forma di kanguri
per giorni un pò futuri [.]
Speriamo non sian duri
sian chiari più che oscuri
l'orecchio non s'otturi
di spettatori impuri [.]
E sempre si maturi
al suono di tamburi

---

6. Note Puccini's use of the unique rhyme on -uri throughout the poem.

Ciao GPuccini
[On verso:] Carlo Zangarini / Via Farini / Bologna
[Postmarked as sent:]
Milano / Partenza
3/01/10 — 2 S[era]
[As arrived:]
Bologna / Centro
4.1.10 — 8

MGC 23

VIA VERDI, 4, MILANO.

Caro Z.

I primi versi dell'atto 3° son versi orbi!
Convien che Zanga rivolga verso Via Verdi – E sgorbi
getti sul foglio che m'è davanti
con mano svelta
(e per ben scriver si levi i guanti)
parola scelta
getti su carta con lesta mano
(carta Fabriano)
                    vieni nel pome-
     riggio qui at home.
          G. P.

     24. I. 10
[On verso:] Carlo Zangarini / 45 Piazza Duomo / Città
[apparently in Zangarini's hand] anche al mattino verso le 10
[Postmarked as sent:]
Milano / Partenza
24/1/10 — 18

MGC 24

VIA VERDI, 4, MILANO.

30. 10

Caro Z
mi occorre un verso che dica:*
Pag: I del 3° atto
Rance – (cupo)
maledetto cane
*parea ferito a morte!

E pensar che da allora
è stato lì <u>curato</u> (priore)
scaldato dal respiro di Minnie, etc.

    ⟨ Guarito poi ⟩

Hai capito?
Bisogna dirlo il <u>parea ferito a morte</u> è necessario – Parti?
    Ciao tuo
    G P
[On verso:] Sig Zangarini / 43 [Piazza] Duomo / Città
[apparently in Zangarini's hand] <u>Da Milano a me in Milano</u>
[No postmarks or stamps]

MGC 25
VIA VERDI, 4, MILANO.
Caro Z
    Ho perduto i foglietti ultimi del libretto dove tu mi avevi fatto
dei versi – erano press'a poco questi – ma due strofe –
    addio mia dolce terra
    addio mia california
    bei monti della sierra
        nevi addio –
        e un'altra strofa sullo stesso metro – La ricordi? Ti prego di
farne un'altra e mandarmela subito – io parto lunedì per Paris Ho-
tel   Westminster   rue de la Paix
    Ciao aff tuo GPuccini
[On verso:] Sig Carlo <u>Zangarini</u> / Via Farini / <u>Bologna</u>
[Postmarked as sent:]
Milano / Partenza
28.5.10.18
[As arrived:]
Bologna / Centro
29.5.10 — 3

MGC 26 [Postcard]
    Torre del Lago
    2. 7 10
    Caro Zanga –
        ricordi tu la strofa d'opposizione coro pag: 13 3° atto—della
quale ti detti il metro? guarda di rintracciarla mi urge – che dis-
grazia fu la perdita dei foglietti!

[On verso:] A Carlo Zangarini / 43 Piazza Duomo / Milano
[Postmarked as sent:]
Torre del Lago / Lucca
2/7/10

MGC 27

TORRE DEL LAGO, TOSCANA.

13 luglio 1910
Caro Zanga
    un gran favore da te – Subito subito mandami ti prego altri
versi della pagina 14 bis dove c'è il recit di Minnie
    "E anche tu lo vorrai,
    Joe etc –
si tratta non di Minnie ma della scena a cotè di Sonora:
    È necessario
    Troppo le dobbiamo –
    deciditi anche tu etc
di questi a parte vorrei trarne un partito maggiore e perciò ti prego
di farmi subito dei versi rotti di Sonora di Joe[,] Happy[,] Harry e
Bello – già alcuni di loro convertiti alla causa che usano insistenze
maggiori sulla massa e sui compagni per ottenere il perdono di
Minnie. – Grazie mandameli subito ti prego urgono 7 o 8 o 10 ver-
setti in più di ciò che è stampato messi nel mezzo oppure in fine.
    Tuo aff Puccini
[On verso:] Carlo Zangarini / 43 piazza duomo / Milano
[Postmarked as sent:]
Torre del Lago / Lucca
14/7/20

MGC 28

TORRE DEL LAGO, TOSCANA.

13. 7. 10
Caro Zanga
2ª lettera
dopo la parola redenzione pagina 14bis – Minnie rimane estatica
e Joh. [sic] s'inginocchia dinanzi a lei ed ella pone la sua mano sulla
testa di lui quasi benedicandolo etc si può far dire a Sonora e agli
altri bois [sic]: guardate e se avete core togliete a Minnie l'uomo che
la fa felice, su via decidetevi tu Harry (che magari sarà restio) oppure
Joe (come vuoi tu)[.] fallo per lei per me, siate uniti nel concedergli

la vita e la felicità etc etc – Siccome dunque dopo la parola <u>reden-zione</u> di <u>Minnie</u> c'è uno strascico orchestrale, su questo farei bruciare le ultime cartucce di Sonora etc[.] Hai ben capito? Io spero

ciao e grazie tuo

GP

[On verso:] a Carlo Zangarini / 43 Piazza Duomo / Milano
[Postmarked as sent:]
Torre del Lago / Lucca
14/7/10

MGC 29

TORRE DEL LAGO, TOSCANA.

31. 7. 10

Caro Zanga

Minnie è pei monti allacciata al suo uomo che s'è conquistato e ci rimarrà fino a dicembre[.] Ho tagliato e ridotto molto il finale – era troppo prolisso. Capirai che a mezzanotte non ci si può perdere in chiacchiere anche se gustose – e la fine è venuta bene ed io spero che il pubblico non pensi al <u>paltò</u> mentre si chiudono i fatti dei miei ragazzi—

"Bois " –

Leggo il <u>Corriere</u> – o perché non dicevi qualche cosa di meraviglioso, per es: che ho scritto l'opera su carta rigata nientemeno con 5 righi e con inchiostro Black-Bleu e che i clarini suonano con Lancia a Benzina?..

Ciao tuo

aff GPuccini

[On verso:] Carlo Zangarini / Piazza Duomo 43 / Milano
[Postmarked as sent:]
Torre del Lago / Lucca
31/7/10
[As arrived:]
Milano / Arrivo
1—8.10.10

*I*talian *T*exts of *Q*uotations

The following original Italian texts were chosen for this section when the cited quotation was not in a readily available source such as *Carteggi pucciniani* or *Puccini com'era*.

1. [Newspaper Article]
    CORRIERE TEATRALE: "*La fanciulla del West* (la prossima opera di Puccini)"

    Puccini, nella sua villa favorita di Torre del Lago, ha avuto, ultimamente ospite Carlo Zangarini, ch'egli conobbe alla lettura d'un suo lavoro, in casa Ricordi. Ora Carlo Zangarini ha avuto incarico di ridurre a libretto il dramma di Davide Belasco, e ha consegnato il lavoro al Maestro, il quale spera di avere pronta la musica per la fine del venturo anno. Il lavoro sarà in tre atti, dei quali l'ultimo pare si discosti dall'originale inglese. . . .
    L'ambiente è la California, il famoso *Eldorado,* la regione della febbre dell'oro, nell'anno 1849.

    Corriere della sera (Milan), 7 November 1907

2. [Newspaper Article]
    NOTIZIE LIRICHE E DRAMMATICHE: "Per un divorzio"

    Si è molto parlato del divorzio Puccini-Illica, il quale ultimo ha legato il suo nome, insieme a quello di Giuseppe Giacosa, alle ultime opere dell'illustre maestro lucchese. . . . Il fatto è vero. Luigi Illica non credette conveniente alla propria dignità artistica, di collaborare con altri al libretto della nuova opera di Puccini. Fin che si trattò di Giacosa, Illica non fece eccezioni. Anzi. . . . Ma sparito Giuseppe Giacosa, Luigi Illica, che rimane sempre non solo il più fecondo, ma il migliore dei nostri librettisti attivi, ha pensato che non era il caso di una collaborazione.

Per questo il librettista della nuova opera di Puccini è Carlo Zangarini; un giovane poeta di serio valore, che non ha bisogno di essere presentato al pubblico.

La sera (Milan), 2–3 December 1907

3. [Newspaper Article]
NOTIZIE TEATRALE—Lirica

. . . L'opera avrà tre grandi parti per soprano, tenore e baritono, nonché una quindicina di personaggi secondari. La protagonista sarà l'unica donna che figurerà sulla scena, poiché mancherà anche il coro femminile. Si avrà soltanto un coro di uomini all'ultimo atto. Puccini è più che mai invaghito del soggetto prescelto, che risponde magnificamente al suo temperamento artistico. Egli sperava che *La fanciulla del West* potesse giungere al fuoco della ribalta verso la fine del 1908, ma ormai si può ritenere che l'opera non potrà essere ultimata prima della primavera del 1909. Naturalmente adesso non è il caso di pensare al teatro dove potrà essere eseguita per la prima volta. Puccini non ci ha nascosto che amerebbe che l'opera avesse il suo battesimo all'estero, per esempio a New York . . . o a Londra. . . . vogliamo augurarci . . . che la nuova creazione pucciniana trovi la sua consacrazione sulle scene d'uno dei più importanti teatri italiani.

Corriere della sera, 30 December 1907

4. [Newspaper Article]
CORRIERE TEATRALE: "Puccini e la sua nuova opera *La fanciulla dell'* [*sic*] *West*"

. . . Mi hanno accusato di pigrizia . . . perché sono rimasto qualche anno in silenzio. Dalle innumerevoli proposte che ho avuto da librettisti anche notissimi, e non d'Italia soltanto ma anche d'Europa e d'America, nessuna corrispondeva a quell'ideale di passione di cui il mio spirito musicale ha bisogno: e le ho tutte scartate. Ma questa *Fanciulla dell' West* mi ha subito trascinato ad amarla: si è impadronita di me, mi ha se-dotto; non avrò pace finché non potrò segnare la parola «fine» all'ultima scena dell'opera.

Corriere della sera, 13 February 1909

5. [Newspaper Article]
   "The Girl of the Golden West: Confessioni e indiscrezioni di un librettista"

   ... Sono stato accanto a lui, per venti giorni del maggio scorso, e per altrettanti dell'ultimo settembre, nel periodo più fervido del suo lavoro, ed ho così avuto la buona ventura di raccogliere i primi vagiti di "Minnie." ... Ma io non dimenticherò mai i giorni del suo nascere ..., la scorsa primavera, nella cerula quiete di Torre del Lago. Carlo Zangarini, che sta diventando il librettista in voga, dopo aver già compiuto gran parte del libretto, chiamato da altri impegni aveva dovuto interrompere il lavoro e correva l'Italia e la Germania a imbastire scene e ricercar belle rime per i suoi innumeri maestri. Ero rimasto solo col maestro, e lavoravamo insieme.

   Corriere della sera, 28 October 1908

6. [Metropolitan Opera Archives, Catalog Entry]
   Paris, 9 June 1910

   È stato convenuto oggi fra la Metropolitan Opera Company di New York ed il Maestro Giacomo Puccini abitante in Torre del Lago ciò che segue:

   1. Il Maestro Giacomo Puccini si obbliga di venire a New York nel mese di Novembre e Dicembre 1910 per trattenercisi quattro settimane di seguito. Resta inteso che, salvo caso di forza maggiore, la prima rappresentazione della "Fanciulla del West" avrà luogo il 6 Dicembre 1910, ed il Maestro dovrà trovarsi a New York due settimane prima dell'andata in scena.

   2. In queste quattro settimane il Maestro Giacomo Puccini assisterà alle rappresentazioni delle sue opere, e si occuperà della mess'in scena della "Fanciulla del West."

   3. La Metropolitan Opera Company si obbliga di far tenere al Maestro G. Puccini un importo di Lire 20,000, dicesi "Lire Ventimila" più il viaggio andata e ritorno per il detto Maestro e la sua signora da Milano, più il soggiorno intero delle quattro settimane a New York.

   4. L'importo di Lire 20.000 sarà rimesso al Maestro in rate di Lire 5.000 alla fine di ogni settimana.

5. Sotto *Soggiorno* è inteso: 1 salone, 1 camera da letto, 1 bagno ed il vitto, *nonchè vetture.*

6. Durante queste quattro settimane il Maestro G. Puccini si obbliga di essere assolutamente alla disposizione della Metropolitan Opera Company per gli impegni sopradetti, e senza il consentimento della detta Metropolitan Opera Company non può assistere a nessuna rappresentazione delle sue opere sia in concerto o teatro.

7. Tutte queste condizioni furono accettate di comune accordo e sono in vigore dal momento della firma della presente da ambo le parti.

METROPOLITAN OPERA COMPANY
[Signature:] *Giacomo Puccini*
Direttore Generale

7. [Newspaper Article]
NOTIZIE TEATRALI—Lirica: *"La fanciulla del West* di Puccini: Qualche indiscrezione"

... E in generale il precipuo carattere della musica pucciniana nel nuovo spartito è questa fusione perfetta, impressionante della parola e della musica, così da fare della *Fanciulla* una creazione che svolga, completandola e rafforzandola [...]. Tra gli spartiti pucciniani è quello che più reca in sè l'orma della sua concezione essenzialmente teatrale.

Corriere della serae, 31 July 1910

8. [Newspaper Article]
CORRIERE TEATRALE—Da Londra: "L'entusiasmo della Destinn per la *Fanciulla del West"*

... La musica è deliziosa. Credo che Puccini non abbia mai raggiunto sino ad ora tale altezza di ispirazione e tanta perfezione nell'adattare la musica alle vicende sceniche.

"Le osservazioni di certi critici, secondo i quali Puccini non avrebbe saputo cogliere lo spirito americano dell'azione, sono erronee. Credo al contrario che egli abbia saputo interpretare l'anima americana in modo prodigioso. La parte di Minnie che io canto è meno faticosa di quella di *Madame Butterfly,* ma è certo la più bella di tutte le parti di prima donna create da Puccini. Quando canto da Minnie mi pare di rivivere i giorni della mia prima infanzia. Mio padre era padrone di miniere in

Boemia. . . . Cantando Minnie mi pare in certo modo di cantare le alle-
gre canzoni della mia prima infanzia."

Corriere della sera, 28 December 1910

9. [Letter, Puccini to Elvira]
New York, 7 dicembre 1910
Carissima Elvira,

. . . Le prove ottime – credo che sarà un successo e speriamo grande –
domani c'è la generale . . . dopo la prima ci sarà un pranzo e ricevimento
da Vanderbilt e forse altri – Che gioia! . . . Tonio sta bene – ma mi pare
in[vagh]ito con una ballerina – certo che quando può se ne va e io mi
trovo un po' solo – ma però è buono e bisogna lasciarlo un po' vivere –
mi ha scritto Fosca una lettera gentile – fosse stata sempre così con me
come avrei di più apprezzato il suo atto – E tu come stai? Spero starai
meglio. . . . L'opera esce fuori splendida un po' lungo il 1° atto ma il 2°
è magnifico e il 3° grandioso – Belasco è stato a tutte le prove con un
amore e un interesse grande – Caruso è magnifico nella sua parte – la
Destinn non male ma ci vorrebbe più energia – Toscanini sommo—
gentile, buono, adorabile – Insomma son convinto del mio lavoro
e spero molto – ma è d'una difficoltà tremenda come musica e come
messa in scena—la quale messa in scena è molto differente (nei det-
tagli) di quello che avevo immaginato io – anche nello strumentale ho
fatto qualche cambiamento—qualche rinforzo—e un piccolo taglio al
1° atto anche perché la Destinn non lo dice come vorrei. . . .

La messa in scena è magnifica – la vedrai a Roma in giugno – Io
non vedo l'ora di rivedere il mio ??? di moglietta (anch'io lo sono) non
t'offendere. Andremo qualche giorno a Torre? Io vorrei andarci[.] Ora
bisogna che io mangi un po' <u>fino</u> pensa ad una buona cuoca sul serio
cercala per tempo trovala e portatela con te. Ciao ti bacio.
tuo Giacomo
[Antonio's postscript:]
Cara Mamma – Ti saluto tanto – Consegno questa lettera a un signore
che parte domani così arriverà più presto.

Museo Casa Natale Giacomo Puccini, Lucca

10. [Newspaper Article]
"Il successo della *Fanciulla del West* al Metropolitan di New York:
cinquanta chiamate a Puccini—100,000 lire d'incasso (per dispaccio
al *Corriere della sera*)"

L'ENTUSIASMO AMERICANO

. . . Avvicinandosi l'ora della rappresentazione, . . . la folla crebbe fino da far sembrare il teatro un grande alveare in piena attività. La ressa era aumentata dalla siepe dei curiosi venuti a vedere l'arrivo delle grandi dame, che però scendono dalle automobili alla porta del teatro tutte avviluppate in manti or pelliccie. Esse non lasciano vedere nulla, fuorchè qualche sprazzo luminoso di brillanti e qualche punta di nasino, emergente da una massa di piume, e arrossato dal vento rigido. . . . La città è avvolta nella neve e nel ghiaccio.

Corriere della sera, 12 December 1910

11. [Newspaper Article]
"Il successo della *Fanciulla del West* al Metropolitan di New York: cinquanta chiamate a Puccini—100,000 lire d'incasso (per dispaccio al *Corriere della sera*)"

LA MUSICA

La musica della *Fanciulla* è profondamente pucciniana. Chi l'udisse senza saperne nulla, non avrebbe difficoltà a trovarne l'autore. L'uso frequente di certi accordi individualissimi, che paion quasi disaccordi, fanno pensare ogni tanto a *Butterfly* e a *Tosca.* . . . Tuttavia la *Fanciulla* rappresenta un nuovo stadio di questa musica pucciniana caratterizzato da un'acutissima armonizzazione, e da un'audacia di orchestrazione, che potrebbe esser pericolosa in altre mani e che rende l'esecuzione e la direzione molto difficili.

Corriere della sera, 12 December 1910

12. [Program Article]
I giudizi della stampa, "Alcune impressioni di autorevoli critici"
From the review of Giovanni Pozza, critic for *Corriere della sera:*

È stato un trionfo. Possiamo dirlo con gioia e senza restrizioni. . . . E l'Italia, da Roma, glielo ha stasera decretato al Costanzi.

La *Fanciulla del West* ha vinto una magnifica vittoria: una vittoria che si è affermata a grado a grado, di atto in atto in un crescendo continuo di commozione e di entusiasmo ed a cui il magnifico teatro che raccoglieva la parte più eletta del pubblico, non solo a Roma, ma di tutta Italia, ha dato un carattere di vera solennità.

Io non so se nella *Fanciulla di West* si debba veramente riconoscere una nuova *maniera* del maestro. Molti lo hanno affermato; io non lo credo.

Certo è che mai come in quest'opera, il Puccini mostrò un più sicuro dominio del suo ingegno e della sua arte.

. . . La nuova opera è senza dubbio quanto di più perfetto ci abbia dato l'odierna musica italiana. . . .

Teatro Grande di Brescia, 1911 production of *La fanciulla del West*

13. [Program Article] *I giudizi della stampa*, "Alcune impressioni di autorevoli critici"
From the review of Alberto Gaseo, critic for the *Tribuna:*

. . . L'opera possiede tutti gli elementi necessari e sufficienti per un successo popolare duraturo; essa è stata scritta per il gran pubblico . . . la comprenderà e l'amerà, così come ha compreso ed amato la *Tosca* e la *Butterfly.*

Una volta di più Giacomo Puccini avrà raggiunto lo scopo ultimo dell'arte sua. . . .

Teatro Grande di Brescia, 1911 production of *La fanciulla del West*

14. [Poem from a Program]
"A Giacomo Puccini"

LUCCA, CITTÀ NATALE.
La melodia, che qui mesta cullava
nella materna voce il tuo vagito,
il tuo genio felice a noi ridava,
fatta più bella via di lito in lito.
Noi la musica tua diciamo ai cieli
e gridiamo il tuo nome a lei da canto;
tale che al mondo insieme si disveli
dolce la patria come dolce è il canto.

Teatro del Giglio di Lucca, September 1911

APPENDIX C

Zangarini's Libretti and Other Works

Italian title/Original title	Composer/Librettist	City: Publisher	Date
I. TRANSLATIONS			
Caino/Kain	D'Albert/Bulthaupt	Bologna: Zanichelli	1901
Hans il suonatore di flauto/ Hans le joueur de flûte	Ganne/Vaucaire, Mitchell	Milan: Ricordi	1907
Pelleas e Mélisanda/ Pelléas et Mélisande	Debussy/Maeterlinck	Milan: Sonzogno	1907
Medea/Medée	Cherubini/Hoffman	Milan: Fantuzzi	1909
La principessa della czarda/ Die Csárdásfürstin	Kálmán/Stein, Jenbach	Milan: Sonzogno	1916?
II. ADAPTATIONS			
Hail Columbia!	Agostini/after Longfellow	Bologna: Neri	1904
La fanciulla del West	Puccini/after Belasco	Milan: Ricordi	1910
La rosiera	Gnecchi/after Musset	Milan: Ricordi	1910
Conchita	Zandonai/after Vaucaire	Milan: Ricordi	1911
Melenis	Zandonai/with Spritini, after Bouilhet	Milan: Ricordi	1912
Capriccio antico	Hartulàry-Darclée/after Bandello	Milan: Sonzogno	1912
Amore in maschera	Hartulàry-Darclée/after ?	Milan: Sonzogno	1913

Italian title/Original title	Composer/Librettist	City: Publisher	Date
L'ultimo dei Moicani	Allen/after Cooper	Milan: Ricordi	1916
Vanda	Azzolini/after Surzycki	?	?
	III. ORIGINAL LIBRETTI		
Berta alla siepe, quadro lirico	Emanuele Gennai	Milan: Bonetti	1908
Terra promessa, poema drammatico	Arrigo Pedrollo	Milan: Poligrafia Italia	1908
Jaufré Rudel, poema drammatico	Adolfo Gandino	Bologna: Neri	1910
Saltarello, dramma lirico	Amleto Zecchi	Bologna: Neri	1910
I gioielli della Madonna, opera, with E. Golsciani	Ermanno Wolf-Ferrari	Milan: Sonzogno	1912
Nido di Falco, idillio drammatico	Oreste Bergami	Milan: Rizzoli	1912
Il santo, tragedia lirica	Ubaldo Pacchierotti	Milan: Sonzogno	1913
Maria sul monte, leggenda lirica	Primo Riccitelli	Milan: Sonzogno	1914
Anthony	Rodriguez Socas	Milan: Sonzogno	1924
Severo Torelli, dramma lirico	Ugo Bottacchiari	Milan: Ricordi	1924?
Le astuzie di Bertoldo, opera giocosa, with O. Lucarini	Luigi Ferrari-Trecate	Bologna: A. Comi	1934?

Zangarini's Other American-Themed Adaptations

In addition to *La fanciulla del West*, Zangarini adapted two other American-themed works for the opera stage: *Hail Columbia!* with music by Mezio Agostini (pub. 1904), and *L'ultimo dei Moicani*, composed by Paul Allen (pub. 1916; see pl. 32).[1] Both were completed before Zangarini's post–World War I disillusionment with the United States and Wilsonian policies in particular. *Hail Columbia!*'s dedication, "To the government and the people of the United

1. In 1909 Agostini succeeded Ermanno Wolf-Ferrari as director of the Liceo Benedetto Marcello in Venice, where he also served as the principal professor of composition.

States of America, country of my mother," reflects Zangarini's friendly prewar disposition.

Although Zangarini's American mother may have introduced him to Longfellow's *Song of Hiawatha* and Cooper's *Last of the Mohicans*, Zangarini's interest in such stories was shared by many artists of his generation who were eager to use American topics as subjects for operas and films. Stories that focused on Native American subjects were particularly appealing to composers and librettists; "exotic" racial difference could be exploited musically, textually, and visually in ways that were ever popular with opera audiences. The project of interpreting American subjects within the western European musical and ideological framework was one that involved Puccini in *La fanciulla del West,* but also captured the imagination of Victor Herbert whose *Natoma* premiered in New York just one year after *La fanciulla del West.* Another composer with whom Zangarini was associated, Luigi Ferrari-Trecate, also composed an "American" opera in 1953, *La capanna dello zio Tom,* adapted from Harriet Beecher Stowe's novel, *Uncle Tom's Cabin.*

Paul Hastings Allen, the only American composer to work with Zangarini, met the librettist when he studied music and worked as a diplomat in Italy.[2] Allen resided in Florence where his *L'ultimo dei Moicani* premiered in 1916. Zangarini's libretto for *Moicani* was published by Ricordi and indicates that this work, unlike most of Zangarini's other adaptations or original libretti, had the backing of Italy's internationally important opera publisher. Zangarini's fluency in English and his familiarity with American literature may have been the reasons Ricordi gave the *Moicani* commission to Zangarini—the same reasons Ricordi recommended him to Puccini years earlier as the librettist for *Fanciulla.*

Song Texts

Copies of these works were not among the papers preserved by the Zangarini family and are known only through references in newspaper articles or entries in Carlo Schmidl's 1928 *Dizionario universale dei musicisti.*

"Amore e Patria," music by Giojer. 1913
"Canzone di Milano," music by Giuseppe Pettinato. 1928.
"Inno al fante" and "Ala imperiale," music by Giuseppe Pettinato, 1927.
Mastro Dill, music by Luigi Gazzotti. 1915.

---

2. Allen (1883–1952), a native of Hyde Park, Massachusetts, lived in Italy from 1903 to 1920.

La mogliettina di carta, music by Enzo A. G. Artioli. 1928.

"Rosa di macchia," music by Elisabetta Oddone. 1908.

L'ultimo chic, music by Luigi Motta, 1915.

Poems, Plays, Essays, and Speeches

Aratrum [set of poems]. Rome: Editrice la Federazione Provinciale Fascista dei Commercianti di Bologna, 1927.

Avanti la Diana [book of poems]. Bologna: Beltrami, 1905.

"Caino" [poem]. 1908.

Camicia Rossa [play]. Editore Oreste Ruggeri, 1904.

Canti del Fronte Interno (1918–1919) : Editi nel decennale della rivoluzione fascista da la rassegna 'il comune di Bologna' [book of poems]. Bologna: Stabilimenti Poligrafici Riuniti, 1932.

Catullo and *Il Conte di Pancalieri* [plays]. Turin and Rome: Casa Editrice Nazionale, 1904.

"Celebrazione del 200 annuale della morte di Adolfo Crescentini (1854 – 1921)" [speech]. Bologna: Tipografia Luigi Parma, 1941.

"Commemorazione del XXXII Anniversario del XX Settembre" [commemorative speech]. Bologna: Stab. Tip. Zamorani e Albertazzi, 1902.

"Di una banca confessionale per artisti" [speech]. Rome: Gaetano Torri, 1927.

Il divino Pierrot [play]. Bologna: Stabilimenti Poligrafici Riuniti B Editori, 1931.

"Elogio del dolore" [speech]. Bologna: Officina Industriale Tipografica, 1902.

Epinicio [poems]. Bologna: Società Tipografica Azzoguidi, 1895.

Frate Francesco [film adaptation]. Milan: Società Italiana Cinematografica, 1927.

"Gustavo Modena" [speech]. Bologna: Tipografia Militare, 1900.

"A memoria le banche consorziate pubblicarono" [poem]. Milan: Bertieri Vanzetti, 1918.

"In morte di Giovanni Bovio" [speech]. Faenza: Premiata Topigrafia Sociale, 1903.

"La morte di Pierrot" [poem]. 1914.

Per gli occhi spenti in guerra [set of publicly recited poems]. Milan: "Orpheus" Casa Editrice in Milano, 1918.

"La psicologia della signorina" [speech]. Bologna: Successori Monti, 1898.

*M*etropolitan Opera *P*erformance *H*istory

1910–11

10 December 1910: World Premiere. All performances in Italian.

Minnie (M)	Emmy Destinn
Dick Johnson (J)	Enrico Caruso
Jack Rance (R)	Pasquale Amato
Joe (Jo)	Glenn Hall
Handsome (Han)	Vincenzo Reschiglian
Harry (Har)	Pietro Audisio
Happy (Hap)	Antonio Pini-Corsi
Sid (S)	Giulio Rossi
Sonora (Son)	Dinh Gilly
Trin (T)	Angelo Badà
Jim Larkens (JL)	Bernard Bégué
Nick (N)	Albert Reiss
Jake Wallace (JW)	Andrés De Segurola
Ashby (A)	Adamo Didur
Post Rider (PR)	Lamberto Belleri (debut)
Castro (C)	Edoardo Missiano

This material is taken from the Metropolitan Opera Archives Database. Unless otherwise indicated, all performances were at the New York Metropolitan Opera House. Please see also chapter 5 for a discussion of selected European and Italian premieres (1910–14).

Billy Jackrabbit (BJ)   Georges Bourgeois
Wowkle (W)   Marie Mattfeld

Conductor   Arturo Toscanini
Director   David Belasco
Director   Edward Siedle (debut)
Set designer   James Fox
Costume designer   Louise Musaeus
Lighting director   Frederick G. Gaus (debut)

—17 December 1910: same cast, conductor, and production as 10 December 1910
—20 December 1910 (Philadelphia): same as 10 December 1910
—26 December 1910: same as 10 December 1910
—*5 January 1911: same as 10 December 1910
—11 January 1911: same as 10 December 1910
—27 January 1911: same as 10 December 1910
—4 February 1911 (matinee): same as 10 December 1910 except Umberto Bedeschi (PR), Elvira Leveroni (W)
—2 March 1911: same as 10 December 1910 except Amedeo Bassi (J; debut)
—18 March 1911 (Brooklyn Academy of Music): same as 2 March 1911
—*27 March 1911: same as 2 March 1911

*Ballet divertissements:
—5 January 1911: Minkus: *Don Quixote Variations* (Mikail Mordkin); Chopin: *Valse in A-flat* (Anna Pavlova); Glazounov: *L'automne bacchanale* (Anna Pavlova, Mikail Mordkin); conductor, Theodore Stier; choreographer, Marius Petipa.
—27 March 1911: Rubinstein: *La nuit* (Anna Pavlova); Glinka: *Mazurka* (Bronislawa Pajitzskaia, Stanislava Kun, Stephania Plaskowietzkaia, Alina Schmolz, Sergei Moroseff, Kyprian Barboe, Alexis Trojanowski, Veronine West); Glazounov: *L'automne bacchanale* (Mikail Mordkin, Anna Pavlova); conductor, Josef Pasternack.

1911–12

—16 November 1911: same as 10 December 1910 except Lambert Murphy (Jo); Jules Speck, director
—13 December 1911: same as 16 November 1911 except Paolo Ananian (C)
—*29 December 1911: same as 13 December 1911
—13 January 1912 (matinee): same as 13 December 1911

—22 January 1912: same as 13 December 1911

*Ballet divertissement: Imperial Russian Ballet.

1912 – 13

—25 November 1912: same as 13 December 1911 except Paolo Ananian (BJ); Giorgio Polacco, conductor

—9 January 1913: same as 13 December 1911 except Paolo Ananian (BJ)

—21 February 1913: same as 25 November 1912 except Arturo Toscanini, conductor

—22 March 1913 (matinee): same as 21 February 1913 except Giorgio Polacco, conductor

1913 – 14

—4 February 1914: same as 25 November 1912

—12 February 1914: same as 4 February 1914

—28 February 1914: same as 4 February 1914 except Riccardo Martin (J)

—14 March 1914 (matinee): same as 25 November 1912.

1929 – 30: New Production

—2 November 1929 (matinee): Maria Jeritza (M), Giovanni Martinelli (J), Lawrence Tibbett (R), Marek Windheim (Jo), George Cehanovsky (Han), Giordano Paltrinieri (Har), Pompilio Malatesta (Hap), Arnold Gabor (S), Everett Marshall (Son), Angelo Badà (T), Millo Picco (JL), Alfio Tedesco (N), Joseph Macpherson (JW), Tancredi Pasero (A), Max Altglass (PR), Paolo Ananian (C), Paolo Ananian (BJ), Pearl Besuner (W); Vincenzo Bellezza, conductor; Ernst Lert, director; Joseph Novak, set designer

—13 November 1929: same as 2 November 1929 except Louis D'Angelo (JL)

—19 November 1929 (Philadelphia): same as 2 November 1929

—25 November 1929: same as 2 November 1929

—3 December 1929 (Brooklyn): same as 2 November 1929 except Louis D'Angelo (JL), Lamberto Belleri (PR)

—5 December 1929: same as 2 November 1929

—27 December 1929 (matinee): same as 2 November 1929 except Louis D'Angelo (JL), Lamberto Belleri (PR)

—10 January 1930: same as 2 November 1929 except Edward Johnson (J), Max Altglass (Har), Giordano Paltrinieri (T), Lamberto Belleri (PR)

—24 January 1930 (matinee): same as 10 January 1930 except Giovanni Martinelli (J), Giuseppe Danise (R), James Wolfe (Hap), Angelo Badà (T), Giordano Paltrinieri (N)

—8 March 1930: same as 2 November 1929 except Leonora Corona (M), Frederick Jagel (J), Giuseppe Danise (R), Alfredo Gandolfi (Son), Louis D'Angelo (A), Lamberto Belleri (PR)

—13 May 1930 (Rochester): same as 2 November 1929 except Leonora Corona (M), Giuseppe Danise (R), Millo Picco (S), Alfredo Gandolfi (Son), Pavel Ludikar (A), Lamberto Belleri (PR); Tullio Serafin, conductor

1930–31

—4 November 1930 (Philadelphia): same as 2 November 1929 except Edward Johnson (J), Giuseppe Danise (R), Alfredo Gandolfi (Son), Louis D'Angelo (A), Lamberto Belleri (PR)

—13 November 1930: same as 4 November 1930 except Giovanni Martinelli (J)

—22 November 1930 (matinee): same as 13 November 1930 except Edward Johnson (J), Tancredi Pasero (A)

1931–32

—9 November 1931: same as 2 November 1929 except Giuseppe Danise (R), Alfredo Gandolfi (Son), Lamberto Belleri (PR); Alexander Sanine, director

—3 December 1931: same as 9 November 1931

1961–62: New Production

—23 October 1961: Leontyne Price (M), Richard Tucker (J), Anselmo Colzani (R), Andrea Velis (Jo; debut), George Cehanovsky (Han), Robert Nagy (Har), Roald Reitan (Hap), Calvin Marsh (S), Clifford Harvuot (Son), Gabor Carelli (T), Theodor Uppman (JL), Paul Franke (N), Ezio Flagello (JW), Norman Scott (A), Frank D'Elia (PR), Louis Sgarro (C), Gerhard Pechner (BJ), Margaret Roggero (W); Fausto Cleva, conductor; Henry Butler, director (debut); Gerald L. Ritholz, designer (debut); Wolfgang Roth, designer[1]

---

1. The sets and costumes were borrowed from the Lyric Opera of Chicago. Arrangement of the physical production—which, in Chicago, had been revised by Gerald L. Ritholz—was supervised by Wolfgang Roth on the Met's stage.

—31 October 1961: same as 23 October 1961 except Leontyne Price (M), acts 1 and 2, and Dorothy Kirsten (M), act 3[2]

—10 November 1961: same as 31 October 1961 except Dorothy Kirsten (M)

—23 November 1961: same as 10 November 1961 except Sándor Kónya (J), Osie Hawkins (Hap), Roald Reitan (JL)

—4 December 1961: same as 23 November 1961 except Leontyne Price (M), Lou Marcella (T)

—30 December 1961: same as 4 December 1961 except Dorothy Kirsten (M), Daniele Barioni (J), Frank Guarrera (R), Roald Reitan (JL)

—6 January 1962 (matinee broadcast): same as 23 October 1961 except Dorothy Kirsten (M)

—14 April 1962 (Boston): same as 4 December 1961 except Dorothy Kirsten (M), Gabor Carelli (T), Joan Wall (W)

—18 April 1962: same as 4 December 1961 except Dorothy Kirsten (M), Walter Cassel (R), Gabor Carelli (T), Joan Wall (W)

—29 April 1962 (matinee, Cleveland): same as 4 December 1961 except Gabor Carelli (T), Joan Wall (W)

—5 May 1962 (Atlanta): same as 23 October 1961 except Dorothy Kirsten (M), Osie Hawkins (Hap), Roald Reitan (JL), Joan Wall (W)

—9 May 1962 (Dallas): same as 23 October 1961 except Osie Hawkins (Hap), Roald Reitan (JL), Joan Wall (W)

—20 May 1962 (matinee, Minneapolis): same as 5 May 1962

1965–66

—1 December 1965: same as 23 October 1961 except Dorothy Kirsten (M), Franco Corelli (J), Russell Christopher (Hap), Robert Goodloe (S), Gene Boucher (JL), Edward Ghazal (BJ), Shirley Love (W)

—7 December 1965: same as 1 December 1965

—17 December 1965: same as 1 December 1965 except Bonaldo Giaiotti (JW); Jan Behr, conductor

—23 December 1965: same as 1 December 1965 except Bonaldo Giaiotti (JW)

—8 January 1966 (matinee broadcast): same as 1 December 1965 except John Macurdy (JW), Raymond Michalski (BJ); Jan Behr, conductor

---

2. Price lost her ability to sing near the end of act 2 and played Minnie in a speaking voice for the remainder of the act. Dorothy Kirsten replaced her in act 3.

—17 January 1966: same as 1 December 1965 except Eleanor Steber (M), Franco Corelli (J) act 1, Gaetano Bardini (J) acts 2 and 3, John Macurdy (JW); Jan Behr, conductor[3]

—8 February 1966 (matinee) student performance: same as 1 December 1965 except Lynn Owen (M), Gaetano Bardini (J), Sherrill Milnes (R), Dan Marek (Jo), Peter Sliker (Han), William Zakariasen (Har), Lloyd Strang (Hap), Paul De Paola (S), Gene Boucher (Son), Lou Marcella (T), J. Robert Dunlap (JL), Charles Anthony (N), Louis Sgarro (JW), Raymond Michalski (C), Carlo Tomanelli (BJ), Dorothy Shawn (W); Jan Behr, conductor

—24 February 1966 (matinee) student performance: same as 8 February 1966

—24 February 1966: same as 1 December 1965 except Richard Tucker (J), Frank Guarrera (R), John Macurdy (JW); Jan Behr, conductor

—28 February 1966 (matinee) student performance: same as 8 February 1966 except Robert Nagy (J), Cesare Bardelli (R), Paul Franke (N)

—18 March 1966 (matinee) student performance: same as 28 February 1966 except Charles Anthony (N), Justino Díaz (JW), Louis Sgarro (C)

—18 March 1966: same as December 1 1965 except Justino Díaz (JW); Jan Behr, conductor

—21 March 1966 (matinee) student performance: same as 8 February 1966 except Justino Díaz (JW), Louis Sgarro (C)

—28 March 1966 (matinee) student performance: same as 8 February 1966 except Beverly Bower (M), Cesare Bardelli (R)

—11 April 1966 (matinee): same as 28 March 1966[4]

1969–70

—11 February 1970: Renata Tebaldi (M), Sándor Kónya (J), Giangiacomo Guelfi (R; Guelfi's last performance), Andrea Velis (Jo), Richard Best (Han), Robert Schmorr (Har), Andrij Dobriansky (Hap; debut), Robert Goodloe (S), Clifford Harvuot (Son), Gabor Carelli (T), Raymond Gibbs (JL) [Debut], Paul Franke (N), John Macurdy (JW), Paul Plishka (A), Frank D'Elia (PR), Louis Sgarro (C), Edmond Karlsrud (BJ), Frederica von Stade (W); Fausto Cleva, conductor; Henry Butler, director; Patrick Tavernia, staging[5]

—21 February 1970: same as 11 February 1970 except Anselmo Colzani (R)

3. Franco Corelli canceled after act 1 and was replaced by Gaetano Bardini as Dick Johnson.

4. This was the first performance in the new Metropolitan Opera House at Lincoln Center, a regularly scheduled student performance sponsored by the Met Opera Guild. It was the first full test of the theater's acoustics.

5. The sets and costumes were borrowed from Lyric Opera of Chicago.

—25 February 1970: same as 21 February 1970

—2 March 1970: same as 21 February 1970 except Bonaldo Giaiotti (JW); Jan Behr, conductor

—5 March 1970: same as 2 March 1970 except Dorothy Kirsten (M), Ion Buzea (J)

—9 March 1970: same as 5 March 1970

—14 March 1970 (matinee broadcast): same as 2 March 1970 except John Macurdy (JW)

1991–92: New Production

—10 October 1991: Barbara Daniels (M), Placido Domingo (J), Sherrill Milnes (R), Michael Forest (Jo), Richard Vernon (Han), Bernard Fitch (Har), Kevin Short (Hap), Perry Ward (S; debut), Bruno Pola (Son), Charles Anthony (T), Kim Josephson (JL; debut), Anthony Laciura (N), Terry Cook (JW), Julien Robbins (A), Michael Best (PR), Vernon Hartman (C), Hao Jiang Tian (BJ; debut), Sondra Kelly (W); Leonard Slatkin, conductor; Giancarlo del Monaco, designer (debut); Michael Scott, designer (debut); Gil Wechsler, lighting director

—14 October 1991: same as 10 October 1991 except James Courtney (S)

—18 October 1991: same as 14 October 1991

—23 October 1991: same as 14 October 1991

—26 October (matinee): same as 14 October 1991 except Vladimir Popov (J)

—29 October 1991: same as 14 October 1991 except George Fortune (R)

—1 April 1992: same as 14 October 1991 except Kim Josephson (Son), Dwayne Croft (JL), Yanni Yannissis (JW; debut)

—4 April 1992: same as 1 April 1992

—6 April 1992 (matinee) student performance: same as 1 April 1992 except Mary Jane Johnson (M; debut), Vladimir Popov (J), George Fortune (R)

—8 April 1992 (simulcast): same as 1 April 1992[6]

—11 April 1992 (matinee): same as 1 April 1992

—16 April 1992: same as 1 April 1992 except Vladimir Popov (J)

1992–93

—22 February 1993: same as 10 Oct 1991 except Ghena Dimitrova (M), Nicola Martinucci (J), Alain Fondary (R), James Courtney (S), Kim Josephson

---

6. This performance was videotaped for the Metropolitan Opera Presents series and first televised over PBS on 19 June 1992.

(Son), David Malis (JL), Joseph Frank (N), Jeffrey Wells (A), Philip Coko-
rinos (BJ); Christian Badea, conductor; Sharon Thomas, staging
—26 February 1993: same as 22 February 1993
—2 March 1993: same as 22 February 1993
—6 March 1993 (matinee broadcast): same as 22 February 1993 except Henry
Grossman (T; debut)
—9 March 1993: same as 6 March 1993 except Anthony Laciura (N)
—12 March 1993: same as 9 March 1993 except Perry Ward (S), Laura Brooks
Rice (W; debut)
—15 March 1993: same as 12 March 1993 except Carol Neblett (M), Sherrill
Milnes (R)
—19 March 1993: same as 6 March 1993 except Sherrill Milnes (R), Raymond
Aceto (Han), Anthony Laciura (N)[7]

7. This is the last performance listed in the Met Archives database.

$\mathcal{D}$iscography and Videography

The following is a selected listing of sound and video recordings of performances of *La fanciulla del West*, chosen for their musical and historical importance. The works are presented in reverse chronological order beginning with the most recent.[1]

Recordings on Major Labels

1992 RCA/BMG 009026-60597-2 (CD): Eva Marton (Minnie), Dennis O'Neill (Johnson), Alain Fondary (Rance), Munich Radio Orchestra and Bavarian Radio Chorus conducted by Leonard Slatkin.

1992 Sine Qua Non 39820212 (CD): Gwyneth Jones (Minnie), Corneliu Murgu (Johnson), Claudio Otelli (Rance), Frankfurt Radio Orchestra and Budapest/Hungarian Radio Chorus conducted by Marcello Viotti.

1991 CBS/Sony Classical S2K47189 (CD): Maria Zampieri (Minnie), Plácido Domingo (Johnson), Juan Pons (Rance), Orchestra and Chorus of the Teatro alla Scala di Milano conducted by Lorin Maazel.

---

1. Centro Studi Giacomo Puccini, ed., *Lirica 2001: La fanciulla del West*, Progetto Puccini nel Novecento 1999–2002 (Lucca: Pubblicazione del Teatro Giglio, 2001), 147–56; *The Metropolitan Opera Guide to Recorded Opera and Guide to Opera on Video*, ed. Paul Gruber (New York: W. W. Norton, 1993); Sandro Cometti, "Discografie," *L'avant-scène opéra: Giacomo Puccini, La fille du Far West* 165 (1995): 117–26; Pierre Flinois, "Vidéographie," *L'avant-scène opéra: Giacomo Puccini, La fille du Far West* 165 (1995): 131; Josée Bégaud, researcher, "L'oeuvre à l'affiche," *L'avant-scène opéra: Giacomo Puccini, La fille du Far West* 165 (1995): 132–38; Fairtile, *Puccini Research*, 340–42.

1978 Deutsche Grammophon 419640-2 (CD): Carol Neblett (Minnie), Plácido Domingo (Johnson), Sherrill Milnes (Rance), Orchestra and Chorus of the Royal Opera House, Covent Garden conducted by Zubin Mehta.

1967 Myto MCD 933-83 (CD): Magda Olivero (Minnie), Daniele Barioni (Johnson), Giangiacomo Guelfi (Rance), Orchestra and Chorus of the Teatro La Fenice conducted by Oliviero De Fabritiis.

1966 Mondo Musica MFOH10131 (CD): Antonietta Stella (Minnie), Pier Miranda Ferraro (Johnson), Giangiacomo Guelfi (Rance), Orchestra and Chorus of the Teatro La Fencie conducted by Oliviero De Fabritiis.

1965 Nuova Era 2324/25 (CD): Magda Olivero (Minnie), Gastone Limarilli (Johnson), Lino Puglisi (Rance), Orchestra and Chorus of the Teatro Communale "G. Verdi" (Trieste) conducted by Arturo Basile.

1964 Melodram MEL 27081(CD): Dorothy Kirsten (Minnie), Franco Corelli (Johnson), Anselmo Colzani (Rance), Orchestra and Chorus of the Philadelphia Lyric Opera Company conducted by Anton Guadagno.

1958 London/Decca 421595-2 (CD): Renata Tebaldi (Minnie), Mario Del Monaco (Johnson), Cornell MacNeil (Rance), Orchestra and Chorus of the Accademia di Santa Cecilia, Rome conducted by Franco Capuana.

1958 EMI/Angel CDMB 63970 (CD): Birgit Nilsson (Minnie), Jão Gibin (Johnson), Andrea Mongelli (Rance), Orchestra and Chorus of Teatro alla Scala di Milano conducted by Lovro von Matacic.

1956 Standing Room Only SRO 506-2 (CD): Gigliola Frazzoni (Minnie), Franco Corelli (Johnson), Tito Gobbi (Rance), Orchestra and Chorus of the Teatro alla Scala di Milano conducted by Antonino Votto.

1954 Arkadia CDHP 565-2 (CD), Centa L 064/3: Eleanor Steber (Minnie), Mario Del Monaco (Johnson), Giangiacomo Guelfi (Rance), Orchestra and Chorus of the Teatro Comunale di Firenze conducted by Dimitri Mitropoulos.

1952 Archivi dell'Opera/BMG 0152-TO (CD): Maria Caniglia (Minnie), Giacomo Lauri Volpi (Johnson), Raffaele De Falchi (Rance), Orchestra and Chorus of the Teatro dell'Opera di Roma conducted by Oliviero De Fabritiis.

1950 Cetra (LP): Carla Gavazzi (Minnie), Vasco Campagnano (Johnson), Ugo Savarese (Rance), Radio Italiana Orchestra and Chorus conducted by Arturo Basile. This was the first and for many years the only recording of *Fanciulla*.

Video (VHS), Laser Disc (LD), and DVD Recordings

1992 Deutsche Grammophon PGD 072 553 (VHS/LD/DVD). Stage performance, stereo, color, subtitled; 140 minutes. Barbara Daniels (Minnie), Plácido Domingo (J), Sherrill Milnes (Rance), Metropolitan Opera Orchestra and Chorus conducted by Leonard Slatkin. Metropolitan Opera: Giancarlo Del Monaco (stage director), Brian Large (video director).

1991 Home Vision (VHS/LD). Stage performance, stereo, color, subtitled; 145 minutes. Mara Zampieri (Minnie), Plácido Domingo (J), Juan Pons (Rance), Orchestra and Chorus of Teatro alla Scala conducted by Lorin Maazel. La Scala: Jonathan Miller (stage director), John Michael Phillips (video director).

1982 Castle Vision CVI 2020 (VHS)/Pioneer (LD). Stage performance, stereo, color, not subtitled; 140 minutes. Carol Neblett (Minnie), Plácido Domingo (Johnson), Silvano Carroli (Rance), Orchestra and Chorus of the Royal Opera House conducted by Nello Santi. Royal Opera, Covent Garden: Piero Faggioni (stage director), John Vernon (video director).

1963 Lyric (VHS). Stage performance, stereo, black and white, Japanese subtitles; 133 minutes. Antoinetta Stella (Minnie), Gastone Limarilli (Johnson), Anselmo Colzani (Rance), conducted by Oliviero De Fabritiis. Opera company, stage director, and video director n.a.

BIBLIOGRAPHY

Abbate, Carolyn, and Roger Parker, eds. "Introduction: On Analyzing Opera." In *Analyzing Opera: Verdi and Wagner*, 1–24. Berkeley and Los Angeles: University of California, 1989.

Adami, Giuseppe, ed. *Giacomo Puccini epistolario*. Milan: Mondadori, 1928. Translated and edited by Ena Makin as *Letters of Giacomo Puccini Mainly Connected with the Composition of His Operas*. Philadelphia: J. B. Lippincott, 1931. Reprint, with revisions and introductions by Mosco Carner, London: Harrap, 1974.

Ahlquist, Karen. *Democracy at the Opera: Music, Theater, and Culture in New York City, 1815–1860*. Urbana: University of Illinois Press, 1997.

Aldrich, Richard. *Concert Life in New York, 1902–1923*, ed. Harold Johnson. 1941. Reprint, Freeport, N.Y.: Books for Libraries Press, 1971.

Altman, Rick. *The American Film Musical*. Bloomington: Indiana University Press, 1987.

———. *Genre: The Musical; A Reader*. London: Routledge and Kegan Paul in association with the British Film Institute, 1981.

André, Naomi. "'Blackface' in Opera and the Politics of Viewing." Unpublished paper read at the annual meeting of the Society for American Music in Lexington, Ky., March 2002.

Arblaster, Anthony. *Viva la Libertà! Politics in Opera*. London and New York: Verso, 1992.

Armitage, Shelley. "Rawhide Heroines: The Evolution of the Cowgirl and the Myth of America." In *The American Self: Myth, Ideology, and Popular Culture*, edited by Sam B. Girgus, 166–81. Albuquerque: University of New Mexico Press, 1981.

Ashbrook, William. *The Operas of Puccini*. New York: Oxford University Press, 1968. Reprint, with foreword by Roger Parker, Ithaca: Cornell University Press, 1985.

Atlas, Allan W. "Belasco and Puccini: 'Old Dog Tray' and the Zuni Indians." *Musical Quarterly* 75, no. 3 (Fall 1991): 362–98.

———. *"Lontano—tornare—redenzione:* Verbal Leitmotives and Their Musical Resonance in Puccini's *La fanciulla del West.*" *Studi musicali* 21, no. 2 (1992): 359–98.

———. "Multivalence, Ambiguity, and Non-Ambiguity: Puccini and the Polemicists." *Journal of the Royal Musical Association* 118, no. 1 (1993): 73–93.

———. "Stealing a Kiss at the Golden Section: Pacing and Proportion in the Act I Love Duet of Puccini's *La Bohème.*" *Acta musicologica* 75 (2003): 269–91.

Atlas, Allan, and Roger Parker. "A Key for *Chi?* Tonal Areas in Puccini." *Nineteenth-Century Music* 15, no. 3 (1992): 229–34.

L'avant-scène opéra: Giacomo Puccini, La Fille du Far West 165 (May–June 1995).

Bastianelli, Giannotto. "Riccardo Zandonai." *Nuova rivista musicale italiana* 6, no. 3 (July–September 1972): 409–18.

Bataille, Gretchen M., ed. *Native American Representations: First Encounters, Distorted Images, and Literary Appropriations.* Lincoln: University of Nebraska Press, 2001.

Baur, Steven. "Music, Morals, and Social Management: Mendelssohn in Post–Civil War America." *American Music* 19 (2001): 64–130.

Bégaud, Josée, researcher. "L'oeuvre à l'affiche." *L'avant-scène opéra: Giacomo Puccini, La Fille du Far West* 165 (May–June 1995): 132–138.

Belasco, David. "Beauty as I See It." *Arts and Decoration,* 23 July. Billy Rose Theatre Collection, New York Public Library for the Performing Arts.

———. *The Girl of the Golden West* [novel]. New York: Grosset and Dunlap, 1911.

———. *The Girl of the Golden West.* In *On Stage America!,* edited by Walter J. Meserve, 490–563. New York: Feedback Theatrebooks and Prospero Press, 1996..

———. *The Girl of the Golden West: A Play in Four Acts.* New York: S. French, 1933.

———. *The Theatre through Its Stage Door.* Edited by Louis V. Defoe. New York: Benjamin Blom, 1969.

Belli, Aldo, ed. *Tramontate stelle.* Viareggio: Pezzini Editore, 1996.

Bellman, Jonathan, ed. *The Exotic in Western Music.* Boston: Northeastern University Press, 1998.

Benjamin, Mary. *Autographs: A Key to Collecting.* New York: R. R. Bowker, 1946. Reprint, New York: Book Craftsmen Associates, 1963.

Betz, Marianne. "Fanciulle del West, Fanciulle dell'Est: Frauenfiguren im Verismo." In *Frauen, Körper, Kunst,* vol. 3, edited by Sibylle Gienger and Martina Peter-Bolaender. Kassel: Furore, 2001.

Bird, S. Elizabeth, ed. *Dressing in Feathers: The Construction of the Indian in American Popular Culture.* Boulder, Colo.: Westview Press, 1996.

Blackmer, Corinne E., and Patricia Juliana Smith, eds. *En Travesti: Women, Gender Subversion, Opera.* New York: Columbia University Press, 1995.

Blair, John. "Blackface Minstrels and *Buffalo Bill's Wild West:* Nineteenth-Century Entertainment Forms as Cultural Exports." In *European Readings of American Popular Culture,* edited by John Dean and Jean-Paul Gabillet, 3—12. Westport, Conn.: Greenwood Press, 1996.

Block, Adrienne Fried. "Dvořák, Beach, and American Music." In *A Celebration of American Music: Words and Music in Honor of H. Wiley Hitchcock*, edited by Richard Crawford, R. Allen Lott, and Carol J. Oja, 256—80. Ann Arbor: University of Michigan Press, 1990.

Blumenberg, Marc A. "Reflections." *Musical Courier* 61, no. 23 (7 December 1910): 21—23.

Bohlman, Philip. "On the Unremarkable in Music." *Nineteenth-Century Music* 16, no. 2 (Fall 1992): 203—16.

Bonaccorsi, Alfredo. "Puccini nella critica d'oggi." *Musica d'oggi* 5, no. 2 (March–April 1962): 70—72.

Bordman, Gerald. *American Operetta: From H.M.S. Pinafore" to "Sweeney Todd."* New York: Oxford University Press, 1981.

Brancaleone, Francis. "Edward MacDowell and Indian Motives." *American Music* 7 (1989): 359—81.

Brèque, Jean-Michel. "Un carrefour de references." *L'avant-scène opéra: Giacomo Puccini, La Fille du Far West* 165 (May–June 1995): 104—9.

Budden, Julian. *Puccini: His Life and Works.* Oxford and New York: Oxford University Press, 2002.

———. "Wagnerian Tendencies in Italian Opera." In *Music and Theatre: Essays in Honor of Winton Dean*, edited by Nigel Fortune, 299—332. Cambridge and New York: Cambridge University Press, 1987.

Burke, Thomas. "The Case of Puccini: A Composer Loved Even by His Detractors." *Musical Courier* 111, no. 2 (13 July 1935): 6.

———. "The Case of Puccini: A Composer Loved Even by His Detractors." *Musical Courier* 111, no. 3 (20 July 1935): 6.

Carner, Mosco. "Giacomo Puccini." In *The New Grove Dictionary of Music and Musicians*, ed. Stanley Sadie, 15:429—40. London: Macmillan, 1980.

———. *Of Men and Music: Collected Essays and Articles.* 3d ed. London: J. Williams, 1944.

———. *Puccini: A Critical Biography.* 3d ed. New York: Holmes and Meier, 1992.

Carr, Helen. *Inventing the American Primitive: Politics, Gender, and the Representation of Native American Literary Traditions, 1789–1936.* New York: New York University Press, 1996.

Casini, Claudio. *Giacomo Puccini.* La Vita Sociale della Nuova Italia 28. Turin: UTET, 1978.

Cawelti, John G. *Adventure, Mystery, and Romance: Formula Stories as Art and Popular Culture.* Chicago: University of Chicago Press, 1976.

———. *The Six-Gun Mystique.* 2d ed. Bowling Green, Ohio: Bowling Green State University Popular Press, 1984.

Centro Studi Giacomo Puccini, ed. *Lirica 2001: La fanciulla del West.* Lucca: Pubblicazione del Teatro Giglio, 2001.

Chase, Gilbert, ed. *The American Composer Speaks: A Historical Anthology, 1770–1965.* Baton Rouge: Louisiana State University Press, 1966.

Chmaj, Betty . "Fry versus Dwight: American Music's Debate over Nationality." *American Music* 3, no. 1 (1985): 63–84.

Citron, Marcia. *Opera on Screen.* New Haven: Yale University Press, 2000.

Civinini, Guelfo, and Carlo Zangarini. *La fanciulla del West* [libretto]. English version by R. H. Elkin. Milan: Ricordi, 1910.

————. *La fanciulla del West, dal dramma per David Belasco* [libretto]. Milan: Ricordi, 1910.

Clark, Robert. *History and Myth in American Fiction, 1823–52.* New York: St. Martin's Press, 1984.

Clément, Catherine. *Opera, or, The Undoing of Women.* Translated by Betsy Wing. Foreword by Susan McClary. Minneapolis: University of Minnesota Press, 1988.

Cleva, Fausto. "Poem of the West." *Opera News,* 8 January 1966, 24–25.

Clifton, James A., ed. *The Invented Indian: Cultural Fictions and Government Policies.* New Brunswick, N.J.: Transaction, 1990.

Cockrell, Dale. *Demons of Disorder: Early Blackface Minstrels and Their World.* Cambridge and New York: Cambridge University Press, 1997.

The Columbia Encyclopedia. 6th ed. New York: Columbia University Press, 2002.

Cometta, Sandro. "Discografie." *L'avant-scène opéra: Giacomo Puccini, La Fille du Far West* 165 (May–June 1995): 117–26.

Conati, Marcello. "'Maria Antonetta' ovvero 'L'Austriaca': un soggetto abbandonato da Puccini." *Rivista italiana di musicologia* 33 (1998): 89–181.

Copland, Aaron, and Vivian Perlis. *Copland: 1900 through 1942.* New York: St. Martin's Press/Marek, 1984.

Corazzol, Adriana Guarnieri. "Opera and Verismo: Regressive Points of View and the Artifice of Alienation." *Cambridge Opera Journal* 5, no. 1 (March 1993): 39–53.

Coward, John M. *The Newspaper Indian: Native American Identity in the Press, 1820–90.* Urbana: University of Illinois Press, 1999.

Crawford, Richard. "Edward MacDowell: Musical Nationalism and an American Tone Poet." *Journal of the American Musicological Society* 49 (1996): 528–60.

Davis, Shelby J. "David Belasco and Giacomo Puccini: Their Collaboration." In *Opera and the Golden West: The Past, Present, and Future of Opera in the U.S.A.,* edited by John L. DiGaetani and Josef P. Sirefman, 129–39. Rutherford, N.J.: Farleigh Dickinson University Press, 1994.

Dean, Winton. "Giacomo Puccini." In *The Heritage of Music,* vol. 3., edited by Hubert Foss, 153–71. New York: Oxford University Press, 1951.

Dellamora, Richard, and Daniel Fischlin, eds. *The Work of Opera: Genre, Nationhood, and Sexual Difference.* New York: Columbia University Press, 1997.

DiGaetani, John Louis. "Comedy and Redemption in *La fanciulla del West.*" *Opera Quarterly* 2, no. 2 (Summer 1984): 88–95.

Döhring, Sieghart. "Puccinis 'Italianità'." In *Nationaler Stil und europäische Dimension in der Musik der Jahrhundertwende,* edited by Helga de la Motte-Haber, 122–31. Darmstadt: Wissenschaftliche Buchgesellschaft, 1991.

Dotto, Gabriele. "Opera, Four Hands: Collaborative Alterations in Puccini's *Fanciulla.*" *Journal of the American Musicological Society* 42, no. 3 (Fall 1989): 604–24.

Dry, Wakeling. *Giacomo Puccini.* London: John Lane, 1906.

Dunn, Leslie C., and Nancy A. Jones, eds. *Embodied Voices: Representing Female Vocality in Western Culture.* Cambridge: Cambridge University Press, 1994.

Enciclopedia della musica. Milan: Ricordi, 1972.

Fairtile, Linda B. *Giacomo Puccini: A Guide to Research.* New York: Garland, 1999.

Farwell, Arthur. "The Music of Puccini's Opera." *Musical America* 13, no. 6 (17 December 1910): 4–5.

Feest, Christian, ed. *Indians and Europe: An Interdisciplinary Collection of Essays.* 1998. Reprint, Lincoln: University of Nebraska Press, 1999.

Finson, Jon W. *The Voices That Are Gone: Themes in Nineteenth-Century American Popular Song.* New York: Oxford University Press, 1994.

Fiorentino, Dante del. *Immortal Bohemian: An Intimate Memoir of Giacomo Puccini.* New York: Prentice-Hall, 1952.

Flinois, Pierre. "Vidéographie." *L'avant-scène opéra: Giacomo Puccini, La Fille du Far West* 165 (May–June 1995): 131.

Fraccaroli, Arnaldo. *Giacomo Puccini si confida e racconta.* Milan: Ricordi, 1957.

———. "Puccini Talks about His New Opera: *The Girl of the Golden West.*" Translation of "Puccini e *La fanciulla del West.*" *Corriere della sera,* 15 October 1910. Undated typescript, Metropolitan Opera of New York Archive.

———. "Puccini e *La fanciulla del West.*" *Corriere della sera,* 15 October 1910.

Freeman, John W. "New Frontier." *Opera News* (6 January 1962): 24–31.

Freund, John C. "First Production of Puccini's Opera." *Musical America* 8, no. 5 (17 December 1910): 1–4.

Gänzl, Kurt. *The Encyclopedia of the Musical Theatre.* 2 vols. Oxford: Blackwell, 1994.

Gara, Eugenio, ed. *Carteggi pucciniani.* Milan: G. Ricordi, 1958.

Gatti-Casazza, Giulio. *Memories of the Opera.* London: John Calder, 1977.

Gavazzeni, Gianandrea. "Introduzione alla critica di Puccini." *La rassegna musicale* 20, no. 1 (January 1950): 13–22.

———. "Nella *Fanciulla del West* protagonista è l'orchestra?" *Musica d'oggi* 1, no. 9 (November 1958): 545–52.

Gerould, Daniel, ed. *American Melodrama.* New York: Performing Arts Journal Publications, 1983.

Giazotto, Remo. *Puccini in Casa Puccini.* Lucca: Akademos and LIM, 1992.

———. "'Puccini nello sgomento' ed altre testimonianze e confessioni inedite dei suoi famigliari." In *Musica senza aggettivi: studi per Fedele d'Amico,* edited by Agostino Ziino, 551–82. Firenze: Olschki, 1991.

Gidley, Mick. *The Vanishing Race: Selections from Edward S. Curtis's "The North American Indian."* Oxford: David and Charles, 1976.

Girardi, Michele. "Il finale de *La fanciulla del West* e alcuni problemi di codice." In *Opera e libretto* II, edited by Gianfranco Folena, Maria Teresa Muraro, and Giovanni Morelli, 417–37. Firenze: Olschki, 1993.

———. *Giacomo Puccini: La vita e l'opera*. Rome: Newton Compton, 1989.

———. *Puccini: His International Art*. Translated by Laura Basini. Chicago: University of Chicago Press, 2000.

Girgus, Sam B., ed. *The American Self: Myth, Ideology, and Popular Culture*. Albuquerque: University of New Mexico Press, 1981.

Goehr, Lydia. "Radical Modernism and the Failure of Style: Philosophical Reflections on Maeterlinck-Debussy's *Pélleas et Mélisande*." *Representations* 74 (Spring 2001): 19–46.

Gossett, Philip. "The Case for Puccini." *New York Review of Books*, 27 March 2003. nybooks.com/articles/16163.

Greenfield, Edward. *Puccini: Keeper of the Seal*. London: Arrow Books, 1958.

Greenfield, Howard. *Puccini: A Biography*. New York: G. P. Putnam's Sons, 1980.

Greenwald, Helen. "Dramatic Exposition and Musical Structure in Puccini's Operas." Ph.D. diss., City University of New York, 1991.

———. "Puccini, *Il tabarro*, and the Dilemma of Operatic Transposition." *Journal of the American Musicological Society* 51, no. 3 (1998): 521–58.

———. "Realism on the Opera Stage: Belasco, Puccini, and the California Sunset." In *Opera in Context: Essays on Historical Staging from the Late Renaissance to the Time of Puccini*, edited by Mark A. Radice, 279–96. Portland, Ore.: Amadeus Press, 1998.

———. "Recent Puccini Research." *Acta musicologica* 65, no. 1 (January–June 1993): 23–50.

———. "Verdi's Patriarch and Puccini's Matriarch: 'Through the Looking-Glass and What Puccini Found There.'" *Nineteenth-Century Music* 17 (1994): 220–36.

Grimshaw, Polly Swift. *Images of the Other: A Guide to Microform Manuscripts on Indian-White Relations*. Urbana: University of Illinois Press, 1991.

Grout, Donald J. *A Short History of Opera*. 2d ed. New York: Columbia University Press, 1965.

Gutiérrez, Ramon A., and Richard J. Orsi, eds. *Contested Eden: California before the Gold Rush*. Berkeley and Los Angeles: University of California Press, 1998.

Hall, Roger. *Performing the American Frontier, 1870–1906*. Cambridge and New York: Cambridge University Press, 2001.

Hamann, Peter, et al. *Ermanno Wolf-Ferrari*. Komponisten in Bayern 8. Tutzing: H. Schneider, 1986.

Harlow, Neal. *California Conquered: War and Peace on the Pacific, 1846–1850*. Berkeley and Los Angeles: University of California Press, 1982.

Haweis, Hugh Reginald. *Music and Morals*. New York: Harper and Brothers, 1874.

Heizer, Robert F., ed. *The Destruction of California Indians: A Collection of Documents from the period 1847 to 1865*. Santa Barbara, Calif.: Peregrine Smith, 1974.

Heller, Adele, and Lois Rudnik, eds. *1915, the Cultural Moment: The New Politics, the New Woman, the New Psychology, the New Art, and the New Theatre in America*. New Brunswick, N.J.: Rutgers University Press, 1991.

Herd, David. *Ancient and Modern Scottish Ballads, etc., 1776.* Edinburgh: Scottish Academic Press, 1973.

Herder, Johann Gottfried. *Outlines of a Philosophy of the History of Man.* Translated by Thomas Churchill. London: J. Johnston, 1800.

Herrera-Sobek, María. *Northward Bound: The Mexican Immigrant Experience in Ballad and Song.* Bloomington: Indiana University Press, 1993.

Hewitt, Vivien A. *The Land of Puccini.* Viareggio: Pezzini Editore, n.d.

Hilger, Michael. *From Savage to Nobleman: Images of Native Americans in Film.* Lanham, Md.: Scarecrow Press, 1995.

Hopkinson, Cecil. *A Bibliography of the Works of Giacomo Puccini, 1858–1924.* New York: Broude Brothers, 1968.

Horowitz, Joseph. "Sermons in Sacred Tones: Sacralization as a Theme in Classical Music." *American Music* 16, no. 3 (1998): 311–40.

———. *Wagner Nights: An American History.* Berkeley and Los Angeles: University of California Press, 1994.

Horwath, Michael. "Tebaldini, Gnecchi, and Strauss." *Current Musicology* 10 (1970): 74–91.

Howard, Rhonda Lane. *Shifting Ground: Transformed Views of the American Landscape.* Seattle: Henry Art Gallery, University of Washington, 2000.

Hubbs, Nadine. *Composing Oneself: Gay Modernist Composers and American Musical Identity.* Berkeley: University of California Press, forthcoming.

Hughes, Spike. *Famous Puccini Operas: An Analytical Guide for the Opera-Goer and Armchair Listener.* 2d rev. ed. New York: Dover, 1972.

Innaurato, Albert. "Heartbreak Saloon: How Puccini Poured Out His Personal Anguish in *Fanciulla.*" *Opera News,* 11 April 1992, 8–12.

Jackson, Stanley. *Monsieur Butterfly: The Story of Puccini.* New York: Stein and Day; London: Allen, 1974.

Keolker, James. *Last Acts: The Operas of Puccini and his Italian Contemporaries from Alfano to Zandonai.* Napa, Calif.: Opera Companion, 2000.

Kerman, Joseph, ed. *Music at the Turn of Century: A Nineteenth-Century Music Reader.* Berkeley and Los Angeles: University of California Press, 1990.

———. *Opera as Drama.* New and rev. ed. Berkeley and Los Angeles: University of California Press, 1988.

Kilpatrick, Jacquelyn. *Celluloid Indians: Native Americans and Film.* Lincoln: University of Nebraska Press, 1999.

Kimbell, David. *Italian Opera.* Cambridge and New York: Cambridge University Press, 1991.

King, C. Richard. *Colonial Discourses, Collective Memories, and the Exhibition of Native American Cultures and Histories in the Contemporary United States.* New York: Garland, 1998.

Koepke, Wolf. *Johann Gottfried Herder: Innovator through the Ages.* Bonn: Bouvier, 1982.

Kolodny, Annette. *The Land before Her: Fantasy and Experience of the American Frontiers, 1630–1860.* Chapel Hill: University of North Carolina Press, 1984.

Lamar, Howard R., ed. *The Reader's Encyclopedia of the American West.* New York: Crowell, 1977.

Lawrence, Vera Brodsky, ed. *The Wa-Wan Press, 1901–1911.* 5 vols. New York: Arno, 1970.

Leukel, Jürgen. "Puccinis kinematographische Technik." *Neue Zeitschrift für Musik* 143, no. 6–7 (1982): 24–26.

Levi, Primo. "*La fanciulla del West* e l'evoluzione del melodramma italiano." In *Paesaggi e figure musicali,* 468–83. Milan: Fratelli Treves, 1913.

Levin, David J., ed. *Opera through Other Eyes.* Stanford, Calif.: Stanford University Press, 1993.

Levin, Gail. "American Art." In *"Primitivism" in Twentieth-Century Art: Affinity of the Tribal and the Modern,* edited by William Rubin, 453–73. New York: Museum of Modern Art, 1984.

Levine, Lawrence W. *Highbrow/Lowbrow: The Emergence of Cultural Hierarchy in America.* Cambridge, Mass.: Harvard University Press, 1988.

Levy, Alan Howard. "The Search for Identity in American Music, 1890–1920." *American Music* 2, no. 2 (1984): 70–81.

Levy, Beth. "'In the Glory of the Sunset': Arthur Farwell, Charles Wakefield Cadman, and Indianism in American Music." *Repercussions* 5, nos. 1–2 (1996): 128–83.

Limerick, Patricia Nelson. "Disorientation and Reorientation: The American Landscape Discovered from the West." In *Discovering America: Essays on the Search for an Identity,* edited by David Thelen and Frederick E. Hoxie, 187–215. Urbana: University of Illinois Press, 1994.

Lindenberger, Herbert. "Opera/Orientalism/Otherness." In *Opera in History from Monteverdi to Cage,* 160–90. Stanford, Calif.: Stanford University Press, 1998.

Lippard, Lucy R., ed. *Partial Recall.* New York: New Press, 1992.

Locke, Ralph. "Constructing the Oriental 'Other': Saint-Saëns's *Samson et Delila.*" In *The Work of Opera: Genre, Nationhood, and Sexual Difference,* edited by Richard Dellamora and Daniel Fischlin, 161–84. New York: Columbia University Press, 1997.

———. "Music Lovers, Patrons, and the 'Sacralization' of Culture in America." *Nineteenth-Century Music* 17, no. 2 (1993): 149–73.

———. "What Are These Women Doing in Opera?" In *En Travesti: Women, Gender Subversion, Opera,* edited by Corinne Blackmer and Patricia Juliana Smith, 59–98. New York: Columbia University Press, 1995.

Lonergan, Walter. "Rome Satisfied with Its *Fanciulla.*" *Musical America* 14, no. 8 (1 July 1911): 18.

Lott, Eric. *Love and Theft: Blackface Minstrelsy and the American Working Class.* New York: Oxford University Press, 1993.

Lowenberg, Alfred. *Annals of Opera, 1597–1940.* 3d ed. London: John Calder, 1978.

Lualdi, Adriano. "Giacomo Puccini, i suoi detrattore l'opera nazionale del '900." *Piazza delle belle arti* 5 (1957–58): 272–306.

Lydon, Sandy. *Chinese Gold: The Chinese in the Monterey Bay Region.* Capitola, Calif.: Capitola Book, 1985.

Maehder, Jürgen. "Giacomo Puccinis Schaffensprozess im Spiegel seiner Skizzen für Libretto und Komposition." In *Vom Einfall zum Kunstwerk: Der Kompositionsprozess in der Musik des 20. Jahrhunderts*, edited by Hermann Danuser and Günter Katzenberger, 35–64. Laaber: Laaber-Verlag, 1993.

———. "Il libretto patriottico nell'Italia della fine del secolo e la raffigurazione dell'Antichità e del Rinascimento nel libretto prefascista italiano." In *Atti del XIV congresso della Società Internazionale di Musicologia: Trasmissione e recezione delle forme di cultura musicale; Bologna, 27 agosto–1° settembre 1987*, edited by Angelo Pompilio, Donatella Restani, Lorenzo Bianconi, and F. Alberto Gallo, 3:451–66. Torino: Edizioni di Torino, 1990.

———. "The Origins of Italian *Literaturoper: Guglielmo Ratcliff, La filia di Iorio, Parisina*, and *Francesca da Rimini*." In *Reading Opera*, edited by Arthur Groos and Roger Parker, 92–128. Princeton, N.J.: Princeton University Press, 1988.

———, ed. *Esotismo e colore locale nell'opera di Puccini: atti del I° Convegno Internazionale sull'opera di Giacomo Puccini, Torre del Lago, Festival Pucciniano, 1983.* Pisa: Giardini, 1985.

Magri, Giorgio. *L'uomo Puccini.* Milan: Mursia, 1992.

Mahar, William J. *Behind the Burnt Cork Mask: Early Blackface Minstrelsy and Antebellum American Popular Culture.* Urbana: University of Illinois Press, 1998.

Mallach, Alan. "Mascagni, *Marat*, and Mussolini: A Study in Ambivalence and Accommodation." *Opera Quarterly* 11, no. 2 (1995): 55–80.

Marchesi, Gustavo. "Puccini l'ultimo signore del melodramma." *Musica e dossier* 42 (July–August 1990): 23–67.

Marchetti, Arnaldo, ed. *Puccini com'era.* Milan: Curci, 1973.

Marchetti, Leopoldo, ed. *Puccini nelle immagini.* Milan: Garzanti, 1949.

Marek, George R. *Puccini: A Biography.* New York: Simon and Schuster, 1951.

Mariani, Renato. "L'ultimo Puccini." *La rassegna musicale* 9, no. 4 (April 1936): 133–40.

Marker, Lise-Lone. *David Belasco: Naturalism in the American Theatre.* Princeton, N.J.: Princeton University Press, 1975.

Marks, Patricia. *Bicycles, Bangs, and Bloomers: The New Woman in the Popular Press.* Lexington: University Press of Kentucky, 1990.

Marnat, Marcel. "La Jeanne d'Arc du Klondyke." *L'avant-scène opéra: Giacomo Puccini, La Fille du Far West* 165 (May–June 1995): 110–12.

Marsh, Robert C. *Dialogues and Discoveries: James Levine, His Life and His Music.* New York: Scribner, 1998.

Martino, Daniele A. *Metamorfosi del femminino nei libretti per Puccini.* Turin: Casa Editrice Books and Video, 1985.

McClary, Susan. *Georges Bizet,* Carmen. Cambridge and New York: Cambridge University Press, 1992.

———. "Structures of Identity and Difference in Bizet's *Carmen*." In *The Work of Opera: Genre, Nationhood, and Sexual Difference*, edited by Richard Dellamora and Daniel Fischlin, 115–29. New York: Columbia University Press, 1997.

McConachie, Bruce A. "New York Operagoing, 1825–50: Creating an Elite Social Ritual." *American Music* 6, no. 2 (1988): 181–92.

Mihesuah, Devon A. *American Indians: Stereotypes and Realities.* Atlanta: Clarity Press, 1996.

Mildenburg, Albert. "True Americanisms in Puccini's Score?" *Musical America* 13, no. 5 (10 December 1910): 1, 36.

Nachbar, John G. *Western Films: An Annotated Critical Bibliography.* New York: Garland, 1975.

Nash, Roderick. *Wilderness and the American Mind.* New Haven: Yale University Press, 1967.

Nelson, Byron. "The Isolated Heroine and the Loss of Community in Puccini's Belasco Operas." *Yearbook of Interdisciplinary Studies in the Fine Arts* 2 (1990): 385–407.

Newlin, Keith, ed. *American Plays of the New Woman.* Chicago: Ivan R. Dee, 2000.

Nicassio, Susan Vandiver. *Tosca's Rome: The Play and the Opera in Historical Perspective.* Chicago: University of Chicago Press, 1999.

Nicolodi, Fiamma. *Musica e musicisti nel ventennio fascista.* Fiesole: Discanto Edizioni, 1984.

O'Connell, Charles. *The Victor Book of Opera.* 9th ed., rev. New Jersey: RCA, 1936. Oesterreicher, Rudolf. *Emmerich Kálmán: Das Leben eines Operettenfürsten.* Rev. ed. Vienna: Amalthea, 1988.

Oja, Carol J. *Making Music Modern: New York in the 1920s.* Oxford: Oxford University Press, 2000.

Osborne, Charles. *The Complete Operas of Puccini: A Critical Guide.* New York: Da Capo Press, 1981.

Panichelli, Pietro. *Il "pretino" di Giacomo Puccini racconta.* Pisa: Nistri-Lischi, 1940.

Perison, Harry. "Charles Wakefield Cadman: His Life and Works." Ph.D. diss., University of Rochester, Eastman School of Music, 1978.

Petrobelli, Pierluigi. "Arrigo Pedrollo: una figura d'artista." *Musica d'oggi* 8 (1965): 82–83.

Phillips-Matz, Mary Jane. *Puccini: A Biography.* Boston: Northeastern University Press, 2002.

Pieri, Marzio. "La maestra cantatrice di Norimberga County." In *Quartetto della maledizione: materiali per "Rigoletto," "Cavalliera" e "Pagliacci," "Fanciulla,"* edited by Gae Aulenti and Marco Vallora, 96–99. Milan: Ubulibri, 1985.

Pilkington, William T., ed. *Critical Essays on the Western American Novel.* Boston: G. K. Hall, 1980.

Pintorno, Giuseppe, ed. *Puccini, 276 lettere inedite: il fondo dell'Accademia d'arte a Montecatini Terme.* Milan: Nuove Edizioni, 1974.

Pisani, Michael. "Exotic Sounds in the Native Land: Portrayals of North American Indians in Western Music." Ph.D. diss. Eastman School of Music, 1996.

———. "From Hiawatha to Wa-Wan: Musical Boston and the Uses of Native American Lore." *American Music* 19, no. 1 (2001): 39–50.

Pizzetti, Ildebrando. *Commemorazione di Giacomo Puccini nel primo centenario della nascita.* Milan: Edizione della Scala, 1958.

———. "Giacomo Puccini." In *Musicisti contemporanei,* 49–106. Milan: Fratelli Treves, 1914.

———. "Omaggio a Puccini." In *Giacomo Puccini,* edited by Claudio Sartori, 123–27. Milan: Ricordi, 1959.

Pollack, Howard. *Aaron Copland: The Life and Work of an Uncommon Man.* New York: Henry Holt, 1999.

Ponzo, Marie. "Homage to the West, Italian Style." *Identity Magazine,* January 1977, 62–65.

Portelli, Alessandro. *The Text and the Voice: Writing, Speaking, and Democracy in American Literature.* New York: Columbia University Press, 1994.

Puccini, Giacomo. *La fanciulla del West: opera completa per canto e pianoforte.* Reduction by Carlo Carignani. Milan: Casa Ricordi, 1910.

Puccini, Simonetta, ed. *Giacomo Puccini: lettere a Riccardo Schnabl.* Milan: Emme, 1980.

Puccini, Simonetta, and William Weaver, eds. *The Puccini Companion.* New York: W. W. Norton, 1994.

Pykett, Lyn. *The "Improper" Feminine: The Women's Sensation Novel and the New Woman Writing.* London and New York: Routledge, 1992.

Radano, Ronald, and Philip V. Bohlman, eds. *Music and the Racial Imagination.* Chicago: University of Chicago Press, 2000.

Radice, Mark A., ed. *Opera in Context: Essays on Historical Staging from the Late Renaissance to the Time of Puccini.* Portland, Ore.: Amadeus Press, 1998.

Ramsden, Timothy. *Puccini and His Operas.* Staplehurst: Spellmount, 1996.

Rao, Nancy Yunghwa. "Gendered Ethnicity and American Musical Modernism of the 1930s." Unpublished paper read at the annual meeting of the Society for American Music in Lexington, Ky., March 2002.

Ricci, Luigi. *Puccini interprete di se stesso.* Milan: Ricordi, 1954.

Rich, Maria. "Opera USA—Perspective: Puccini in America." *Opera Quarterly* 2, no. 3 (Fall 1984): 27–45.

Rinaldi, Mario. *Giacomo Puccini: 'La fanciulla del West.'* Guide musicali 3. Milan: Istituto di Alta Cultura, 1943.

———. "Puccini e la sua maniera." In *Musica e verismo: critica ed estetica d'una tendenza musicale,* 249–91. Rome: Fratelli de Santis, 1932.

Rogin, Michael. *Blackface, White Noise: Jewish Immigrants in the Hollywood Melting Pot.* Berkeley and Los Angeles: University of California Press, 1996.

Rohrbough, Malcolm. *Days of Gold: The California Gold Rush and the American Nation.* Berkeley and Los Angeles: University of California Press, 1997.

Rollins, Peter C., and John E. O'Connor, eds. *Hollywood's Indian: The Portrayal of the Native American in Film.* Lexington: University Press of Kentucky, 1998.

Rosenthal-English, Miriam. *Giacomo Puccinis La fanciulla del West: Eine neue Opernkonzeption im oeuvre des Komponisten.* Musicologica Berolinensia 3. Berlin: Verlag Ernst Kuhn, 1997.

Ross, Peter, and Donata Schwendimann Berra. "Sette lettere di Puccini a Giulio Ricordi." *Nuova rivista musicale italiana* 13, no. 4 (October–December 1979): 851–65.

Rossi, Nick. "At Home with Puccini." *Opera Quarterly* 2, no. 3 (Fall 1984): 72–88.

Russo, John Paul. "Puccini, the Immigrants, and the Golden West." *Opera Quarterly* 7, no. 3 (Fall 1990): 4–27.

Sachs, Harvey, ed. *The Letters of Arturo Toscanini.* New York: Alfred A. Knopf, 2002.

———. *Music in Fascist Italy.* New York: Norton; London: Weidenfeld and Nicolson, 1987.

Sadie, Stanley, ed. *The New Grove Dictionary of Opera.* 4 vols. London: Macmillan, 1992.

Said, Edward. *Culture and Imperialism.* New York: Knopf, 1993.

———. *Orientalism.* New York: Pantheon, 1978.

Sartori, Claudio, ed. *Puccini.* Milan: G. Ricordi, 1959.

Schatt, Peter W. *Exotik in der Musik des Jahrhunderts: Historisch-systematische Untersuchungen zur Metamorphose einer ästhetischen Fiktion.* Munich: Emil Katzbichler, 1986.

Schickling, Dieter. *Giacomo Puccini: Biographie.* Stuttgart: Deutsche Verlags-Anstalt, 1989.

Schmidl, Carlo, ed. *Dizionario universale dei musicisti.* 2 vols. Milan: Sonzogno, 1928.

Seligman, Vincent. *Puccini among Friends.* New York: Macmillan, 1938.

Severgnini, Silvestro. *Invito all'ascolto di Giacomo Puccini.* Milano: Mursia, 1984.

Sheppard, Alice. *Cartooning for Suffrage.* Albuquerque: University of New Mexico Press, 1994.

Smith, Sherry L. *Reimagining Indians: Native Americans through Anglo Eyes, 1880–1940.* New York: Oxford University Press, 2000.

Speck, Jules. *La fille du West: opéra en trois actes (du drame de David Belasco), livret de Guelfo Civinini et Carlo Zangarini, musique de Giacomo Puccini, mise en scène de Jules Speck, régisseur de la scène du Metropolitan Opera New York.* Paris: Ricordi, [c. 1912].

Solie, Ruth. "Fictions of the Opera Box." In *The Work of Opera: Genre, Nationhood, and Sexual Difference,* edited by Richard Dellamora and Daniel Fischlin, 185–208. New York: Columbia University Press, 1997.

Specht, Richard. *Giacomo Puccini: The Man, His Life, His Work.* Translated by Catherine Alison Phillips. New York: Alfred A. Knopf, 1933.

Stuart, Roxana. "Uncle Giacomo's Cabin: David Belasco's Direction of *La fanciulla del West.*" In *Opera and the Golden West: The Past, Present, and Future of Opera in the U.S.A.* Rutherford, N.J.: Fairleigh Dickinson University Press, 1994.

Szasz, Ferenc. "The American Quest for Religious Certainty, 1880–1915." In *The American Self: Myth, Ideology, and Popular Culture,* ed. Sam B. Girgus. Albuquerque: University of New Mexico Press, 1981. 88–104.

Tambling, Jeremy. *Opera and the Culture of Fascism.* Oxford: Clarendon Press, 1996.

———. *Opera, Ideology, and Film.* New York: St. Martin's Press, 1987.

Tarozzi, Giuseppe. *Puccini.* Translated by John W. Freeman. New York: Treves, 1985.

Tickner, Lisa. *The Spectacle of Women: Imagery of the Suffrage Campaign, 1907–14.* Chicago: University of Chicago Press, 1988.

Timberlake, Craig. *The Bishop of Broadway: The Life and Work of David Belasco.* New York: Library Publishers, 1954.

Todd, Ellen Wiley. *The "New Woman" Revised: Painting and Gender Politics on Fourteenth Street.* Berkeley and Los Angeles: University of California Press, 1993.

Tomlinson, Gary. *Metaphysical Song: An Essay on Opera*. Princeton, N.J.: Princeton University Press, 1999.

Tompkins, Jane. *West of Everything: The Inner Life of Westerns*. New York: Oxford University Press, 1992.

Torrefranca, Fausto. *Giacomo Puccini e l'opera internazionale*. Turin: Fratelli Bocca Editori, 1912.

Trachtenberg, Alan. *The Incorporation of America: Society and Culture in the Gilded Age*. New York: Hill and Wang, 1982.

Trafzer, Clifford E., and Joel R. Hyer, eds. *Exterminate Them: Written Accounts of the Murder, Rape, and Slavery of Native Americans During the California Gold Rush, 1848–1868*. East Lansing: Michigan State University Press, 1999.

Traubner, Richard. *Operetta: A Theatrical History*. Garden City, N.Y.: Doubleday, 1983.

Tsou, Judy. "Gendering Race: Stereotypes of Chinese Americans in Popular Sheet Music." *Repercussions* 6, no. 2 (1997): 25–62.

Tuggle, Robert. *The Golden Age of Opera*. New York: Holt, Rinehart, and Winston, 1983.

Turner, J. Rigbie. *Four Centuries of Opera: Manuscripts and Printed Editions in the Pierpont Morgan Library*. New York: Pierpont Morgan Library in association with Dover Publications, 1983.

Valleroni, Aldo. *Puccini minimo*. Turin: Priuli e Verlucca Editori, 1983.

Waterhouse, John C. G. "Italy from the First World War to the Second." In *Modern Times: From World War I to the Present*, edited by Robert P. Morgan, 111–27. London: Macmillan, 1993.

Weaver, William. *The Golden Century of Italian Opera from Rossini to Puccini*. New York: Thames and Hudson, 1980.

———. *Puccini: The Man and his Music*. New York: E. P. Dutton, 1977.

Weissmann, Adolf. "Puccini and Our Present Times." Translated by G. A. Pfister. *Sackbut* 3, no. 10 (May 1923): 291–95.

Weston, Mary Ann. *Native Americans in the News: Images of Indians in the Twentieth Century Press*. Westport, Conn.: Greenwood Press, 1996.

Williamson, John. "Eugen d'Albert: Wagner and Verismo." *Music Review* 45, no. 1 (February 1984): 26–46.

Wilson, Conrad. *Giacomo Puccini*. London: Phaidon Press, 1997.

Winter, William. *The Life of David Belasco*. 2 vols. New York: Moffat, Yard, 1918.

Wright, Will. *Six Guns and Society: A Structural Study of the Western*. Berkeley and Los Angeles: University of California Press, 1975.

Zangarini, Carlo. "Vigilia pucciniana." *Il resto del carlino* (Bologna), 20 September 1910.

———. "Un carteggio inedito del Maestro per La fanciulla del West." *Il resto del carlino* (Bologna), 29 November 1928.

Zondergeld, Rein. "Riccardo Zandonai: the Master of Fake Emotion." *Opera* 35 (1984): 1191–96.